CW00606399

LE CORBUSIER AND THE MAISONS JAOUL

LE CORBUSIER AND THE MAISONS JAOUL

Caroline Maniaque Benton

PRINCETON ARCHITECTURAL PRESS | NEW YORK

PUBLISHED BY
Princeton Architectural Press
37 East Seventh Street
New York, New York 10003

For a free catalog of books, call 1 (800) 722-6657.
Visit our website at www.papress.com.

Printed and bound in China
12 11 10 09 4 3 2 1 First edition

Published with the support of the Graham Foundation for Advanced Studies in the Fine Arts

Published with the support of the Ministère de la Culture et de la Communication (Centre national du livre and Direction de l'architecture et du patrimoine), Paris.

Translated from the original French by Barbara Shapiro Comte. Chapter 3 translated by Tim Benton.

EDITOR: Lauren Nelson Packard
DESIGNER: Paul Wagner

SPECIAL THANKS TO: Nettie Aljian, Sara Bader, Dorothy Ball, Nicola Bednarek, Janet Behning, Becca Casbon, Carina Cha, Penny (Yuen Pik) Chu, Russell Fernandez, Pete Fitzpatrick, Wendy Fuller, Jan Haux, Clare Jacobson, Aileen Kwun, Nancy Eklund Later, Linda Lee, Laurie Manfra, Katharine Myers, Jennifer Thompson, Arnoud Verhaeghe, Joseph Weston, and Deb Wood of Princeton Architectural Press
—Kevin C. Lippert, publisher

Library of Congress Cataloging-in-Publication Data
Maniaque, Caroline.
[Le Corbusier et les maisons Jaoul. English]
Le Corbusier and the maisons Jaoul / Caroline Maniaque.
p. cm.
Includes bibliographical references and index.
ISBN 978-1-56898-800-9 (hardcover : alk. paper)
1. Le Corbusier, 1887-1965—Criticism and interpretation.
2. Jaoul family—Homes and haunts—France—Neuilly-sur-Seine.
3. Neuilly-sur-Seine (France)—Buildings, structures, etc.
I. Le Corbusier, 1887-1965. II. Title.
NA1053.J4M3614 2009
720.92—dc22

2008042217

Fig. 1 (overleaf)
House B, as it appeared when Michel and Nadine Jaoul lived there in 1986.

CONTENTS

ACKNOWLEDGMENTS

This work could not have been accomplished without the support of numerous friends and colleagues. To them, I offer my warmest thanks: Michel and Nadine Jaoul for their encouragement as well as their intellectual stimulation. Tim Benton, Anne Debarre, Joan Ockman, and François Perot gave me invaluable advice, enabling me to enrich the content. Wilma Wols submitted the text to close scrutiny and Stefan Zebnowski-Rubin edited the notes and bibliography. I would like to extend my deep thanks to Barbara Shapiro Comte for her lucid and attentive translation.

Bernard Welcomme, Director of the École d'architecture de Lille, kindly granted me leave of absence to prepare the manuscript of this book at the Getty Research Institute from January to April 2003. A Fulbright fellowship made this possible. Additional financial assistance from the Centre national du livre, the Graham Foundation, and Michel and Nadine Jaoul was also indispensable to the publication of the book. I would like to thank Eric Lengereau and Anne Laporte for making possible financial aid from the Ministère de la Culture et de la Communication. For the English edition, I am grateful to Jean-Louis Cohen, Sarah Goldhagen, Pat Kirkham, Andrew Morrall, Mary McLeod, Stanislaus von Moos, and Wim de Witt for their support, and to Philippe Boudon who followed the first phase of this project.

This book greatly benefited from encounters with Le Corbusier's clients, collaborators and artisans, and from research in the Fondation Le Corbusier (FLC) archives, for which I thank Évelyne Tréhin, former director, Michel Richard, present director, Isabelle Godineau, and Arnaud Dercelles, whose professionalism and assistance facilitated the completion of this book. My thanks go to Giuseppe Nieddu for having introduced me to Salvatore Bertocchi. I am grateful to Lord Palumbo and his wife Hayat, together with Sophie Chevalier and Gaëlle Rio, who graciously allowed me access to their houses.

INTRODUCTION

Fig. 2 (opposite)
House A, the large living room, 1986.

Less than a half-mile from the Place de l'Étoile on the Champs-Elysées, in Neuilly-sur-Seine, a suburb to the west of Paris, Le Corbusier designed two houses for the Jaoul family. An intimate space composed of warm materials and multicolored wall surfaces, vaulted in brick and naturally lit through carefully placed bay windows, with a handsome fireplace surrounded by niches for cherished works of art and crafts, the Maisons Jaoul hardly conform to the conventional image of the architect's 1920s *machine à habiter* (machine for living in). Nor do they reflect the preconceived idea of their architect as cold, austere, and puritanical. The historiography of Le Corbusier's works has justly acknowledged the spatial richness and formal plasticity of the architect's postwar years, in buildings such as the pilgrimage chapel at Notre-Dame-du-Haut at Ronchamp (1955), the Monastery of Sainte-Marie de La Tourette (1959), and the major buildings at Chandigarh (High Court, Palace of Assembly, and Secretariat, 1955–58). Yet, despite the fact that the Maisons Jaoul could rightfully be celebrated among these masterpieces of his mature years, little mention to date has been made of this largely neglected work upon which Le Corbusier nonetheless devoted four intensive years, from 1951 to 1955. Testimonies gathered here of the warm, amicable collaboration between the architect and the Jaoul family give unique insight into that period, establishing the background and design evolution of their houses.[1]

Close examination of the associated visual documents and building files allows us to retrace the genesis and history of the project[2] and to study the design process. It confirms that here Le Corbusier was reappraising the fundamental bases of the art of living, putting forward alternative models to improve upon the lifestyle within. Right from the outset of discussions with the Jaouls, however, Le Corbusier insisted on one condition that came to dominate the entire project: the incorporation of Catalan vaults into the houses, an architectural feature he deemed essential to the desired effect of well-being that he strove to create.

Le Corbusier benefited from the Jaoul commission to modify his approach toward construction. By the 1930s, he had already explored the potential of organic materials such as stone, wood, and brick. For the erection of the Neuilly houses, a genuine dialogue was established between the building contractors, including the Corsican carpenter and the Sardinian mason. This dialogue, demonstrating the architect's wealth of creative ideas (although, at the time, misunderstood and criticized) is reconsidered in light of new research findings at the Fondation Le Corbusier (FLC) and recent interviews with a number of Le Corbusier's artisans and collaborators involved in this quest for materiality. In his article published in *The Architectural Review* (1955), James Stirling observed that, "frequently accused of being 'internationalist,' Le Corbusier was, in fact, the most regional of architects."[3] The Brutalist finish, which seemed to shock the young Stirling, was deliberately thought out and adopted by Le Corbusier who was mindful to send his artisans a selection of photographs of vernacular walls as a reference to how he wanted the Jaouls' homes to be built, after testing out different types of joints in full-scale trials.

Visitors to the Maisons Jaoul are often very startled at the contrast between the rough Brutalism of the exposed concrete-and-brick exterior walls and the superb smooth finishes of the interior walls. The latter explode with vigorous bright colors and vibrate with contrasting textures, such as varnished wood, painted concrete, and ceramic kitchen tiles. The built-in furniture—the shelves, desks, and buffets covered with a slab of waxed or stained concrete—is itself embellished with inlaid ceramic chips, like so many personal touches, the stamps of artisan fabrication. Le Corbusier's vigilant attention to such detail throughout the design process and his frequent site visits attest to the importance he accorded to this work. The Jaoul project is a prime example of the architect's deliberate desire to synthesize two opposing approaches: the artisanal in his use of the Catalan vault, and the industrial in his recourse to prefabricated wood and glass end walls set in the structure. Rather than searching for absolute perfection, Le Corbusier sought to express the "human hand," in the spirit of sculpting a unique object. This attitude was already manifest in his work on the Maison Errazuris in Chile, as early as 1930, where in a letter to his clients accompanying his plans, he ended with a final admonition:

> Don't be surprised by what seems like a rather traditional look to our proposal, for it's not only the external appearance that counts. We renounced all construction that presented technical difficulties and decided to concentrate solely on traditional masonry and carpentry procedures. Using this as a starting point, we accentuated the true nature of the selected materials. We therefore thought that you could use stone found directly on your plot of land, to create a rustic sort of masonry. As for the carpentry, we simply used some round wooden logs, stripped of bark, and painted them white.... I hope that our proposal will please you. I myself would be delighted to live in such a house. I'm telling you all this to point out that the enclosed plans truly represent a viable architectural solution, despite appearances to which I referred at the beginning of this letter.[4]

It is a well-known fact that Le Corbusier was attracted to primitive and vernacular architecture.[5] In fact, without calling into question his own contribution to developments in spatial experiments from the 1920s onward, Le Corbusier predicted that "the rusticity of materials would in no way prove a hindrance to the expression of a clear plan and modern aesthetic."[6] More and more conscious of the role of materials in modern architecture, he sought to ally techniques commonly referred to as "primitive" with so-called cutting edge techniques, without nonetheless ever renouncing his commitment to modernity.[7]

In effect, from a broader viewpoint, one could argue that the conceptual process developed by Le Corbusier at the Maisons Jaoul was representative of a pervasive postwar European quest that was expressed, on the one hand, by Existentialist philosophers (such as Jean-Paul Sartre) and, on the other hand, by artists of the Art Brut movement (such as Jean Dubuffet).[8] The Jaouls were art connoisseurs who counted many artists among their closest friends. They frequented René Drouin's gallery in the Place Vendôme where Wols (Alfred Otto Wolfgang Schulze), Jean Dubuffet, and Jean Fautrier, among others, were often exhibited. The Jaoul's art collection closely adhered to dominant artistic currents, at once harkening back to a lost primitive innocence and expressing the need for a concrete reality characterized by the taste for authenticity. These qualities of deep-rootedness in the Maisons Jaoul bear witness to this tendency.

How did Le Corbusier succeed in ascribing a certain monumental grandeur to a domestic brief, while providing a private and intimate environment? How did he respond to technical and economic criteria while considering essential human qualities? An analysis of conceptual drawings from the early phases of the design process addresses the dialogue between these contrasting demands, "this mixture of intimacy and grandeur," as Jean-Jacques Duval so justly apprehended during his visit to the Maisons Jaoul in 1955.[9] In fact, one could argue that all Le Corbusier's houses manifest a balance between these two extremes—"monumental" or "grand" and "private" or "intimate"—and support his fundamental research on the concept of the *machine à habiter* and the *coquille de l'escargot* (snail's shell). On the one hand, through the rationalist thread linking the Maison Domino (1914) to the Cité Frugès at Pessac (1924–28), Le Corbusier tackled the double issue of "how to be modern" and how to offer this modernity to the general public through standardized, mass-produced design solutions. On the other hand, through designing houses at a more intimate scale, like the Villa Fallet (1907), his mother's small house in Vevey (1925–26), or the Petite Maison de Weekend (Villa Félix) in La Celle-Saint-Cloud (1935), Le Corbusier deliberated over questions on the art of living.

From 1929 onwards, Le Corbusier made every effort to exploit diverse materials, such as rough stone, plywood facings, and exposed brick at the Villa de Mandrot (1931), and to incorporate the vault to convey a sense of intimacy, as in the Villa Félix in La Celle-Saint-Cloud, for example.[10]

In the Jaoul project, underway by 1951, Le Corbusier examined the art of living, while simultaneously offering a critique of rationalist modernity, for which he himself had played a key role as protagonist for over thirty years. Did the idea of a modern lifestyle inherently imply the renouncement of a more sensual way of life? A dilemma arises out of these two orientations, since the former favors standardization, industrialization, and the universal, while the latter searches for uniqueness, craftsmanship effects, and a personal statement of individualism. Does the emphasis on standardization and uniformity automatically exclude the expression of the individual? Does mechanization or industrialization always conflict with craftsmanship? Does the search for the universal automatically eliminate the need for the specific? Why is it so difficult to resolve the conflict between intimacy and grandeur?

This study aims to respond to such questions. After a photographic promenade through the two houses, the first chapter evokes the artistic milieu shared by the Jaouls and Le Corbusier during the 1940s and '50s, followed by a description of the history and genesis of the project, and phases of the design process, from Le Corbusier's preliminary site sketches to his detailed proposals, plans, and invitations to bids. The second chapter considers the amicable relations that Le Corbusier cultivated with his collaborating teams of artisans and the adventurous climate of the construction world in those days. The third chapter addresses the art of living as a general theme and raises the issue of intimacy. The fourth chapter covers the critical reception of the houses, mainly in the Anglo-American press of the fifties and sixties, and concludes with a summary of the various renovations and changes that have taken place up to the present day.

If, indeed, in *The New Brutalism* (1966), Reyner Banham highlighted the risks and challenges raised by the Maisons Jaoul, by the 1980s during the worldwide centennial celebrations of Le Corbusier's birth, hardly any of the associated exhibitions and publications even bothered to mention the work. Neither the Karlsruhe exhibition catalogue, *Synthèse des Arts, Aspekte des Spätwerks, 1945–1965* (1986), nor the Centre Georges Pompidou exhibition catalogue, *Le Corbusier, une encyclopédie* (1987) features specific entries on the houses.[11] To the contrary, the Arts Council of Great Britain exhibition catalogue, *Le Corbusier: Architect of the Century* (1987) did publish an analytical illustrated text on the project.[12] Since that time, and after their sale in 1988 and subsequent restoration, the Maisons Jaoul are once again cited as crucial landmarks within Le Corbusier's oeuvre.

This book relies predominantly on written, iconographic, and oral sources. They originate primarily from the personal archives of the Jaoul family, as well as the archives of the FLC, at a time when the original files were still directly accessible to researchers.[13]

The term "fabrication" used in the French title makes specific reference to Francis Ponge's *La Fabrique du Pré* (1971) in which the author sets out an archaeology of the foundations of his poetry. His idea of presenting a poem not in its perfected, definitive form, but rather in a series of multiple sketches or drafts, ruptures the silence of his writing, thus rendering it transparent and explicit, and conferring on it a status beyond that of a mere preparatory phase. This book explores and accounts for the creative process underpinning the Maisons Jaoul and the labor invested in the "fabrication" of this architecture.

THE PROMENADE

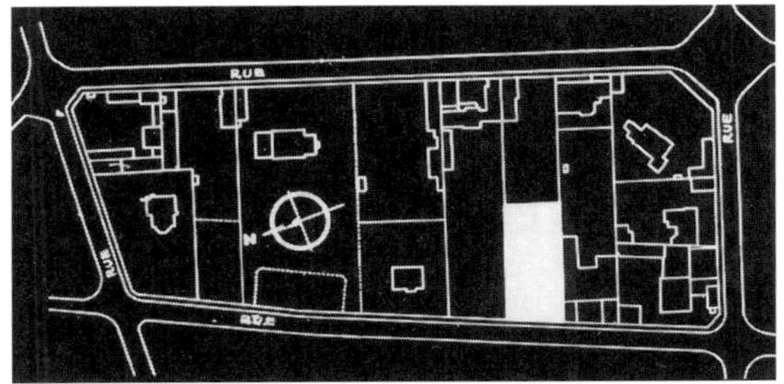

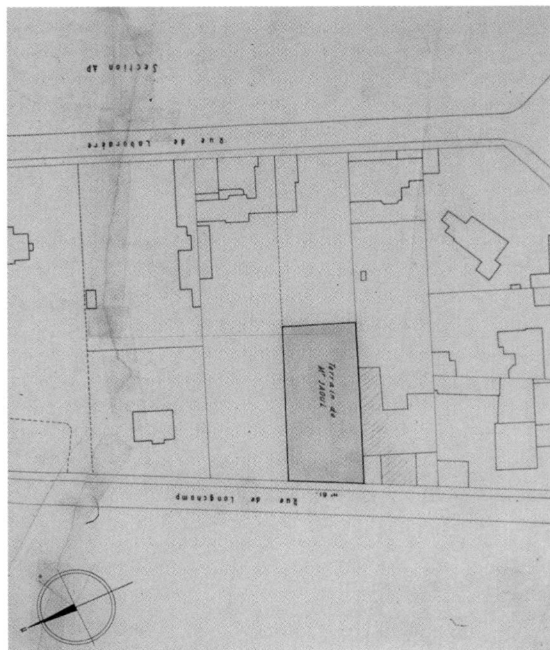

The neighborhood

In the 1950s, the neighborhood adjacent to Parc Saint-James in Neuilly-sur-Seine, where the Maisons Jaoul were built, still retained its countrified atmosphere, dotted with single-family houses set back from the street, surrounded by private, often fenced-in gardens. By 2004, most of these housing types had been replaced by rectangular apartment blocks with continuous balconies running along their facades, enclosed by manicured lawns and shrubbery, typical of sixties suburban residential neighborhoods to the west of Paris.

The Jaoul lot is located at 81 *bis*, rue de Longchamp, one in a row of parallel rectangular subdivisions within the city block, oriented longitudinally to the northwest and southeast. The perimeter of the block is bordered by rue de Longchamp to the west, rue du Centre to the south, rue de Labordère to the east and rue du Bois de Boulogne to the north. Measuring 150.42 feet and 156 feet in length along its north and south sides, respectively, and 70.53 feet in width across its west front facing rue de Longchamp, the 3280.84-square-foot plot is reinforced by a natural 6.56-foot slope, which descends roughly eastwest from the back to the front of the lot. To the south, a four-story 1930s brick building, set back 24.6 feet from the street, abuts the property, and to the north, the once empty lot in the early days of the Jaoul project, is also built-up with an apartment block. A neighboring garden adjoins the property to the east.

Fig. 3
Site plan. The Jaoul plot (denoted by solid white) is located between rue de Longchamp and rue de Labordère in Neuilly-sur-Seine.

Fig. 4
Plan of the plot, March 19, 1952. FLC 9905 (detail).

The plot and house position

Fig. 5 (top left)
Access to the houses is provided by a bifurcating ramp with one slope descending to the garage and the other mounting to a platform or terraced court that anchors the two houses, set at right angles. Creating a discrete passageway between the public street and the more intimate domestic space, the ramp operates as a control device, reinforced by the fortified character of the first house (House A), with its semi-blind gable end and rainwater downspouts. Its three-story longitudinal side elevation, distinctly parallel to Rue de Longchamp, is set back from the street by a softly undulating garden, dampening the ambient street sounds.

Fig. 6 (top right)
House B, whose longitudinal elevation lies perpendicular to that of House A, is located at the far end of the site. Its two gable ends are composed of wood panels and a variety of glazed elements: "Thermopanes," double glazing, plate glass or frosted glass.

Fig. 7 (right)
Bird's-eye view over the grass-and-turf covered roofs of the two houses, which appear to be set in a grove of trees. Le Corbusier intentionally borrowed familiar features of the suburban house type for the Maisons Jaoul, being partially detached from the property lines and removed from the street to protect their quiet isolation. Of the hundreds of photographs that the photographer Lucien Hervé sent to or archived at Le Corbusier's Rue de Sèvres office between 1953 and 1956, not one captures the street, ramp, and houses in one frame, implying that the successful integration of these design features within the neighborhood had not been one of the architect's main concerns. Nonetheless, Le Corbusier did search for continuity within the built environment, especially evident in his choice of red brick to complement the adjacent brick facade of the 1930s apartment block just south of the Jaoul property.

The court and the garden

Fig. 8
The exterior square court, positioned between the two houses, functions as a filter between the shared family area and the private, individual spaces, working as a semi-private terrace to receive guests, while simultaneously protecting the intimacy of the home interior. The court also serves as the pivotal point for the distribution of space.

Fig. 9
Perspective drawing of the two houses on the lot, as seen from the street. (Perspectives, sections, and plans in figures 9–14, 21, and 34 were executed by Pierre Henon.)

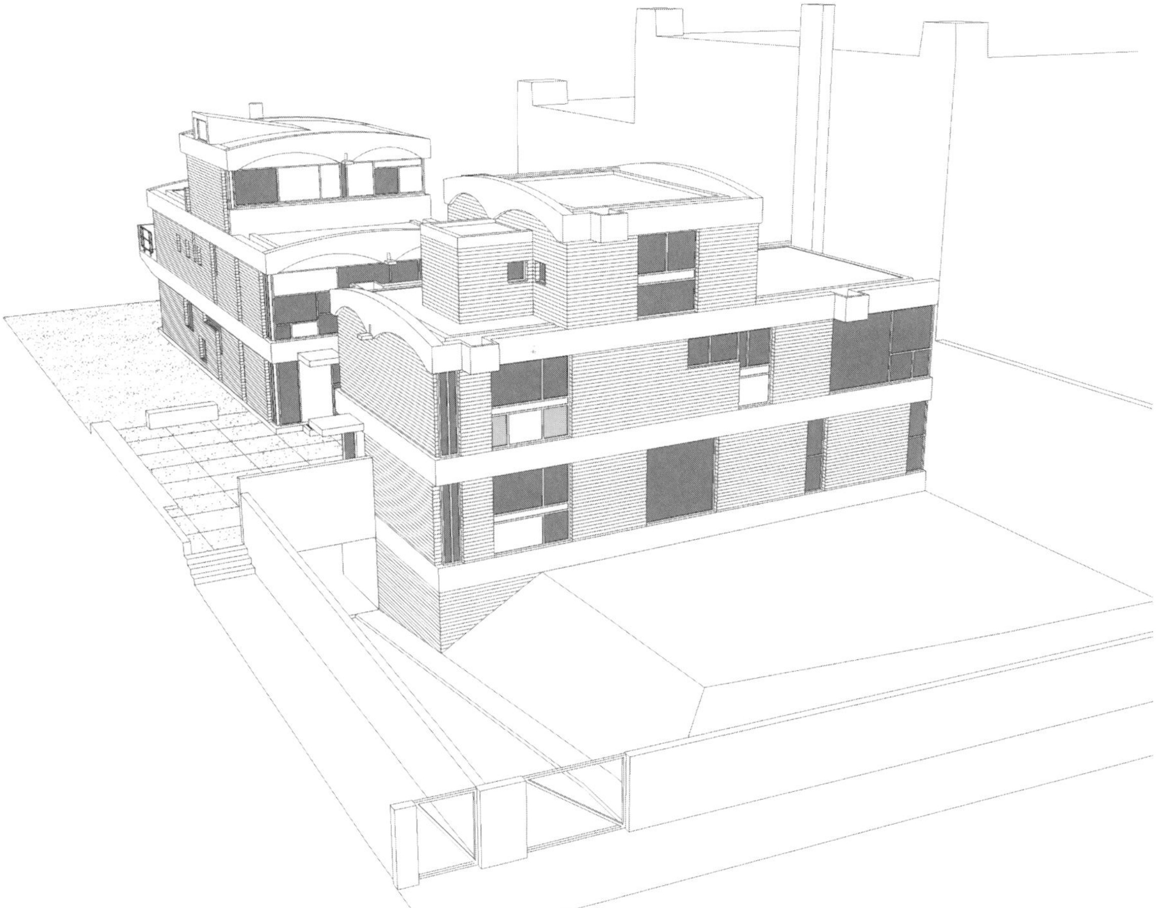

The layout

Fig. 10
Plan of the existing ground-floor level. The habitable surface area of House A and House B is 252 square meters (826 square feet) each. The terraces occupy a surface area of 63 and 70 square meters (207 and 230 square feet), respectively. The two houses share a common basement, serviced by two staircases, where the garage, boiler room, and cellars are located. Each house is designed with a ground floor, first floor, and a partial second floor, with each ground floor containing an entrance hall, a large reception area serving as both dining and living room, and a kitchen.

Fig. 11
Perspective view of the two houses, seen from the garden.

Fig. 12
Houses A and B, first-floor plans, existing conditions. The master bedroom in each house opens onto a recessed balcony on the east facades. House A contains three bedrooms with sinks and showers and separate toilets; a small chapel extends from Madame Jaoul's first-floor bedroom. House B contains four bedrooms, one with a full bathroom and the others with a sink and shower and separate toilets on the first floor.

Fig. 13
Houses A and B, second-floor plans, existing conditions.

Fig. 14
Longitudinal section of the two houses on the lot, existing conditions.

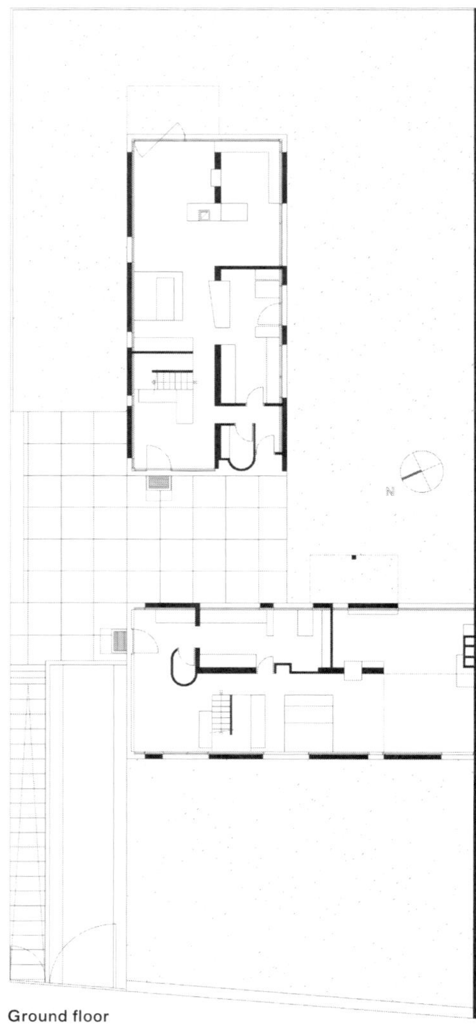

Ground floor

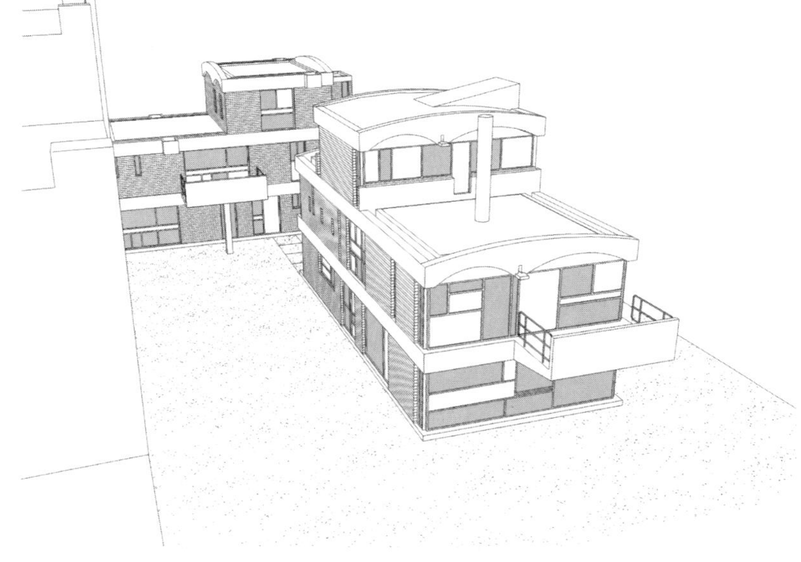

1st floor

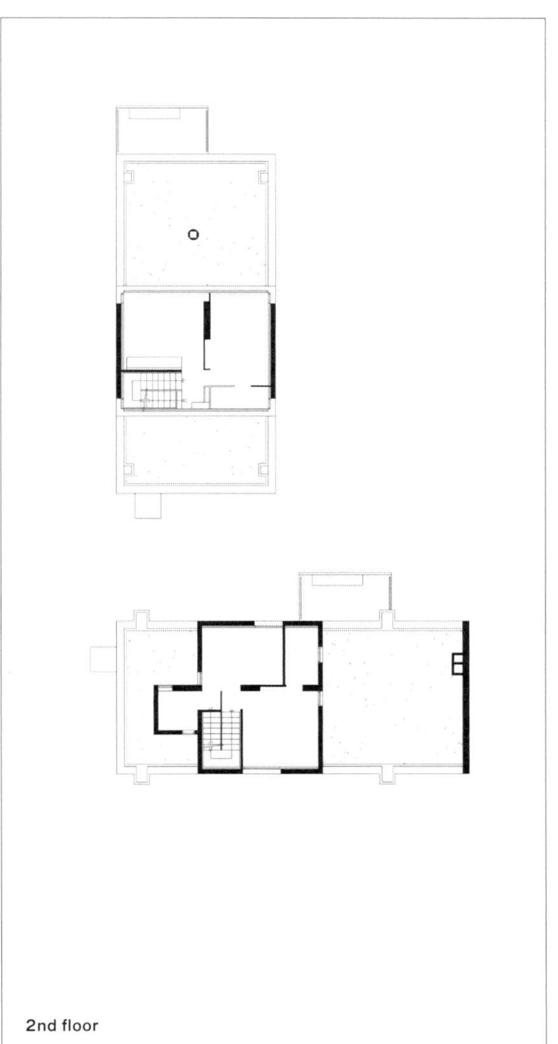

2nd floor

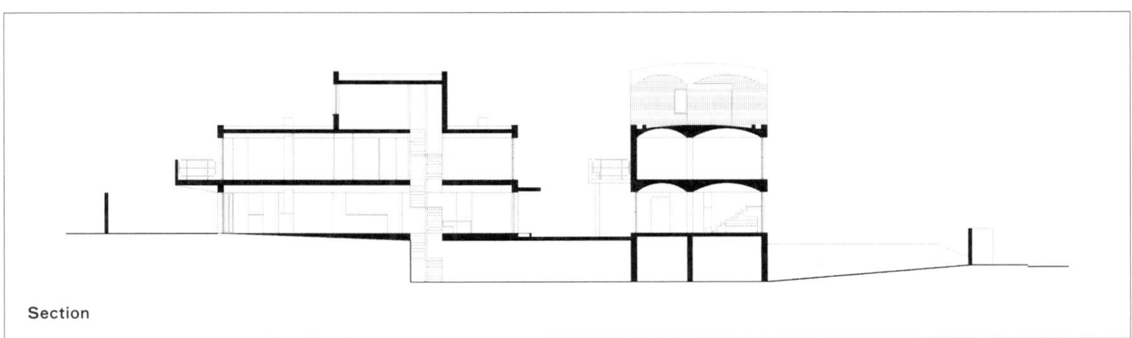

Section

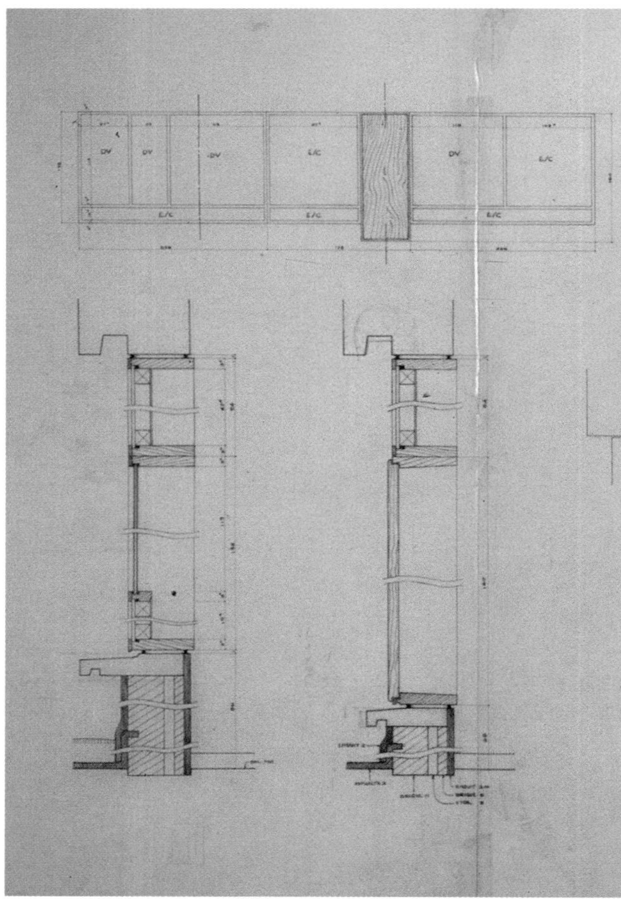

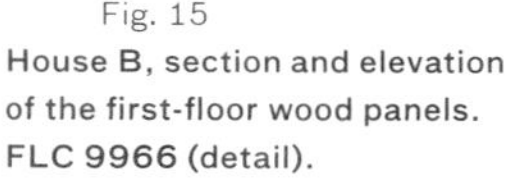

Fig. 15
House B, section and elevation of the first-floor wood panels. FLC 9966 (detail).

Fig. 16a, b, c
House B under construction (photography by Lucien Hervé). Each house is composed of two bays, one with a 11.8-foot span and the other with a 7.4-foot span, covered by one Catalan vault.

Fig. 17
House B. The walls of the houses are framed by continuous reinforced concrete beams (27.5 inches high and 13 inches thick) at each floor level. These beams simultaneously form the structure for the entire building and form the lintels above the bays. The depth of the lintels serves to contain the section of the vaults there. The perforated openings on the facades are arrhythmic. They express the internal organization of the houses and are therefore neither set along a vertical alignment nor organized according to a predetermined rhythm.

Fig. 18
View of House A showing the concrete beams that contain the catalan vaults. The facade walls are treated in exposed brick without revetment.

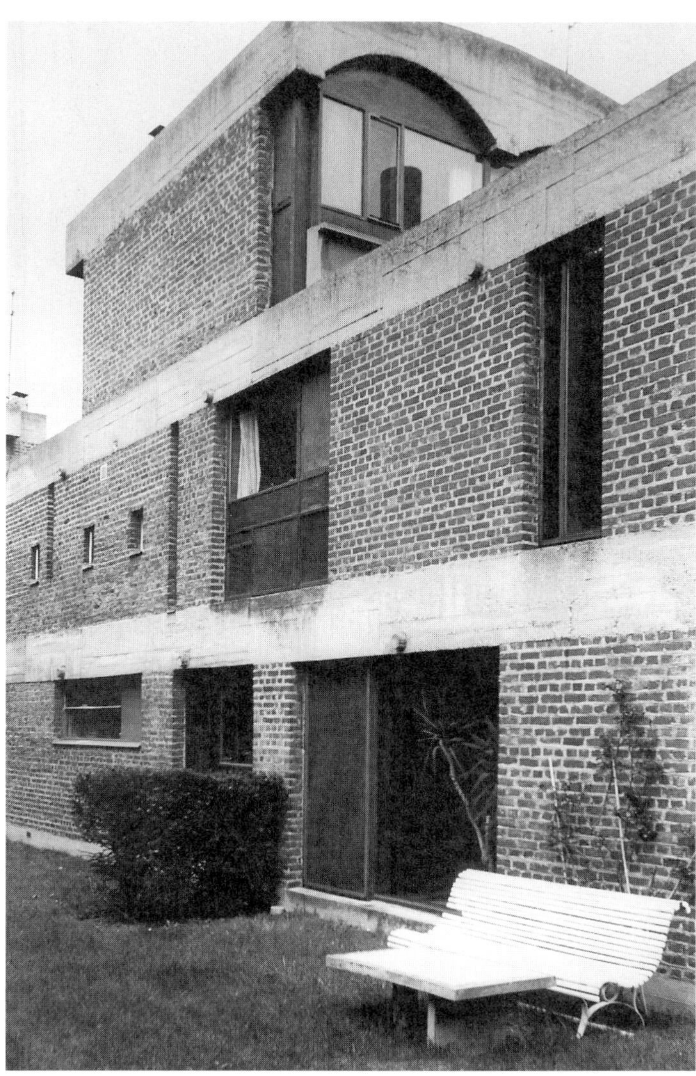

Fig. 19
Entrance to House B, 1986. Linked to the vertical circulation, the staircase is located within the 12-foot-wide bay, along one-third of the longitudinal axis.

Fig. 20
Salon, House B, 1992. The circulation and composition—a play of polychromy, solids, and voids—are controlled by visual framing. Perception of the vaulted horizontal module is accentuated by the fact that the space is freed of all wall partitions, thus opening up a clear perspective view across the entire house. Within the interior, the central spine wall (13 inches thick) between the two bays, as well as the double-wall of the facade is plaster finished. Exposed terra-cotta tile vaults cover all the ground-floor rooms.

Fig. 21
House B, axonometric perspective.

Fig. 22
In House A, a pass-through facilitates service between the kitchen and dining room, while in House B, the kitchen communicates directly with the dining room through a half-wall forming a bar, equipped with a hinged horizontal wooden shutter to seal the space when required. These details illustrate sensitive design solutions to distinguish the two houses in response to the separate and contrasting lifestyles of their resident families.

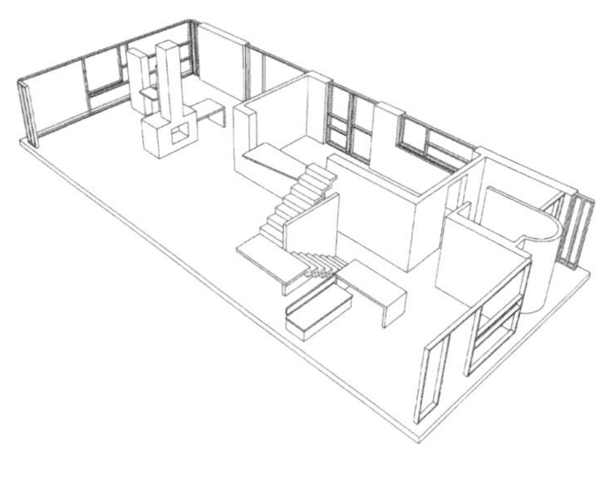

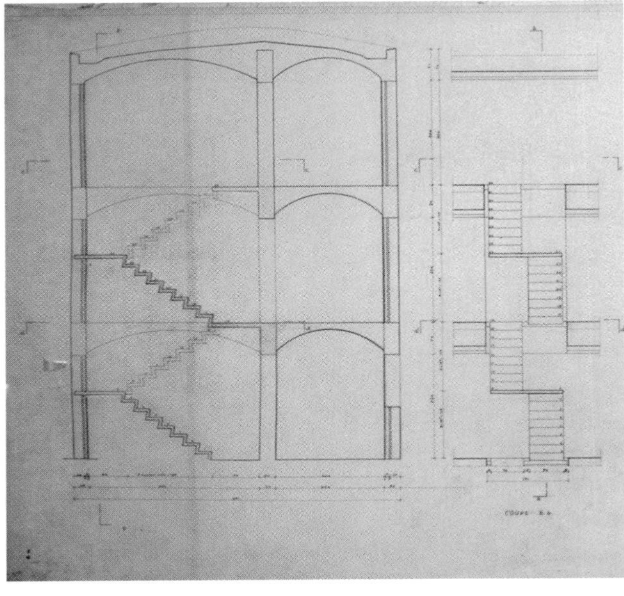

Fig. 23
Staircase in House B, looking down from the second floor. The juxtaposition of the staircase and flanking wall accentuates the play of light, channeled here from the overhead skylight, thereby emphasizing the narrow interstice between the wall and the steps.

Fig. 24
The staircase, looking up from the first floor toward the second floor.

Fig. 25
House B, sections of the staircase. FLC 9973 (detail).

Fig. 26
House B. Bedroom on the first floor, 1986.

Fig. 27
In House B, the circulation space is clearly demarcated on the first floor. Inserted within the 12-foot-span bay, a hallway distributes the bedrooms on either side. The bright-green chimney conduit, traversing the master bedroom, interrupts the longitudinal axis of this hallway and articulates the merging of two bays making up this bedroom. It also contributes to the delineation of a more intimate space.

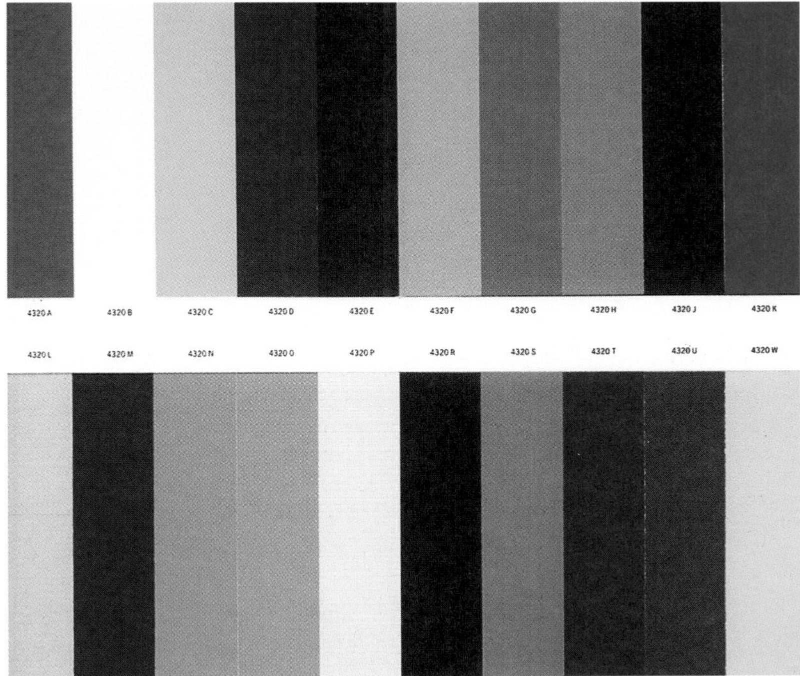

The polychromy

Fig. 28
Extract from *Claviers de couleurs*, Basel, Salubra, 1959. The two Salubra albums (1931 and 1959) assemble wallpaper samples designed by Le Corbusier and offer the possibility of choosing color combinations with the help of special eyeglasses and a "keyboard of colors."

Fig. 29
Living room in House A, 1986. By the late 1920s, Le Corbusier had understood that "color modifies space, classifies objects, stimulates physiological reactions and has a strong effect on our sensibilities."[1] In the 1950s, he called to mind the role of polychromy: "You divide up the habitable spaces into compartments as you see fit, according to gestures that are useful to quotidian behavior and that are linked by independent circulation systems. This gives you the free plan. Once the mason has finished his work, it is this free plan that gives you walls that appear incoherent at first glance. They are gray or white, depending on the circumstances, and then you might find that this scheme creates monotony, which might bother some people, although I myself am not in the least bothered by it, as I find white agreeable. But, in any case, you resort to using color, to arrange things according to an order. You classify and put events into hierarchies, you give them purposes."[2]

Fig. 30
Salon in House B, 1986. The variety of colors and materials in the house interiors contrasts with the austerity of the rude brick exterior. Each space is qualified by a color and particular atmosphere. As such, in House B, at the point where the central spine wall stops, to allow a fluid passageway between the 12-foot and the 7.4-foot bays, it is not treated in the same way on each of its sides. The side facing the fireplace is painted in yellow and bright green, while the side facing the library is painted in grayish-blue and the wall end section in white.

Fig. 31
Detail, colored walls of the second-floor bedroom, House B, after restoration in 1992.

Fig. 32
Detail, colored walls of the first-floor master bedroom, House B, after restoration. The square wood insets in the wall correspond to the closing plugs of the rainwater downpipes.

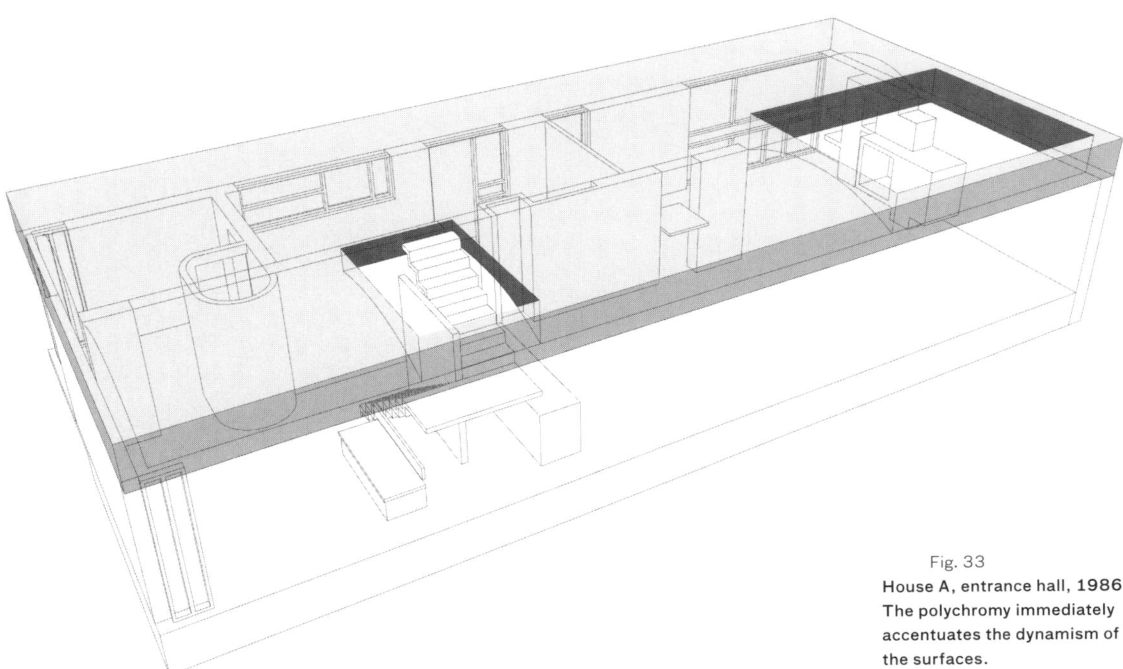

Fig. 33
House A, entrance hall, 1986. The polychromy immediately accentuates the dynamism of the surfaces.

Fig. 34
The perspective drawing of House A shows the floor openings and space dividers, accentuating the rhythm on the ground level from the entrance to the living room.

Chapter 1

IN SEARCH OF AUTHENTICITY: THE GENESIS OF THE PROJECT

As soon as I am entrusted with a job, I tend to store it away in the back of my mind, that is to say, I do not allow myself to draw a single sketch for many months. The human brain is made up in such a way that it has a certain autonomy: it is a container into which one can pour all the ingredients of a problem jumbled together. There one leaves them to "float," "simmer" [and] "ferment." Then suddenly a spontaneous inner drive causes everything to fall into place; one picks up a lead pencil, a stick of charcoal, some colored pencils (color being the key to the process) and one is able to come up with something on paper: the idea emerges—the child emerges, he comes into the world, he is born.

—Le Corbusier, *L'Atelier de la recherche patiente*, Paris, 1960

Architect and client in the artistic milieu of postwar Paris

In 1951, Le Corbusier received a commission to build two houses for an extended family: one for André Jaoul, his wife Suzanne, and their younger son Bruno, and the other for their older son Michel Jaoul, his wife Nadine, and their three children.

André Jaoul was born in 1894 in Saint-Hippolyte-du-Fort where his father ran a small furniture manufacturing company. In 1910, at sixteen years old, he left to acquire business training in England, but four years later, when war was declared, he signed up for the French commando. After being wounded at the Front, he was sent to convalesce in the Savoy region, not far from a small arms-production factory in Gifre. As he was bilingual, it was not long before Jaoul was hired by the director of this factory (a subsidiary of the Société d'Electro-Chimie d'Ugine group) to develop the international sales and copyright division of their products, including specialized steels, chemical products, ferro-alloys, aluminium, and light metals. Named director of Ugine's foreign relations department by the late twenties, on one of his trips to New York between October 16 and 21, 1935, Jaoul encountered Le Corbusier on board the ship *Normandie*.[1] The two men got along well. Le Corbusier was attracted to Jaoul's complex personality, an unconventional combination of athletic risk taker, art lover, autodidact, fluent English-speaker, and Americanophile. "My father, who had trained in England from 1910 to 1914, also played center-forward on a football team and boxed as a sparring partner with Georges Carpentier," recalled Michel Jaoul.[2]

A mutual interest in establishing a professional collaboration reinforced their friendship. Le Corbusier was convinced that industrialists had a central role to play both in the cultural combat of the architectural avant-garde and in the infrastructure and social changes to industrial society. In a letter dated February 6, 1937, Jaoul congratulated Le Corbusier on his recently published book *Quand les cathédrales étaient blanches*:[3] "Your book has brought me more than just a breath of fresh air from the USA. It [also] clarifies several points that remained obscure to me despite my numerous trips over there."[4] In the United States, Jaoul facilitated contacts between

Fig. 35
André and Suzanne Jaoul, 1949.

Fig. 36
Michel and Nadine Jaoul, c. 1965.

Fig. 37
Nadine Jaoul, *Réunion de famille* (Family Reunion), oil on canvas, 1946. In the background of this domestic scene, one can distinguish (top right) Dubuffet's *Essayeuse de chapeau* (*Woman Trying on a Hat*), painted in 1943 and (top left) the cropped bottom edge of Le Corbusier's *Tête* (Head), a gift he offered to Suzanne Jaoul.

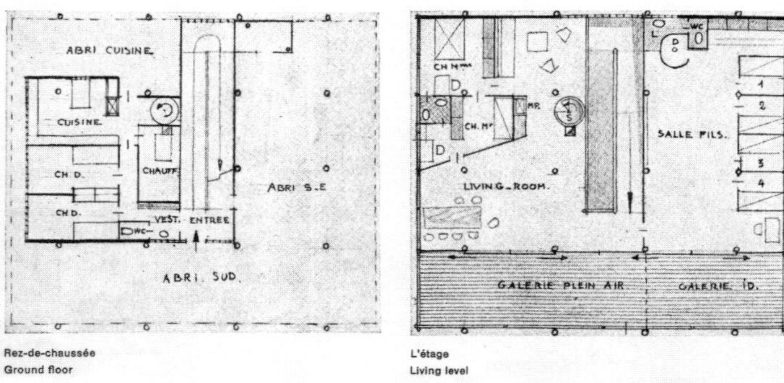

Fig. 38a, b
Le Corbusier and Pierre Jeanneret, a weekend house proposal for André Jaoul, 1937; ground-floor and upper-floor plans, and perspective. These drawings were executed by Pierre Jeanneret on November 29, 1937. FLC.

Le Corbusier and various industrialists whom the architect was keen to meet during his sojourn. Among other events, he scheduled a luncheon at the Plaza Hotel where Corbusier was introduced to James A. Rafferty, president of the Carbon and Carbide Chemical Corporation, and to George Davison, one of the directors of Union Carbide.[5]

Shortly afterwards in the same year, responding to Jaoul's request, Le Corbusier drew up a proposal for a family weekend house with independent structure, pilotis, pine-log timber work, and a double sloping roof, all regulated by a standard module (Fig. 38 a, b).[6] This unexecuted project precipitated a series of proposals for dry-assembled house types, elaborated at the outbreak of World War II (1939–40), in collaboration with his cousin Pierre Jeanneret and French designer and engineer Jean Prouvé in the context of the architect's research on rapidly assembled temporary constructions and proposals for engineers' and foremen's housing in Lannemezan in the High-Pyrenees (Fig. 39 a, b), supported by Jaoul.[7] The original Jaoul weekend house proposal can also be traced back to a group of earlier country houses that the architect had designed around organic materials in the spirit of vernacular architecture, such as the unbuilt Maison Errazuris in Chile (1929–30) and the Maison Peyron aux Mathes in the Charente-Maritime region (1935). Embodiments of a Corbusian Eden, these small retreats were conceived as domestic environments for a simplified, rural way of life, reliant on readily available regional materials for their construction.

Le Corbusier remained in contact with Jaoul during the troubled years of Occupation in France. In 1940, the architect installed himself temporarily at Ozon in the Pyrenees[8] and, despite his precarious financial situation, conducted research for Ascoral, subsidized by the Société Ugine.[9] Results of this work were eventually published in 1945 under the title *Les trois établissements humains* (Fig. 40).

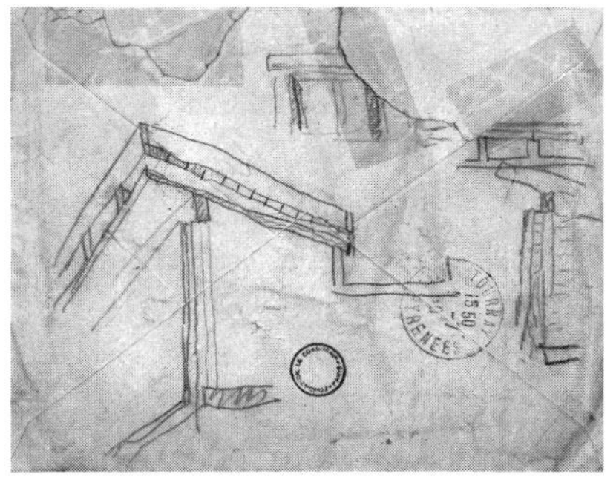

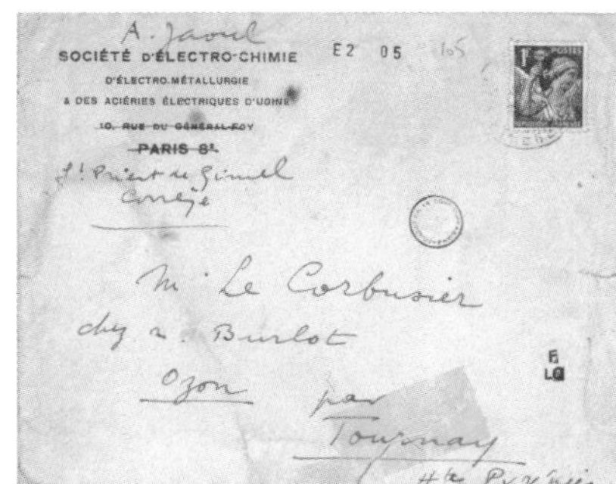

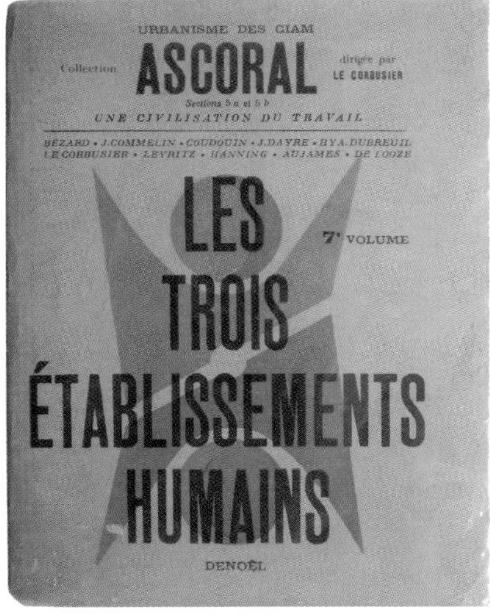

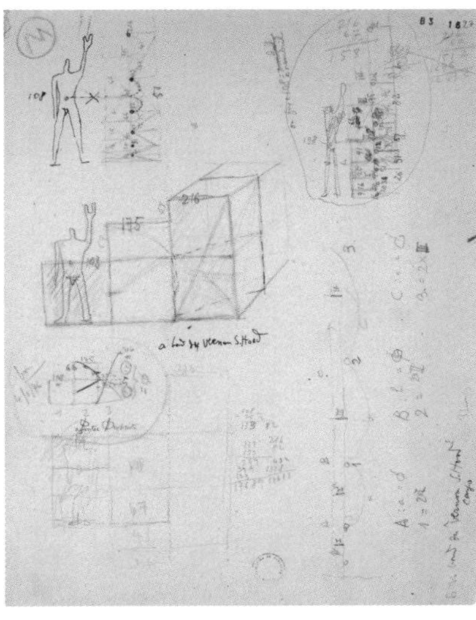

Fig. 39a, b (top)
Letter from André Jaoul to Le Corbusier, July 7, 1940. On the back of the envelope, the architect penciled in several thumbnail construction details of the houses for engineers and foremen in Lannemezan. FLC E2 (5) 105.

Fig. 40 (left)
Front cover of Le Corbusier's book, *Les trois établissements humains* (Three Human Settlements), Denoël, 1945.

Fig. 41 (right)
Le Corbusier, colored pencil sketch study on Modulor dimensions, dated January 4, 1946, executed on board the cargo ship *Vernon S. Hood*. FLC B3 (16) 27.

After the war, the two men met up again in the United States, Jaoul having traveled there to sell his company's metallurgy processes, Le Corbusier to conduct a fierce and frustrating battle to impose his design for the United Nations headquarters and to promote his touring exhibition of paintings, drawings, and sculpture in various galleries and museums. On this occasion, the architect specifically credited Jaoul's role in launching the Modulor in North America (Fig. 41), as a "tool to place on the drawing table alongside a compass."[10]

It appears that a mutual taste for paintings also united the two men, and even implicated the two Jaoul families. Like his father, Michel Jaoul worked in the sales division of techniques and procedures for Ugine and Pechiney (specialists in chemicals, steel, and aluminium), responsible for establishing several factories abroad (notably in India and Australia). In a letter to the author he emphasized his family's interest in contemporary art and Le Corbusier's role in establishing a network of contacts: "Le Corbusier introduced us to René Drouin whose gallery was located in the Place Vendôme during the war, probably the sole person in Paris to exhibit avant-garde painting, specifically by Dubuffet, Wols [and] Singier. Michel Tapié was one of his inspirations, before he became associated with Daniel Cordier. There was also the Galerie Jeanne Bucher where works by the

Fig. 42
A basalt stone, part of Le Corbusier's private collection. FLC.

painter Hans Reichel were shown.... Afterwards we met Pierre Soulages, from whom we bought a painting at his studio in 1950, forming the basis of a friendship. All these people knew one other."[11] Le Corbusier had, in fact, consigned several paintings to René Drouin's gallery from July 1944 onward, but he broke their contract in April 1946 due to a lack of exhibitions organized by the gallery dealer (Fig. 42).[12]

René Drouin's role in recognizing and exhibiting artists such as Jean Dubuffet, Jean Fautrier, and Wols was altogether remarkable.[13] Drouin had originally been trained as an architect and furniture designer before opening his gallery in collaboration with Leo Castelli in the late 1930s.[14] In 1941, when Castelli left France for the United States, the astute Drouin remained in Paris, pursuing his role as gallery owner, while instinctively following his friends' advice and his own passions. The author Jean Paulhan introduced him to Dubuffet's studio in 1944; the poet H. P. Roché initiated him into Wols's work. Such connections led Drouin to sponsor Dubuffet's first exhibition in October 1944.

Two years later, Dubuffet again showed at the Drouin gallery. In the accompanying catalogue entitled *Mirobolus, Macadam et Cie: Hautes Pâtes de J. Dubuffet* (Fig. 43), the artist comments on the extreme poverty and disparate nature of his materials: "... true that lines are not executed with care or attention to detail, but to the contrary give an impression of negligence, which at first glance can be disconcerting, because the means employed appear to go entirely beyond conventional norms. One sees straightaway that in some places I have worked with my finger, in other places with a spoon or the tip of a scraper."[15] In reference to this period, Max Loreau emphasizes in his 1966 catalogue that Jean Dubuffet took even greater pleasure in accentuating the "processes of execution to endorse the conceptual character of the figurative objects, resorting to the most cursory, abbre-

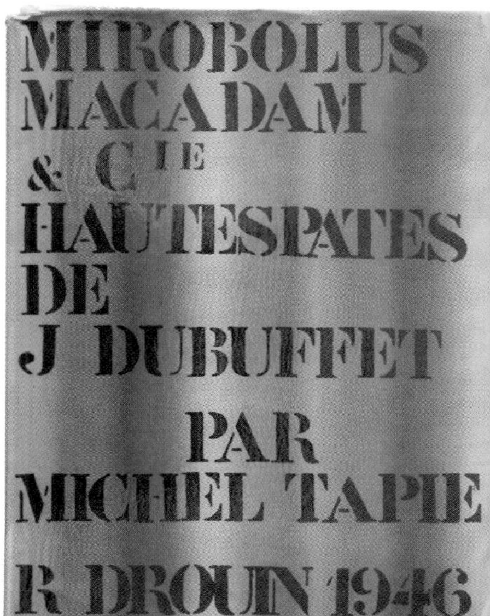

Fig. 43
Michel Tapié, *Mirobolus Macadam & Cie. Hautes Pâtes de J. Dubuffet* (Fantastic Macadam & Co.: Thick Paste Works of J. Dubuffet), Galerie R. Drouin, 1946. M. and N. Jaoul archives.

Fig. 44
Jean Dubuffet, *Sauteuse de corde* (Girl Skipping Rope), oil on canvas, dated February 1943. Dubuffet offered this painting to Le Corbusier as a gift. Private collection.

viated means, using crude lines and coarse surfaces in shrill, juxtaposed and contrasting colors that seem altogether gauche and clumsy."[16]

Even if critical and public reactions to Dubuffet's work were largely negative—some students even slashed two of his canvases—discerning viewers were quick to perceive the originality of his work, comparing it to current literary sensibilities, in particular Existentialist literature. It was in this light that certain poets and authors, including Francis Ponge, Paul Éluard, Eugène Guillevic, Jean Paulhan, Georges Limbour, and Michel Tapié, had already begun to comment on his work by 1947.[17]

Le Corbusier, too, very closely identified with this artistic and literary sensibility. He was probably well aware of Dubuffet's work by the mid-1920s when both men had been in the company of the Swiss writer-editor (1883–1949).[18] Whatever the exact circumstances of this encounter, by 1943 their relationship was firmly established during the architect's visit to Dubuffet's studio on the rue Lhomond in Paris, accompanied by Jean Budry, Paul's brother. On that occasion Le Corbusier had been highly attracted to a painting called *Girl Skipping Rope*[19] (Fig. 44) and expressed an interest in purchasing it. Instead, Dubuffet counteracted by offering it as a gift:

> It struck me as indecent to make a business out of this. My pleasure was in giving paintings to those who appreciated them. I felt that distributing them freely was the only healthy [thing to do] and also the only way to remain unfettered.[20]

Soon after, Le Corbusier invited Dubuffet for Sunday lunch at his apartment on the rue Nungesser-et-Coli in the 16th arrondissement of Paris. Dubuffet later mailed the following note:

I want to thank you again for our enchanting Sunday; my thoughts constantly fly up to the heights of Paris where everything is so unusual and so very attractive; now the world has two levels for me: the bottom where I am, where I rush about all over the place on my bicycle, and the top, on another plane, all in glass, wind, whiteness, garden and terraces, from where I return, altogether refreshed and regenerated. There, up above, everything is in the process of change![21]

In July 1945, invited by Paul Budry, Dubuffet departed for two weeks to Switzerland, accompanied by Jean Paulhan and Le Corbusier, where they visited Geneva, Lausanne, and Saint Moritz. During this sojourn, in pursuit of his growing interest in a form of artistic expression that he already qualified "art brut," Dubuffet visited several psychiatric hospitals to collect drawings of interned patients.[22] Discussions between artist and architect on the subject of this "art of the insane" must have been fascinating because, from 1927, Le Corbusier had also become extremely aware of and personally implicated in the importance of this type of art. His first cousin, Louis Soutter, who had spent many years in an insane asylum (he died in 1942),[23] was himself an Art Brut painter. In 1936, Le Corbusier dedicated an article to his work in the review *Le Minotaure*, which served as the impetus for his first exhibition in the United States at the Wadsworth Atheneum Museum of Art in Hartford, Connecticut.[24]

Fig. 45
Jean Dubuffet, *Mur à l'oiseau* (Wall with Bird), plate II, black-ink lithograph, dated March 17, 1945. Dubuffet was a regular in the studio of Fernand Mourlot who produced fifteen lithographs for Guillevic's book *Les Murs* (The Walls), published in 1950. Le Corbusier also relied on Mourlot to produce his prints and lithographs.

On the occasion of two lithographic exhibitions called Matière et mémoire (Material and Memory) and Les Murs (The Walls) (Fig. 45) organized by Michel Tapié at the Galerie André in 1945, Dubuffet wrote: "[I]nvention, new imagery, is born directly out of the material."[25] In his *Notes pour les fins-lettrés* (*Notes to the scholarly*) of 1946, the artist speaks of material as the message or medium through which a painter expresses himself. No longer the artist's interest to make "beautiful painting," he argues instead that:

The essential gesture of a painter is to smear. Not to smooth in with a tiny feather or strand of hair [and] some tinted water, but to plunge his hands into buckets or basins full of clays and paints and, with his palms and fingers, to fill the wall space in front of him. With naked hands or assisted by the most rudimentary available instruments as good conductors—whatever blade might be lying around or stub of a stick or stone shard—that neither interrupt nor weaken the wavelengths, to knead body to body, there to imprint the most immediate traces that he may have of his thoughts and rhythms and impulses coursing through his arteries and running along the length of his nerve endings.[26]

Art Historian Sarah Wilson suggests a connection between the artist's reflections on materials and methods and those of Gaston Bachelard on clay in *L'Eau et les rêves: essai sur l'imagination de la matière*, published in

Fig. 46
Front cover, Pierre Seghers, *L'Homme du commun ou Jean Dubuffet* (The Common Man or Jean Dubuffet), Paris, Éditions Poésie 44, 1944. M. and N. Jaoul archives.

1942, without overlooking the possible impact of Maurice Merleau-Ponty's *Phénoménologie de la perception*, published in 1945.[27] These authors all searched for authentic experiences, real and tactile, as though to purge the anguish accumulated during the wars. The materiality of the work to which Dubuffet lays claim reveals a discourse that characterizes an era, from literature to philosophy.[28] Sartre's Existentialism had impregnated both the artistic milieu and the architectural avant-garde, in France as well as in England.[29]

Having spoken enthusiastically about Dubuffet's work, Le Corbusier invited André Jaoul to visit his atelier (first located in the rue Lhomond and later in the rue de Vaugirard). There, between 1946 and 1950, the Jaouls encountered Dubuffet's friends and fellow painters. Works acquired, either as purchases or gifts during the course of these years, already formed an ensemble of pictures that were eventually to hang on the walls of their new houses (Figs. 46–48; 52–54). It is clear that the dialogue between Le Corbusier and the Jaouls was facilitated by a mutual sensitivity toward an artistic gesture allied to the authentic texture of materials, a prevalent trait among the painters and sculptors shown at the Galerie René Drouin. The evocation of this intellectual landscape provides the fundamental basis to capture those critical exchanges occurring during the 1950s, across artistic as well as architectural worlds.

Le Corbusier's postwar artistic output reflects this atmosphere. Already by the late 1920s, he had started to assemble a personal collection of shells and found objects.[30] During the 1940s, he increasingly committed himself more profoundly to exploring the material substance of objects, which, by 1946, had led to his carving a series of sculptures in

Fig. 47 (top)
Jean Dubuffet, *Bord de mer* (By the Sea), gouache, c. 1946. M. and N. Jaoul collection.

Fig. 48 (middle)
Jean Dubuffet, *Essayeuse de chapeau* (Woman Trying on a Hat), oil on canvas, 1943. Private collection.

Fig. 49 (bottom left)
"Reconstruction France 1950," *L'Architecture d'aujourd'hui* (Architecture Today), n° 32, October–November 1950. This issue covers various reconstruction projects in Le Havre, Amiens, Dunkerque, and Maubeuge.

Fig. 50 (bottom middle)
"Habitations individuelles," *L'Architecture d'aujourd'hui* (Architecture Today), N°44, September 1952. The journal offers a panorama of French and international constructions, the United States being represented by the work of Richard Neutra and Marcel Breuer, among others, highly appreciated if judged by the choice of images for the cover and the three selected houses.

Fig. 51 (bottom right)
"Contribution française à l'évolution de l'architecture," *L'Architecture d'aujourd'hui* (Architecture Today), n° 46, February–March 1953, in which an article is devoted to the Unité d'Habitation in Marseilles.

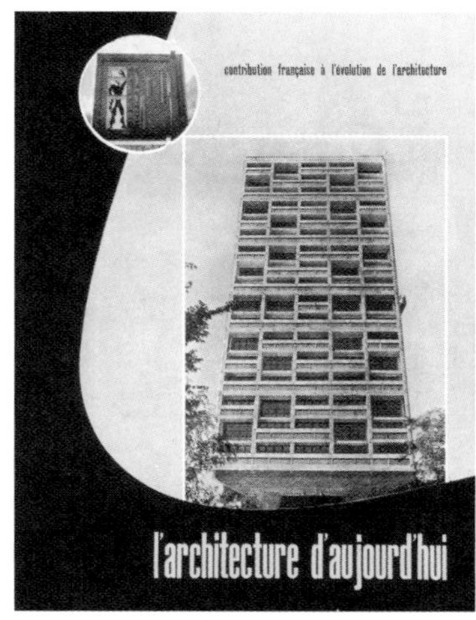

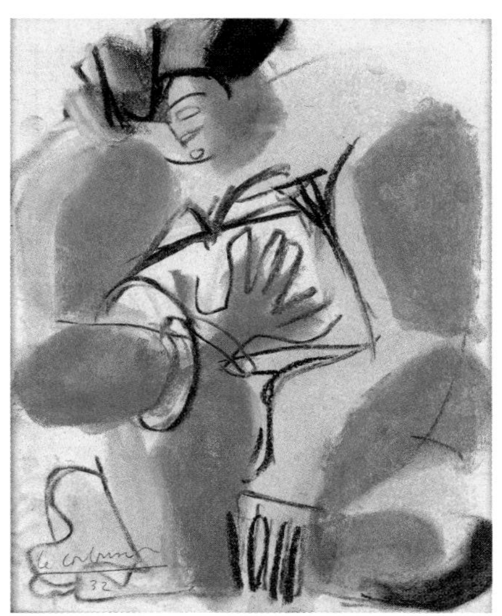

Fig. 52 (top)
Le Corbusier, *Couple à l'apéritif* (Couple with Aperitifs), oil pastel and ink, 1938. Le Corbusier offered this drawing to Michel and Nadine Jaoul as a marriage gift on February 25, 1943. M. and N. Jaoul collection.

Fig. 53 (left)
Le Corbusier, *Femme lisant* (Woman Reading), pastel, 1932. M. and N. Jaoul collection.

Fig. 54 (right)
Le Corbusier, *Repasseuse* (Woman Ironing), gouache and ink, 1938. M. and N. Jaoul collection.

Fig. 55
Michel and Nadine Jaoul and an Indian friend, Suman Benegal, near a low vault in Chandigarh, c. 1960. During one of their trips to India, they were startled to come across a vault similar to those in their Neuilly house.

collaboration with Joseph Savina. Shortly thereafter, he executed an ensemble of sand-cast plaster sculptures on the beaches of Long Island, New York, with his Sardinian friend, the sculptor Nivola. These developments induced him to reconsider the rough tactility of his buildings, notably the Unité d'Habitation in Marseilles. From that moment, sculpture and art were to enter, literally, into his architecture.[31] Elsewhere the integration of the plastic arts into his architecture formed the subject of a proposed exhibition at the Porte Maillot in Paris (1950), for which the architect adopted the title *Synthèse des arts*.[32] Christopher Pearson emphasizes that Le Corbusier was not the sole architect interested in this issue. Proceedings from the CIAM VI congress in Bridgewater (1947) and those from CIAM VII in Bergamo, Italy (1949) confirm that the concept of the integration of the arts and architecture had become a major preoccupation of numerous architects, a subject widely discussed in the professional press, notably by André Bloc, editor of *L'Architecture d'aujourd'hui* (Figs. 49–51).[33]

This orientation had repercussions on Le Corbusier's new commission in Neuilly where the Jaoul families had lived since 1931 at 26, rue Parmentier. The neighborhood attracted an artistic crowd, valued by the Jaouls. Michel Jaoul thus describes the personal relationships established in the quarter:

> My father often traveled to Germany on business for Ugine. There he had a friend who was a great art lover. Through him he made the acquaintance of Jean Crotti,[34] the Swiss painter who lived in Neuilly and had married Suzanne Duchamp (sister of Marcel Duchamp), herself a painter and friend of Raoul Dufy. The Crottis were not only our friends, but also our neighbors. The immediate circle of painters and devotees of art in the Crottis

circle grew rapidly to take in a number of foreign artists (English, American, Polish, German refugees). Doctor Fraenkel, who treated many artists in the Surrealist circle, was our family physician.[35]

Le Corbusier too was well acquainted with the Neuilly scene, having designed four projects for the Meyer family during the years 1924 and 1925, on a site situated close to the local Parc Saint-James.[36]

Two houses and their vaults

When the Jaouls purchased a plot on the rue de Longchamp, their objective was to resolve the immediate housing problem facing Michel Jaoul and his family from 1946 onward. As their situation was urgent, they were ready to accept "a provisional wood construction similar to a self-built Austrian chalet."[37] Having assumed that Le Corbusier was far too engrossed in his worldwide projects to take an interest in this simple domestic program, they originally contacted the English architect Clive Entwistle. In point of fact, Le Corbusier was indeed preoccupied with a number of ongoing undertakings at that moment:[38] the Unité d'Habitation in Marseilles (1945–52) and the Indian projects in Ahmedabad and Chandigarh where, in collaboration with Pierre Jeanneret, Maxwell Fry, and Jane Drew, he had accepted to direct a team to design the capital of the Punjab (a city of 500,000 inhabitants) and to execute the main urban infrastructures. For this project, Le Corbusier had committed himself to spend one month in India twice a year, which amounted to a total of twenty-three visits from 1951 through 1964. In 1950, Le Corbusier also took on the urban design proposals for Bogotá, the capital city of Colombia.[39] The year 1951 was equally consecrated to the detailed elaboration of his illustrated manuscript called *Le Poème de l'angle droit*, (The Poem of the Right Angle) ultimately published in 1955.[40]

It was through Le Corbusier as intermediary that the Jaouls first encountered Clive Entwistle. Michel Jaoul stayed at his house in London during 1945.[41] Correspondence in the Fondation Le Corbusier archives clarifies the relationship between Entwistle and the Paris architect in the late 1930s when the Englishman had initiated the idea of a collaboration.[42] In 1947–48, Entwistle translated Le Corbusier's *Propos d'urbanisme* under the title *Concerning Town Planning*.[43] During June 1951, in response to André Jaoul's request, Entwistle drew up a proposal for a residential building to accommodate his two families.[44] The scheme involved the arrangement of lodgings on two superimposed levels, united to form one small block (designated "R+3"), set back from the rue de Longchamp (Figs. 56 and 57). His proposal combined familiar Corbusian motifs and a rational modular system, a rather widespread phenomenon in works by contemporary British architects.

Entwistle submitted his proposal in June 1951. But it seems that Le Corbusier's voyage to New York, coinciding with André Jaoul's own trip, put an end to this project, as did subsequent meetings there on May 29 and

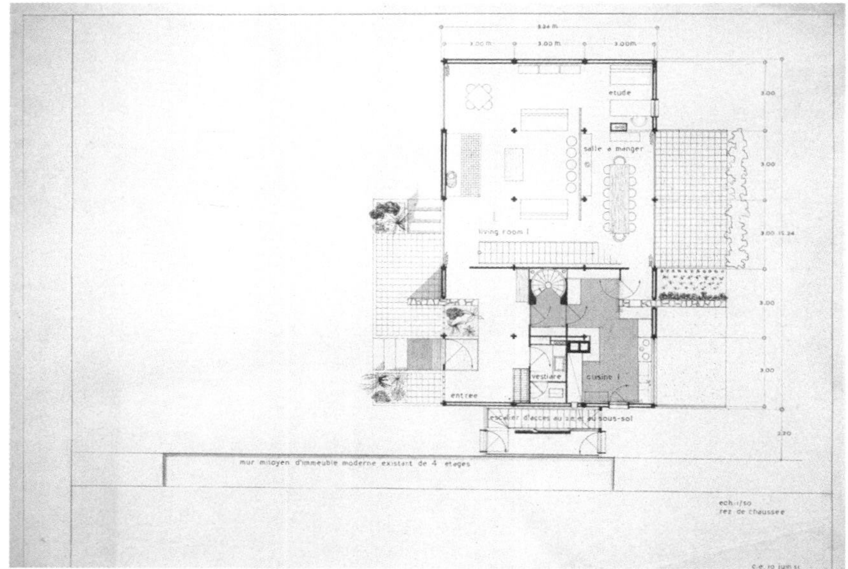

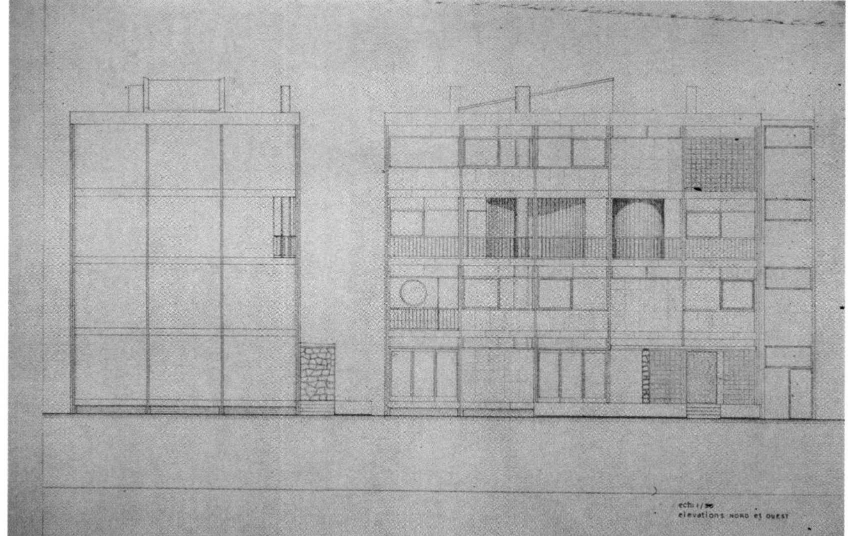

Fig. 56
Ground-floor plan, June 8, 1951. FLC 10077.

Fig. 57
West elevation, June 28, 1951. FLC 10044.

June 5, 1951.[45] During these trips, in conversation with Le Corbusier, Jaoul had broached the subject of his purchase of the Neuilly site and his intention to build, requesting that he examine the Englishman's plans. On June 27, Le Corbusier again met with Jaoul in Paris, taking advantage of the occasion to criticize his colleague's proposal to unify the two dwellings within a single three-story building: "For this price, you could make two houses out of it! And you could have some vaults [as well]!"[46] Three days later, on a Saturday afternoon, Le Corbusier paid a visit to the rue de Longchamp site.[47]

"And you could have some vaults!" he had proclaimed. The vaults in this case implied a symbolic space connoting the image of the first human habitation within a rocky crevice, the very essence of a shelter (Figs. 58, 59, 61). As for the economic strategy, "two houses for the price of one," such

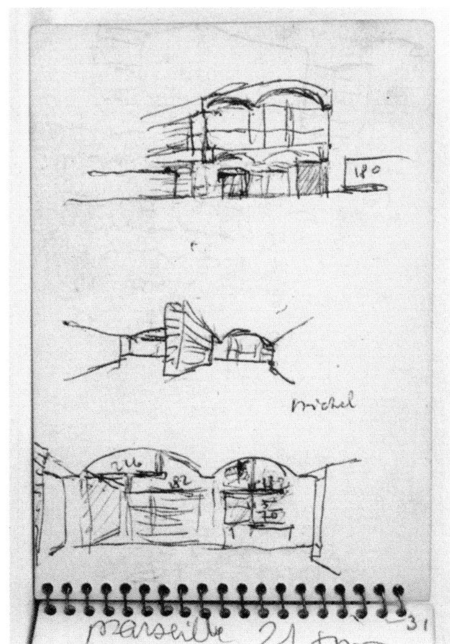

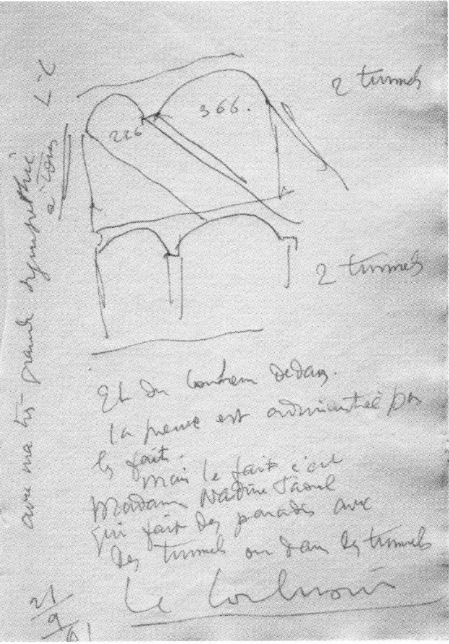

Fig. 58
Le Corbusier, *Sketchbooks*, vol. 2, 1950–1954, Sketchbook E22, sheet 576, February–March 1952.

Fig. 59
Le Corbusier's dedication evoking "the tunnels," written in the Maisons Jaoul guest book, dated September 21, 1961. M. and N. Jaoul archives.

Fig. 60
The railway freight car might also have served as a source of inspiration for the longitudinal arched module in the Maisons Jaoul.

was, by now, a familiar tactic that Le Corbusier habitually used with his clients in his arguments over size. It reiterates a letter [see Appendix] that he had sent earlier to Professor Fueter on March 17, 1950, also proposing vaults and brick walls while simultaneously arguing for a reduction of 20 percent on expenses:

> "...those damned Swiss irritate me with their exaggerated notions of architectural finish. You are an intelligent person and so am I. We're not bourgeois; we appreciate the rough texture of exposed brick, joints coarsely mortared by the mason, whitewash laid over the brickwork, etc. I'm convinced that your house will be much better in its rude state, and you'll economize at least 20 percent on expenses, well worth your while.[48]

Corbusian references typically derive from a wide range of eclectic sources. In this case, the low, barrel-arch profile of railroad freight cars (Fig. 60), the Pullman or sleeping cars and couchettes with buffet cars serving numbers of travelers—all of which struck Le Corbusier as successful designs adapting minimal spaces to accommodate maximum overlapping activities—might possibly have served as inspirational models, along with the multifunctions of the Train Bleu. Fascinated by this luxury train, in 1929 the architect had asked the young Catalan architect Domènec Escorsa (who had once worked for him) to prepare some measured drawings of its sleeping car and restaurant carriage.[49]

For the Jaoul families, therefore, he straightaway proposed a new design of two *unités d'habitation* or juxtaposed dwelling units under one shared vault, represented as a strange and enhancing characteristic, the leitmotiv of the composition. Predictably, his double-house scheme contrasted radically with Entwistle's rectilinear unitary design proposal.

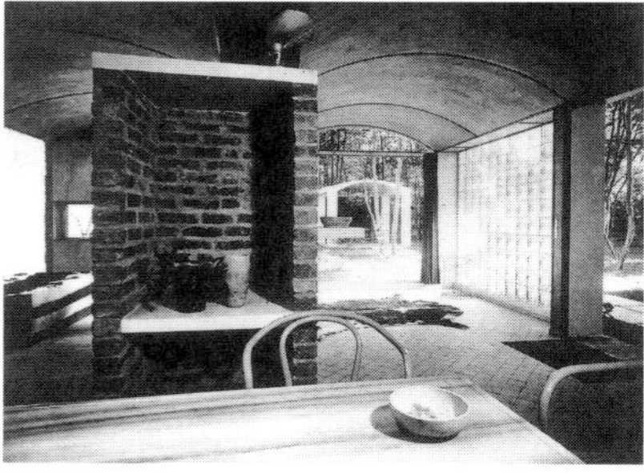

Fig. 61
The vault and the rubble-stone party wall of Le Corbusier's atelier (1931–1934), rue Nungesser-et-Coli, Boulogne-sur-Seine.

Fig. 62
Le Corbusier, *Ma Maison* (My House) atelier and dwelling. In this 1929 sketch, the habitable section is treated in a Purist style, while in the studio, the vault symbolizes a creative space. FLC 33413.

Fig. 63
Interior of the Petite Maison de Week-end (Little Weekend House), La Celle-Saint-Cloud, 1935.

What value did Le Corbusier attach to the vault? His interest in vaulted structures (notably the Catalan vault) as a design solution for covering a span, and his use of the lowered vault employing traditional materials (like exposed brick) recall some of the diverse aspects of his architectural culture. In fact, as Stanislaus von Moos carefully points out, the vault encompasses two of Le Corbusier's dominant themes. On the one hand, he admired the industrial vault: the Hennebique or Freyssinet shed-type, the Auguste Perret thin concrete shell (used on the Casablanca docklands, familiar to the young Charles-Édouard Jeanneret) and the Monol-type (for which the young Jeanneret-Le Corbusier had applied for a patent in 1919).[50] On the other hand, he was fascinated by the warmth of the welcoming arch, a receptacle of light, like those he designed for his atelier on the rue Nungesser-et-Coli (1931–34), (Fig. 61) and the Petite Maison de Week-end (or Villa Félix) at La Celle-Saint-Cloud (1935), (Figs. 63 and 64). Considered as an ensemble, these vaults symbolize the artist's atelier (Fig. 62).[51] Among these diverse vault types, Le Corbusier also classified other categories, distinguishing those that provide or bring in light (the shed vault) from those that demarcate a space (for example, the "nave" of the Weekend house). All these aforementioned projects, like the Maisons Jaoul, made the

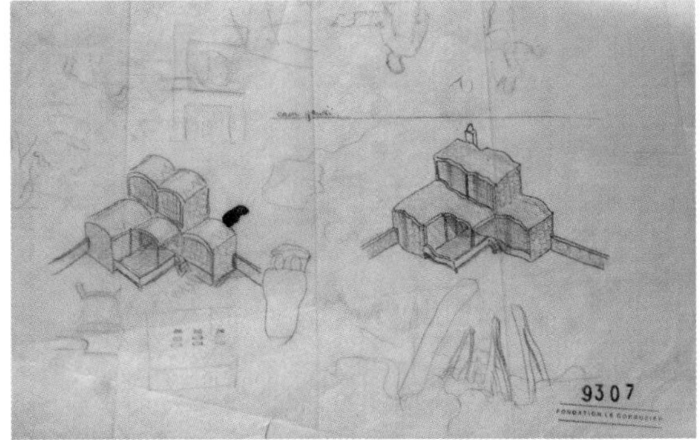

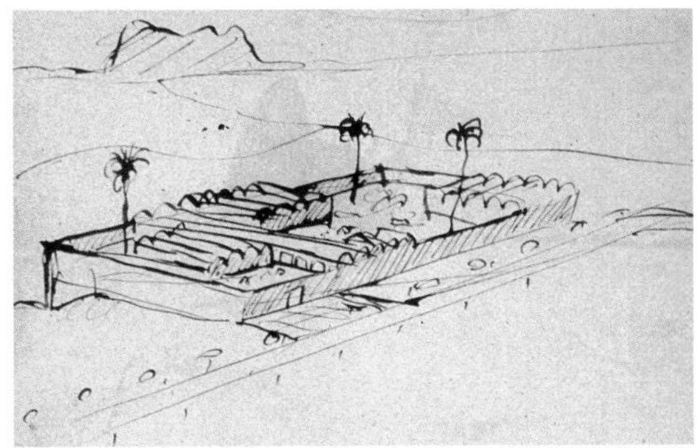

architecture of this "cell-unit which has many applications" more precise, refined, and complex, as the architect explained in relation to his "Roq et Rob" projects at Cap-Martin in 1949.[52]

If, in the 1920s, the 16.4-foot span bay with "*planchers éclairés* (illuminated floors)" and the *fenêtre en longueur* had become fixed elements in his vocabulary, after the Second World War, Le Corbusier had gradually given more importance to the vaulted bay and specific perforated openings to illuminate and ventilate each room. The vault imposed itself as the ubiquitous module for every house type, "from peasant to upper-middle class."[53] To the architect it symbolized the foyer, the central hearth, a notion of well-being, improving upon the deficiencies of his 1920s *machine à habiter*. For his Mediterranean projects—Maison Cherchell in North Africa, 1940 (Figs. 65-67) and the "Roq et Rob" vacation complex on the Côte d'Azur (1948–50), (Fig. 68)—the vault appeared as a "natural" element, complementing the landscape and incorporating the cellular unit at a human scale. For the Maisons Jaoul, Le Corbusier also saw this solution as a biographical reference to his client André Jaoul, who originated from the remote and mountainous region of the Cévennes. This fact was sufficient to justify the use of Catalan vaults as a signifier of his identity conveyed through a primitive architectural language. In the architect's mind, despite the fact that Jaoul was a great industrialist, he also represented the image of a peasant who constructed his own homestead. Le Corbusier's "*recherche patiente*" led him to explore the vault both as a form and as a metaphor of a habitus.[54]

Fig. 64 (top left)
The vault and the space: Petite Maison de Week-end (Little Weekend House), La Celle-Saint-Cloud, 1935. FLC 9307.

Fig. 65 (top right)
Proposal for the Peyrissac agricultural domain, Cherchell, 1940. FLC 29995C.

Fig. 66 (bottom left)
Elevation of the cross-walls for the agricultural domain at Cherchell, 1940, *Oeuvre Complète*, vol. 4, 1938–1946, 122.

Fig. 67 (bottom right)
Proposed vaults to be used as roofs for the Peyrissac agricultural domain, Cherchell, 1940. FLC 29994D.

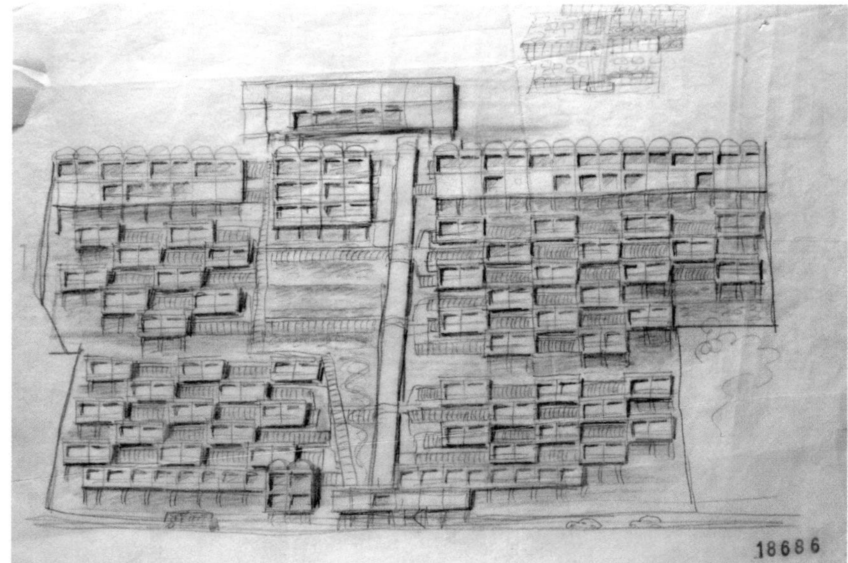

Fig. 68
Study sketch and elevation for the "Roq" project, c. 1949. FLC 18686. The atelier assistants R. Salmona and G. Samper, both Colombians, were responsible for the preliminary study, along with one for the Maisons Jaoul.

The site and its restrictions

Nevertheless, the initial task was a delicate one, provoking overt complaints from Le Corbusier: "The regulations concerning the site were contradictory, the programme was complicated, and the budget was unavoidably limited by the outrageous cost of private building."[55]

Established in 1951, the official Neuilly-sur-Seine town plan controlled all new construction in the district. The rue de Longchamp neighborhood came under regulations pertaining to Sector HR1 (Residential Dwellings 1) that limited houses and apartment blocks to a ground floor surmounted by three stories ("R+3," allowing a height below or equal to 39 feet) and by a land use coefficient of 1.30.

Regulations for the placement of new constructions stipulated that they be set back at least 13 feet from the street, with the building footprint not exceeding 32 percent of the land surface. Constructions at the limit of the setback were not permitted unless they abutted structurally sound existing walls on the adjacent property. If the construction was set back, this margin had to be equal to the height of the building, provided that the facade here made up the principal views, or one-sixth the width of the plot if this facade included secondary bays. The distance between the building and the rear property line had to be equal to the height of the building divided by two. However, if this margin could not be respected, an agreement on a common court could be established between neighboring property owners.[56]

Very soon after studying Entwistle's plans, Le Corbusier paid a visit to the Jaoul site. He made a few sketches and roughed out his preliminary architectural concepts. Sheets in his sketchbook contain annotations on sun angles that dictated the configuration of future plans and sections. Le Corbusier analyzed the site, its exposure and orientation, and the control of

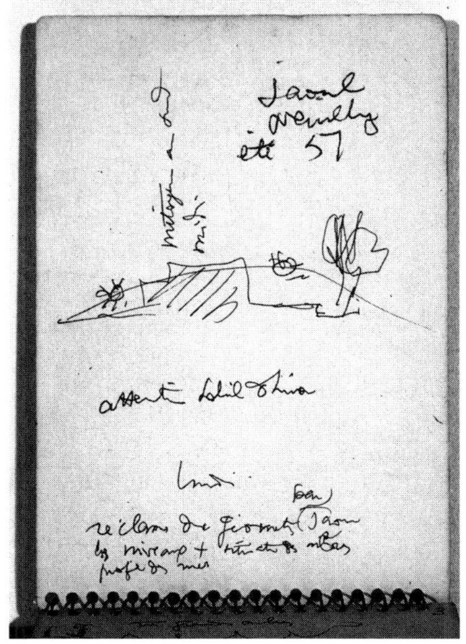

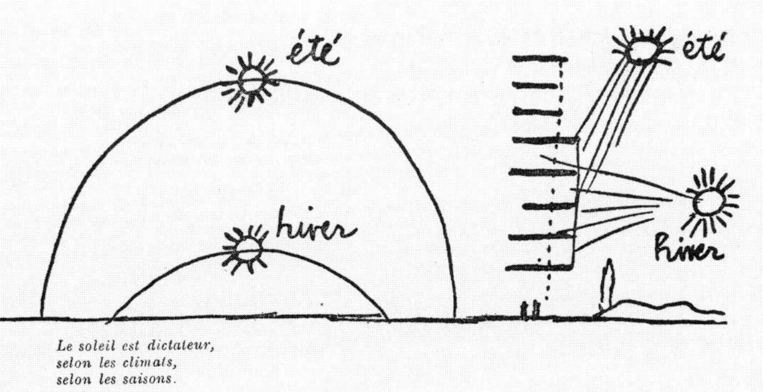

the light, before he developed an elevation.[57] He began by evaluating the surface area of the lot (3,280.84 square feet), oriented longitudinally northwest/southeast. The site measured 150.43 feet by 70.25 feet at its upper portion and 156 feet by 70.24 feet at its lower end (Le Corbusier rounded it off to 72 feet). The geometric configuration intrigued the architect as it closely approximated to a perfect double square. To the south, the site was closed off by Worth House, a four-story brick building in a composite 1930s style, set back 24.6 feet from the street. To the north lay an open lot, to the south the demarcation of the rue de Longchamp, and to the east a neighboring garden.

Fig. 69
Le Corbusier, first sketch of the site labeled "été 51 (summer 51)," Sketchbook E22, sheet 549, from F. de Franclieu, ed., *Le Corbusier. Sketchbooks vol. 2, 1950–1954.*

Fig. 70
Le Corbusier, research on the *brise-soleil* (sunbreaker).

To execute his first sketch, labeled "summer 51" (Fig. 69), the architect oriented himself to the southwest and outlined a profile of the neighboring wall. He traced the course of the sun during the summer months, east to west, illuminating the whole property. However, as he noted, when the sun's curve was at its lowest during the winter months, the south party wall would act as a screen casting a shadow across the Jaoul property. Le Corbusier had discussed the concept of the sun's trajectory as a design strategy during countless lectures, as an act of faith in the sun (Fig. 70). In asking the land surveyor for precise measurements of the ground levels, the implantation of the trees and the profile of the streets, he seemed to be searching, right from his earliest sketches, for the exact footprint of the volumes exposed to the greatest amount of sunlight.

On a rough plan oriented to the southeast, in the middle of sheet 550 (Fig. 71), Le Corbusier outlined the rectangular lot, noting its dimensions, natural slope and cardinal points, along with rough elevations of the heights of neighboring trees and shadows cast on the terrain. In the northwest sector, he recorded several inconveniences: "shade (quite dark hole)" and "noises from the street." He envisaged a vertical screen isolating the

Fig. 71
Le Corbusier's sketch showing the rectangular site, with indications on its dimensions, natural slope, and cardinal points. Sketchbook E22, sheet 550.

Fig. 72
Plan sketch showing various locations for the house volumes. Le Corbusier, Sketchbook E22, sheet 551.

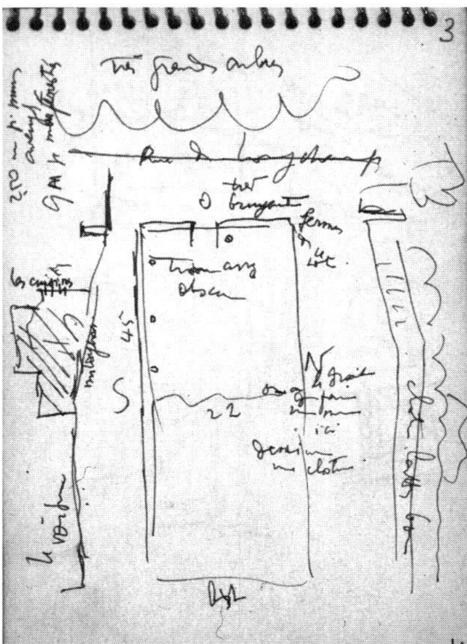

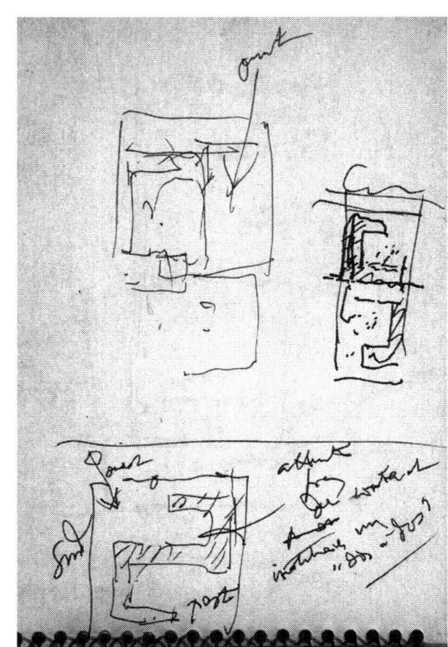

parcel from the street and a wooden lattice fence at the north edge of the property. He recalled the administrative constraints regarding the setback zones and party walls: a margin of 8.2 feet for the construction of a blind wall and a margin of 29.52 feet for a wall with window openings. The remarkable effort he put into the elaboration of this early sketch clearly shows his concentration on sunlight factors in order to maximize their effects on the initial design.

On sheet 551 (Fig. 72), Le Corbusier executed three thumbnail plan studies of the disposition of volumes. He sketched in possible responses to problems of natural light exposure and the differentiation between two separate family units. After having conceived two concave forms, one facing north, the other south (an unworkable solution in terms of light exposure), he tried an alternative version by reversing the options. This time around, one of the houses captured sun from the east, while the other from the west. He continued to investigate possible responses to the linked investigation as to how to associate the two residences while situating them in such a way that they would both profit simultaneously from a satisfactory exposure to the sun. The architect probably assumed that this double configuration directly responded to the client's demand, a universe for two generations of families. Even if this precise configuration was not explored further, nevertheless from this point onward, the layout of the two houses in the form of a right angle had already been evoked as a design possibility.

The longitudinal sketch on sheet 552 (Fig. 73) shows his intention to implant the house on the highest point of the terrain, facing onto the street. It indicates a hollow space, under the proposed cantilevered volume, to bury the cars. This solution responded to his ofttimes-repeated formula: "The aspect of the sun dominated the lay-out of the plans and sections."[58] The strategy employed here to raise the body of the building was also a

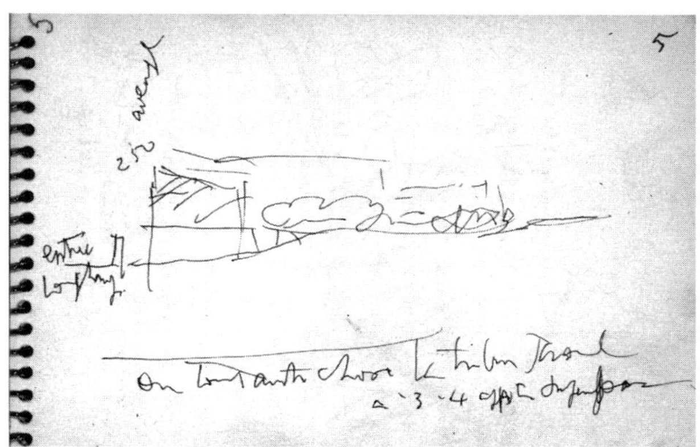

familiar Corbusian idiom. He had already experimented with the same idea for the artisan-sculptor Antonin Planeix's house-cum-studio (1924–28) on the Boulevard Masséna in Paris. There, right from the very earliest concept sketches, he had proposed a construction raised up on four pilotis, a design that freed up the ground floor as an open area for a garage and a few storerooms.[59] This solution removed the Maison Planeix from the humid ground plane, resolved the car problem, and increased the opportunities for good natural light. On this Jaoul sheet, Le Corbusier added the following remark: "Or something quite different for the Jaoul clan. 3–4 superimposed apartments." The following sheet 553 (Fig. 74) effectively summarizes natural light exposures.

Fig. 73
"Or something quite different for the Jaoul clan. 3-4 superimposed apartments." Le Corbusier, Sketchbook E22, sheet 552.

Fig. 74
The direction of the sun, Le Corbusier, Sketchbook E22, sheet 553. "Plan for an enclosure wall here to the east = shaded in the/ morning/reflecting sun in the afternoon."

In conclusion, what emerged out of Le Corbusier's first site visit were four central lines of inquiry that came to dominate the design process: the disposition of two closely interconnected volumes; the alignment of four parallel bays along the same northwest/southeast axis, giving an "a/b/b/a" rhythm to the plan according to a proportional scheme; close attention to sun exposure; and the advantageous use of the natural slope of the terrain. At this point, it is possible to speculate that the parallel bays had already been conceived as vaulted or arched elements, even though not a single elevation precisely indicating this feature exists from this initial phase. In retaining these central concerns throughout all the phases of the composition, Le Corbusier demonstrates his attachment to the principles of the technical aesthetic of the Modern movement. He maximizes the nonconstructed area on the site as well as the penetration of natural light within the houses. In playing with the double form, he also reveals his attachment to the issues of intimacy and privacy. Here, from the earliest sketches, is the affirmation of the strength of the proposal, which relies on an a priori synthesis of the orientation of volumes. Subsequent slow elaborations disclose a myriad of tiny adjustments required before he arrived at the ultimate satisfactory design configuration.

In search of technical solutions

Later sheets in the same sketchbook contain numerous annotations concerning the Unité d'Habitation construction site at Marseilles, the Modulor, site planning at Sainte-Baume, the 226 x 226 cellular unit, and the Cabanon at Cap-Martin. Evidence suggests that Le Corbusier had kept this pocket sketchbook with him during summer visits to Cap-Martin because numerous recognizably repetitive motifs crop up in these diverse contemporary projects, such as his characteristic attention to site, research on the Modulor, and observations on window details and shapes.

Throughout the early 1950s, Le Corbusier traveled extensively, predominantly in India where in 1951 he remained throughout February, March, April, and November; in 1952 throughout March, April, and November; and in 1953 during May and June. He also visited Colombia in February and September 1950, as well as in May 1951. Captivated by the unique environments of these countries, the architect attentively jotted down observations in his sketchbooks, such as characteristics of the design of wood panels and natural ventilation systems. Such observations would eventually inform his rue de Longchamp design.

The first drafted plans issued from the rue de Sèvres atelier from July 25 through October 1951 defined the design proposal: a juxtaposition of long naves covered by low vaults, deep dwellings delineated by parallel brick walls, with proportions regulated by the Modulor (that is, two bays with, respectively, 7.4- (2.26 m) and 12-foot (3.66 m) spans). Such features provided the basis of the spatial elaborations to which Le Corbusier remained faithful to the end. The Jaoul file contains some five hundred drawings (sketches, plans at various scales, sections, details), witness to the slow and deliberate evolution of the project up to its final execution.

Le Corbusier already had a firm idea of his precise intentions for the built form. During his journey to Bogotá in September 1950, he had observed some Catalan vaults at the home of the architect Francisco Pizano de Brigard, noting down technical details on the system of construction.[60] His pocket notebook from July 1951 also contains precious information on these low vaults constructed without coffering[61] (Figs. 75 and 76). This time he obtained information from his Catalan architect friends José Luis Sert and Domènec Escorsa, whom he encountered on July 9, 1951, in Hoddesdon, England, during the CIAM VIII conference.[62] In his sketchbook, Le Corbusier drew a section of a Catalan vault composed of three layers of bricks,[63] recording the dimensions of the plaster-jointed brick member (11.41 x 5.51 x 0.59 inches) and indicating the construction detail that consisted in displacing, at each level, the arch center that held up the bricks and the necessity of inserting some iron tie-rods (Fig. 77). His friends also pointed out to him that non-mortared or dry bricks could also be laid down either lengthwise or in

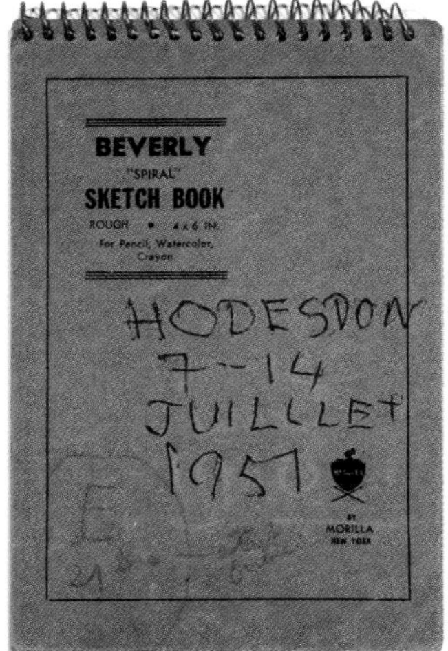

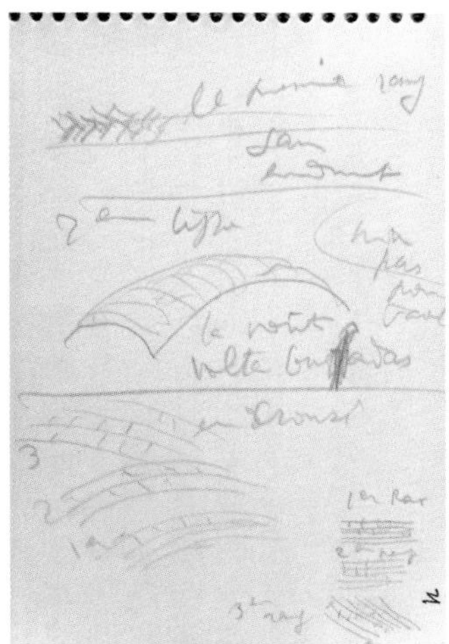

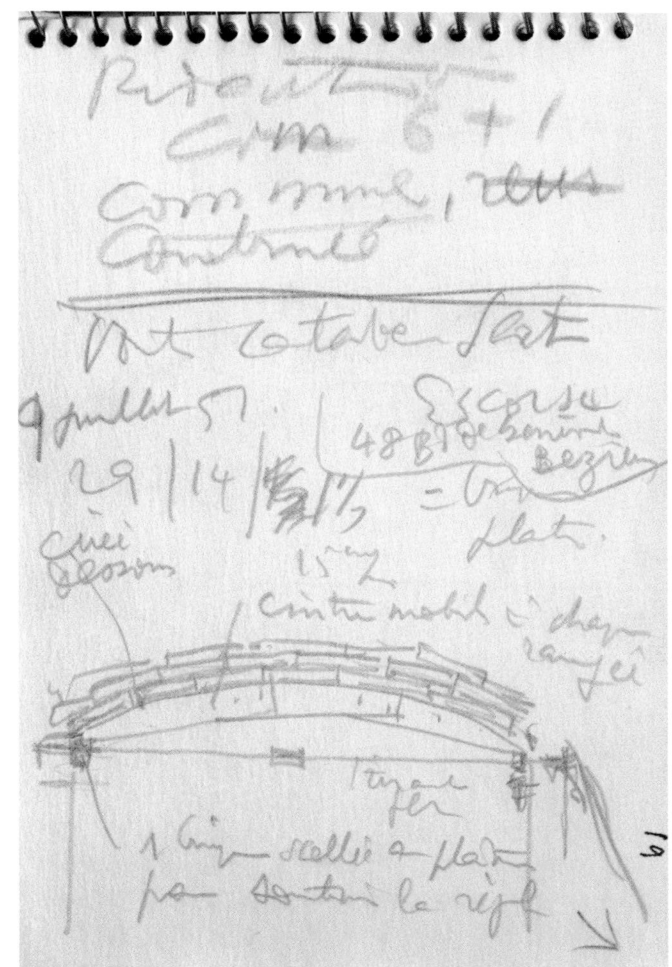

Fig. 75
Cover of Le Corbusier's Sketchbook E21, July 1951.

Fig. 76
Le Corbusier's sketch for other types of vaults. Sketchbook E21, sheet 513.

Fig. 77
Le Corbusier's schema for a Catalan vault. Sketchbook E21, sheet 512.

a herringbone pattern. Pursuing additional information, Le Corbusier corresponded with Escorsa on July 26, 1951, attaching to his letter a plan and section at one-tenth scale. Here he emphasized the strong features already determined for his project:

> This is what I want: I would like some beams or springers at 7.41 feet (2.26 m) from the space above the floor; French bylaws require a ceiling height of 8.53 feet or 9.51 feet; thus the arcs of the vaults are more or less predetermined. I think that the 8.53 feet or 9.18 feet concern both the 12-foot-wide vaults and the 7.41-foot-wide ones; consequently those at 7.41 feet will be more pronounced as arches than those at 3.66 meters.[64]

Here he cites his references: "This year the Colombian architect Pisano [Pizano] in Bogotá made some exposed brick vaults polished with transparent wax; could one do the same here with French materials?" He then posed a number of very specific questions regarding the technical aspects of vault construction:

Fig. 78
Advertisement for *Le Modulor* in *L'Architecture d'aujourd'hui*, n° 30, 1950.

How does the vault react on the supporting walls?.... What is the effect of the vault at the abutment of the vaults spanning the voids measuring 1.13 m, 2.16 m, 1.83 m or 3.66 m?.... What is the most practical slab and the minimum allowable thickness of a floor under live load at the apex of the vault?[65]

He also enquired after traditional craftsmen: "Do you know of any Catalan masons who could carry out the work in Paris and who could be hired by a general contractor?"[66] Escorsa sent him all the necessary details to construct the vaults and was present during preliminary on-site tests. With regard to the use of brick and concrete, Joseph Abram points out that:

[T]he use of exposed brick-and-concrete wall sections was not new in Modern architecture. In Perret's work from the twenties onward, in the industrial hangars (Atelier Durand, 1922, Copeau factory, 1925), but also in the artists' ateliers (such as those of Georges Braque, 1927, Mela Mutter, 1928, Dora Gordine, 1929), one notices that they are often constructed with rudimentary means. Paul Nelson's houses in Paris (Maison Brooks, 1929) and Ernö Goldfinger's Hampstead house (1937) belong to the same lineage, which derive from [Perret's] garage on the rue de Ponthieu (Paris, 1906).[67]

Fig. 79
The Modulor system, "a tool for measure based on the human scale and mathematics."

As for his proportional measurement system for the Jaoul design, Le Corbusier heralded the Modulor which he "... used to determine the principle dimensions, spans of 12 feet (3.66 m) and 7.4 feet (2.26 m) and a height to the soffit of the vault-carrying lintels of 7.4 feet (2.26 m)[68] (Figs. 78 and 79). Here once again the two major notions explored by Le Corbusier, on how to be modern and how to be sensitive to the human scale, are implicit in his Modulor system. However, it seems that this system of measurement nonetheless played a double role, that of harmonizing and uniting the design, and integrating the contribution of various collaborators who intervened on the Neuilly houses. In fact, a large portion of the initial studies were drawn up by the Colombian architect Germàn Samper,[69] although during the first year of research, other foreign architects working at the rue de Sèvres atelier also contributed to the project: Balkrishna V. Doshi from India,[70] Georges Sachinidis from Greece, Rogelio Salmona from Colombia,[71] Kim Chung-up from Korea, along with those from France, including Jacques Mériot, Guy Lemarchand, Jacques Masson, André Wogenscky, Fernand Gardien, André Maisonnier, and Jacques Michel, the last directly responsible for supervising the Jaoul building site (Fig. 81). While mostly contributing to progress on the Neuilly project, Samper, Salmona, Doshi, and Michel also worked simultaneously on the Indian houses in Ahmedabad, the Villa Sarabhai (1951–56) (Figs. 80 and 82), and the Villa Shodhan (1951–56), with Jean-Louis Véret assuring on-site supervision.

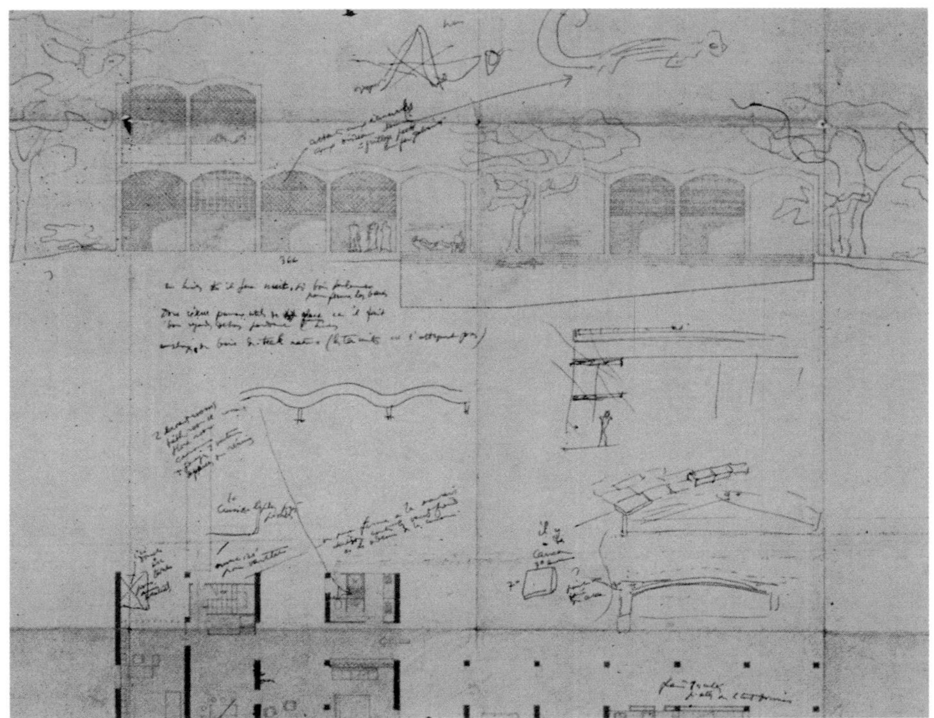

Fig. 80
Sketch, plan, and elevation for the Villa Sarabhai in Ahmedabad, 1951, FLC 6676 (detail).

Fig. 81
Group portrait c. 1956, Le Corbusier's atelier at 35, rue de Sèvres. Ivan Žaknić identified those present. Front row, from left to right: Iannis Xenakis, Olek Kujawski, Jeannette Gabillard (secretary), Jeanine Dargent (secretary), Balkrishna V. Doshi, Jeanne Heilbuth (Le Corbusier's personal secretary), and Le Corbusier. Second row: Jacques Michel, Georges Sachinidis, Jacques Mériot, Kim Chung-up, Augusto Tobito, Henri Bruaux, Roggio Andréini, Jacques Masson, André Maisonnier, and Fernand Gardien.

Fig. 82
Le Corbusier with Doshi, c. 1955.

Various phases of the design process

From July 1951 to July 1952, attempting to grapple with the difficult terrain, Le Corbusier and his collaborators explored four different options (and their variants) based on interconnected construction principles: bays with unequal spans (7.4 feet and 12 feet) covered by Catalan vaults supported by solid brick walls.[72]

First phase

Following Le Corbusier's indications, a series of unsigned plans were drafted in the atelier on July 25, 1951, covering various parts of the composition. They show four major and minor parallel bays (Figs. 83–86), scanned according to an a/b/b/a proportional rhythm (a=7.4-foot (2.26 m) span; b=12-foot (3.66 m) span), juxtaposed and shifted to the northwest/southeast axis of the parcel. The strategy consisted in raising the living area of the first house situated toward the northwest, plunged into shadow cast by the neighboring wall, while pushing back the second house toward the south part of the site. Within the shadiest section, the architect located the maids' bedrooms.

The ground-floor plan FLC 10199 (Fig. 83) shows that the three-car garage occupies the first two bays (7.4 feet + 12 feet) of the ground level. A common entrance hall leads from one section of the ground level toward the house on the left and its living areas, while the staircase allows access to the first level of the house on the right. It is immediately evident that the shift of levels of the two houses, due to the placement of the garage underneath the house to the right, makes room for three habitable levels in the first house but only two in the second house. Much importance has been placed on the terraces that punctuate the development of the plans. The alternating rhythm of 7.4 feet and 12 feet (2.26 m x 3.66 m) in the bays is maintained from this point onwards, and already within the articulation of the interiors, the main kernel of the final design is perceptible.

The northwest cross-section (Fig. 86) simplifies the configuration thus achieved. This first proposal allows us to appreciate, in hindsight, the greatest difficulties still to be resolved: the interdependence between the two houses (the shared entrance hall) and the disposition of the garage.

Second phase

Subsequent months of studies brought about the separation of the two houses, designated henceforth by the letters A and B, even though the common garage still occupied the ground level of one of the houses. The colored plan proposition (dated November 12, 1951) develops a diagonal implantation of volumes across the site (Fig. 87). The two dwellings, still parallel, each composed of two bays (12f. x 7.4f.), are linked by an intermediary space with the same character as that in the first phase, serving as the shared ground-floor hallway. Here the rhythm of the vaults changes according to an a/b/b/a/b sequence.

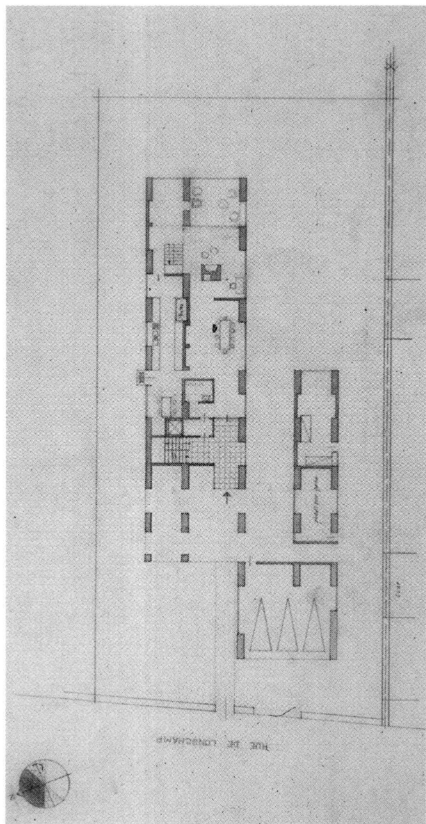

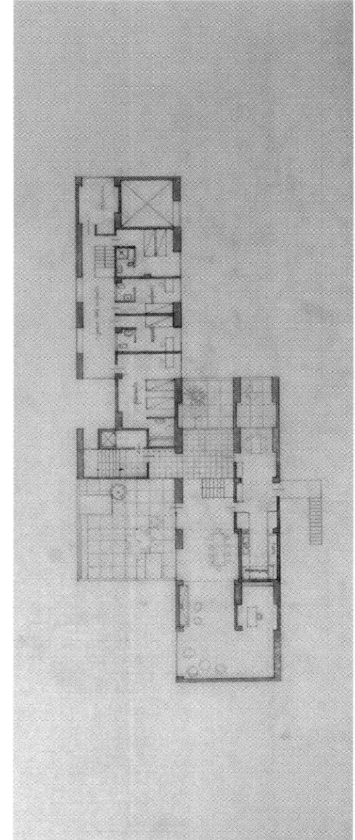

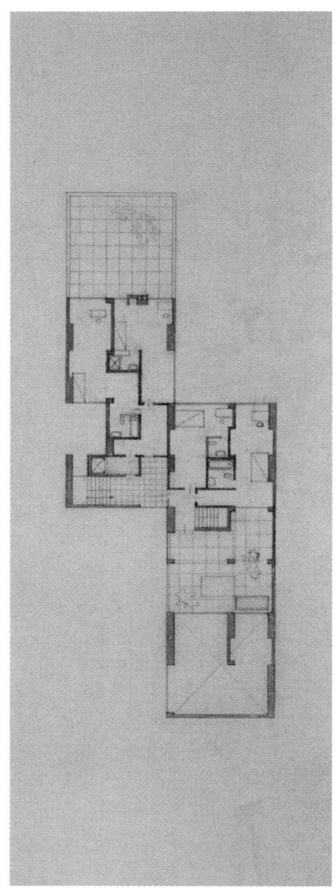

Fig. 83
Plan FLC 10199, ground floor, first proposal, July 25, 1951.

Fig. 84
Plan FLC 10200, first proposal for the first level, July 25, 1951.

Fig. 85
Plan FLC 10201, first proposal for the second level, July 25, 1951.

Third phase

On November 30, 1951, frustrated by the constraints of the Jaoul property, Le Corbusier envisaged an entirely new emplacement, extending his design beyond the legal limits to include the adjoining plot (Fig. 88). Samper developed this option from December 5 to 10, producing a dozen alternative plans, sections, and elevations.[73] He explored an alternative whereby the longitudinal axis of the vaults ran parallel to the street and the houses were divided into two separate entities. Here a new option came to light, that of one shared elevated exterior terrace, accessible from the street by an upward sloped ramp over the subterranean garage. The idea of burying the garage had already cropped up in a number of forays in phase one (Fig. 86), but the consequences of such a scheme—each house having its separate ground level—was not elaborated. The necessity to overcome an obstacle often triggered Le Corbusier's imagination. Venturing into the speculative possibility of an alternative design on a plot of land that flagrantly ignored the Jaouls' real site constraints was altogether consistent with his habitual strategies, for the discrepancy between the existing narrow lot and the fictive enlarged site freed the architect's creative powers to solve the problem at hand from a completely new perspective. This tack forced him slowly but surely to find a new solution that he had been searching for during the previous six months.

FONDATION LE CORBUSIER 10100

Sup. 625 M²

Fig. 86
Cross-section FLC 10206, first proposal, July 25, 1951.

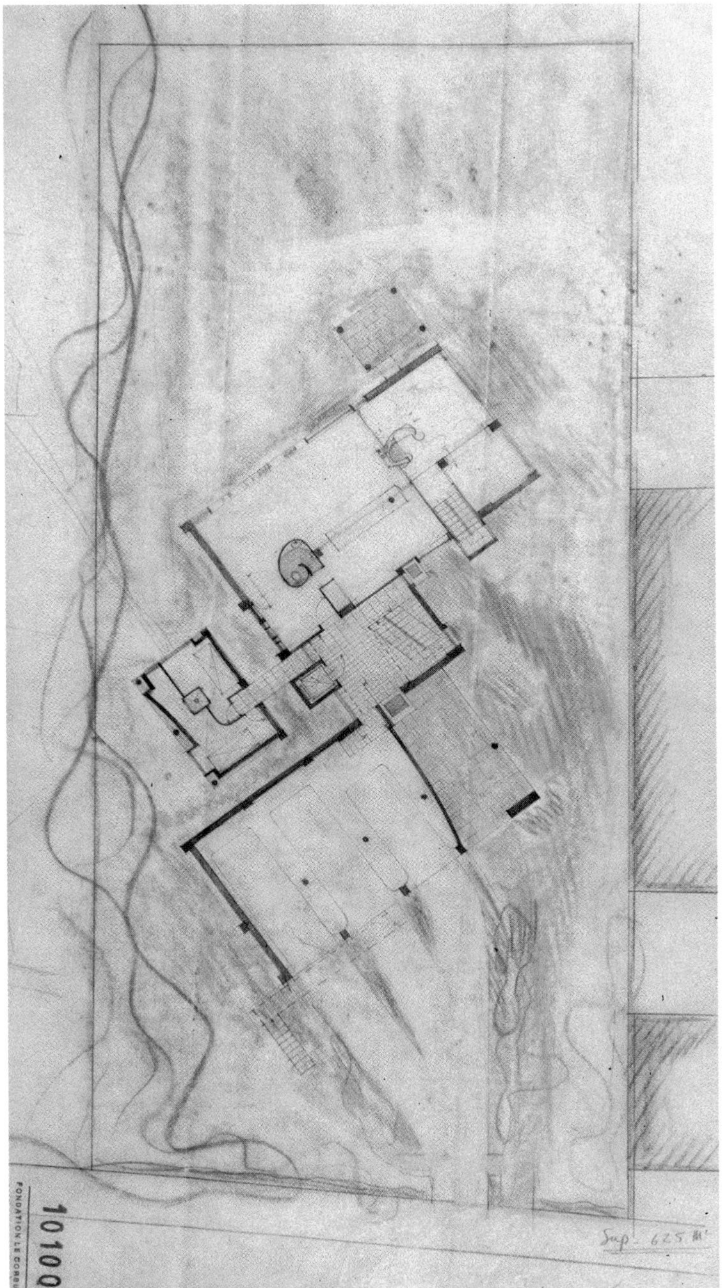

Fig. 87
Plan dated November 12, 1951, with the house plans oriented diagonally. FLC 10100.

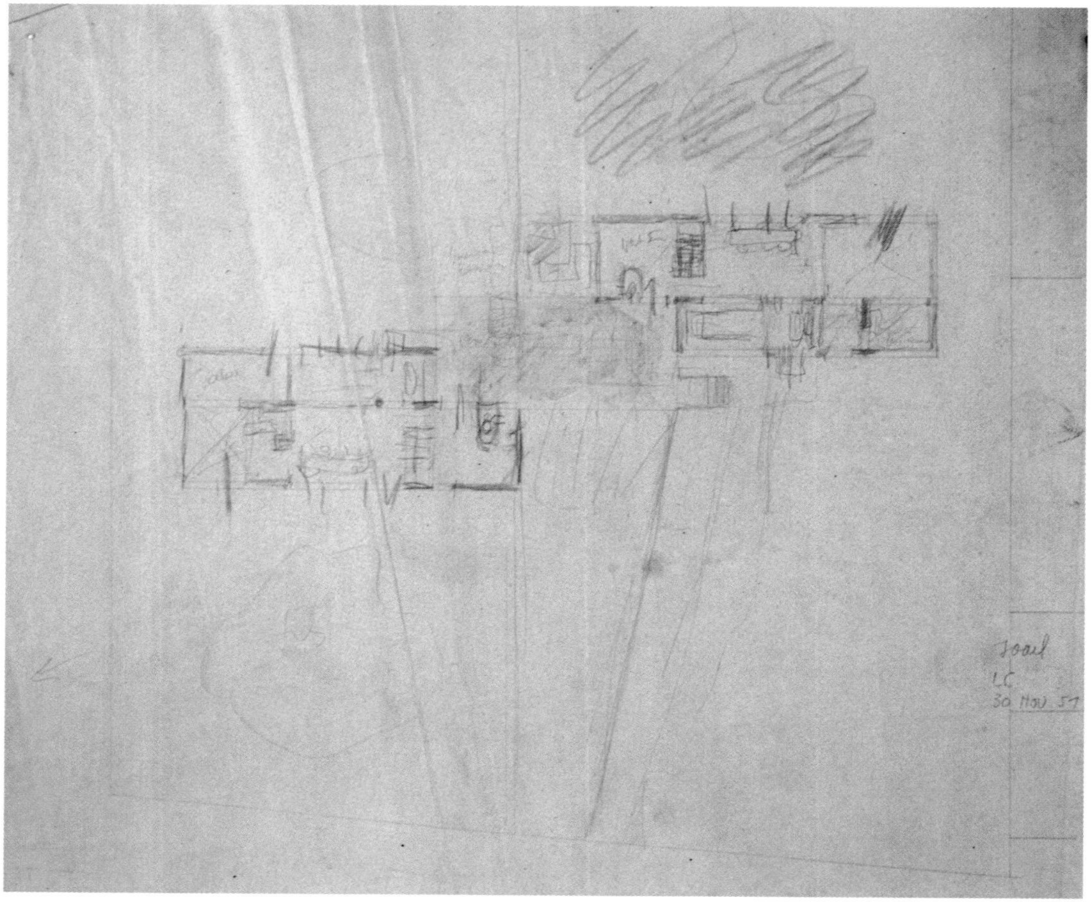

Fig. 88
On November 30, 1951, Le Corbusier decided to extend his proposal across the adjacent plot. Plan FLC 10027.

Fig. 89a, b, c
Farmhouses of the Dordogne region. Travel sketch by German Samper, January 1952.

Fig. 90
In early 1952, for the first time, the houses are shown at right angles, separated by an exterior terrace. The ramps extend along the southeast property line. Ground-level plan. FLC 10103.

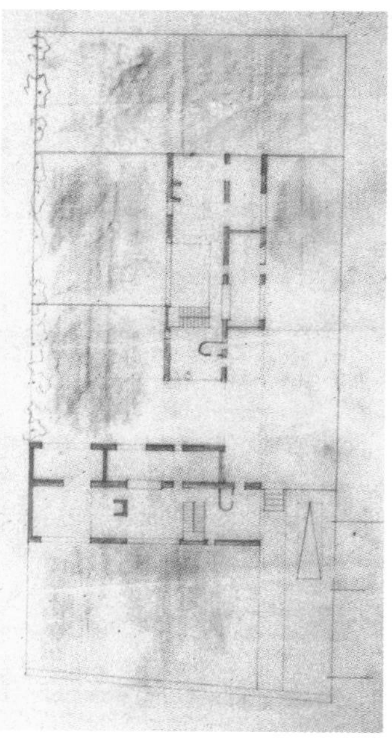

A mirror-image layout plan of two similar houses (with the exception of the fireplace positions) clearly emerged (Fig. 88). One of the houses benefited from a sun-exposed, illuminated living room to the south, while the other suffered the consequences of a shady living room to the northwest. The vaults adopted a new b/a/a/b rhythm.

Ultimately, in retreating to the legal borders of the lot, Le Corbusier had few options but to pivot one of the houses around the axis of the common platform or raised terraced entrance area. His initial wager upon taking on the commission—that of proposing not one but two houses—here starts to find a satisfactory resolution.

Fourth phase

During January 1952, Samper profited from a few days vacation in the Dordogne region of southwest France to observe and sketch some vernacular farmhouses, built with a characteristic access ramp leading up to their entry (Fig. 89 a, b, c).[74] This utilitarian feature might possibly have prompted the young architect to suggest an analogous solution for the Neuilly project.

Dating from this period, a drafted ground plan of the two houses in colored pencils (Fig. 90) indicates that the Jaoul property has been altogether reintegrated within its original footprint. It also reveals, for the first time, the two houses set perpendicularly to each other, with the resulting right angle pulled apart by an exterior terraced area slipped between the houses. Here, House A, parallel to rue de Longchamp, has been slid over by a few meters to abut the adjacent property line to the north, while House B, placed to the rear of the terrain, remains at right angles to it. Ramps run along the southeast property line. Le Corbusier's freehand colored pencil plan study (Fig. 91) advances on this scheme, by offering an innovative adjustment, reversing the disposition of the two houses: House A now moves toward the property's south border, while House B is pushed upward to the north, thereby relocating the two access ramps to the northeast, or left side of the property (when viewed from the rue de Longchamp).

From the street entry, a clear distinction is made between the walking and the driving circulation, emphasized by the directional opposition between the two access ramps along the north edge. The cars drive directly down into the underground garage situated beneath the houses, while the pedestrians mount the ramp to a terrace from which the separate house entries are reached (Fig. 92). The court and garden to the south of the terrain are shared by the two houses and, by extension, the two families. This platform court functions as a pivotal point for the distribution of spaces within the two houses. It proves to be the critical design element; it resolves the superposition or stacking of the houses and the distinction between pedestrian and car circulation. In this instance, Le Corbusier combines an architectural question (the conception of a house) with a planning question (the qualification of an exterior space by the rapprochement of two distinct

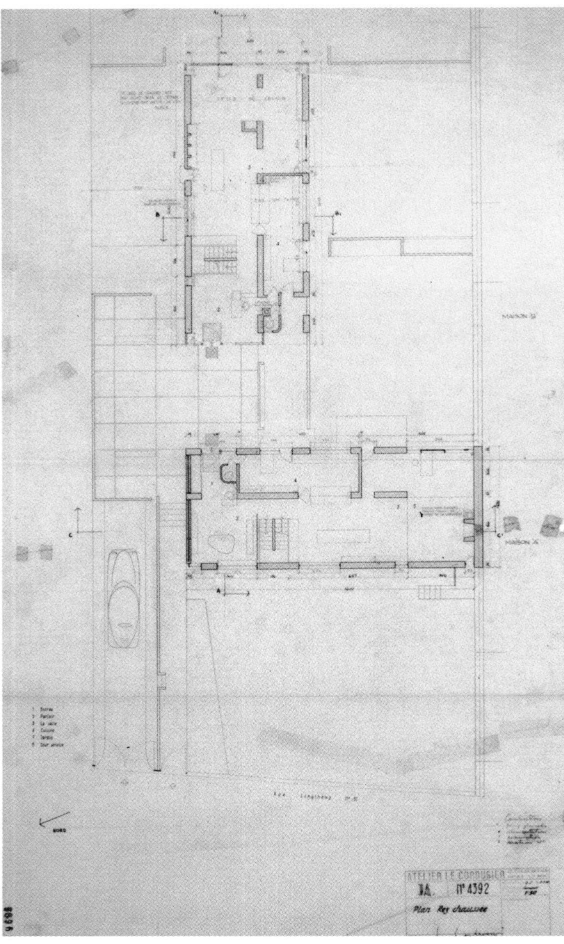

Fig. 91
The houses are set at a right angle, separated by an exterior terrace. The garden is compartmentalized by low walls. Study sketch drawn by Le Corbusier in early 1952. FLC 10170.

Fig. 92
Ground-level plan, March 7, 1952.

volumes). The wager developed here applies to observations made by Jacques Lucan:

> The existence of a building, absolutely isolated, can only be left to architecture; the moment that two buildings are present, a relationship is established, a grouping emerges,... Relationship and assemblage signify rapprochement, possibilities of proximities and contiguities: they lead to the constitution of a concave space.[75]

Plans from March 1952, published in the *Œuvre Complète 1946–1952*, do not entirely correspond to the built work (Figs. 93, 94, 122), the most significant evolution in the plan involving the placement of the entrances to the two houses. In the first hypothesis, the front doors of the two houses faced each other directly. This meant placing the entrance to House A in the side wall, rather than the gable wall. In the second hypothesis, the front door to House A was moved round onto the gable wall (Fig. 95). This solution was adopted on September 11, 1952. (Fig. 109). It underscores the role of the vault as a means to signal, in a rational manner, both the entry facades and the

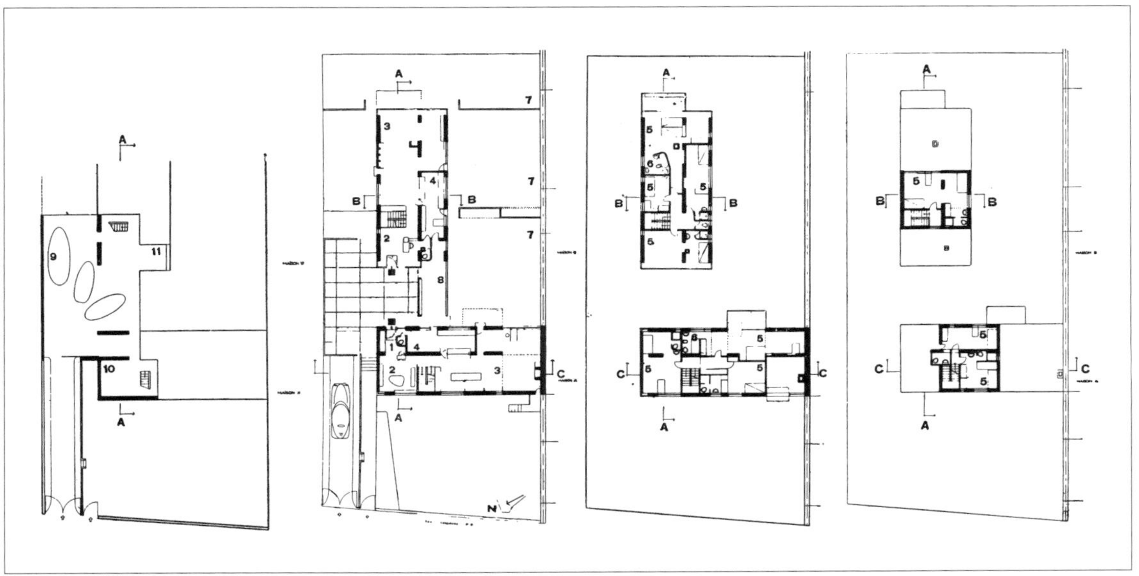

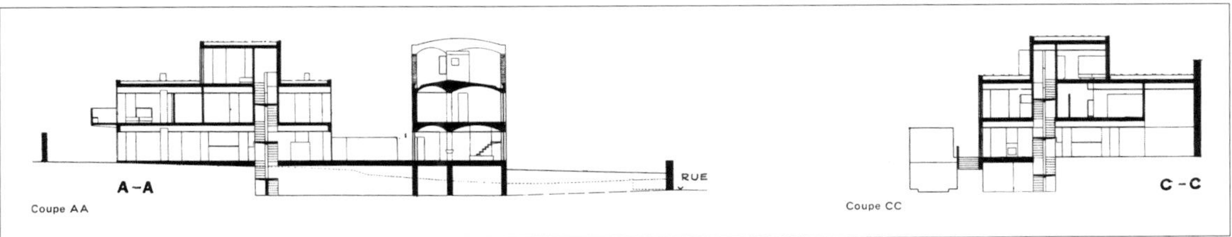

Fig. 93
Overall plan of the two houses on the site (March 7, 1952), as it was published in the *Œuvre Complète*, vol. 5, 1946–1952, 175.

Fig. 94
Sections, Maisons Jaoul, February 1952.

Fig. 95
Bird's-eye view of the two houses, FLC 10061, 1952.

directional unfolding of each house.[76] This layout, moreover, allowed for a clearer distinction between the two buildings and demarcated the independence of the two households, each given a discrete entrance out of sight from the other.

During the evolution of various stages of their work, Le Corbusier's collaborators more than likely considered the design from different cardinal orientations (northeast, southwest, east, and west). The French architect Édith Girard points out "an old trick" that was undoubtedly used in the atelier:

> When drawing up a plan ... one designs by subconsciously orienting one's own body into this space, by drawing, for example, the trajectories that one would spontaneously follow. Now this effect of lateralization is arbitrarily deployed

from one single point: one draws by placing one of the four sides of the paper in front of oneself and this choice, seemingly innocuous, contains a multitude of presuppositions that will have major repercussions on the invention of forms.... But regarding a plan, it is very clear that the drawing is going to represent a space that is practicable from every direction, and not at all oriented in reality according to the orientation that I give it on my drafting table. In conclusion, it is necessary to turn one's drawing in every direction: start to work on it from one direction, for example, the top oriented to the north, then from the opposite direction by looking at it from the south, then seeing it from the sky, and from the other two sides, from the east and from the west... a plan is good [only] if it holds up when seen from no matter what point of view.[77]

If nothing precisely indicates that Le Corbusier also adopted this "trick" himself, he was nonetheless clearly attentive to the diversification of forms and the methods of representing his architecture.

Conceptual ambiguities

Briefly summarizing some five hundred existing drawings and visual documents in the Jaoul file does not entirely account for the complexity of Le Corbusier's conceptual process. They cover an astounding diversity of proposed solutions, along with a wide heterogeneity of representational forms drawn by his various assistants. It appears that the Jaoul house commission represented for Le Corbusier the occasion to ask himself profound questions on the very nature of the house itself, provoking responses that seemed to pull him in two different directions, divided between several conflicting desires, difficult to reconcile. While he wanted to execute a simple, economical house for the industrialist Jaoul, he also strove to endow the house with a vernacular expression worthy of a peasant from the Cévennes, or, in other words, by exploring a type of monumentality of forms, he simultaneously attempted to develop a human approach to the domestic spaces.

To appraise the balance between these two tendencies—between a simple, economical house and a formal monumentality—and the conflicts that resulted throughout the entire design process, a close analysis of several drawings executed between September 18 and October 1951 proves useful. Apart from some decisive decisions already pointed out—the alignment of four parallel bays along the same northwest and southeast axis, the scanning of the plans of the two houses according to an a/b/b/a proportional rhythm, the attention to natural light, the use of the natural slope of the terrain, and the vault motif—multiple questions arose out of the struggle between the modern options and the vernacular choices. Plans produced on the very same day reveal solutions of a very different nature. Their graphic representation is also very diverse. Two examples, the first a cross-section, the second a front elevation, illustrate this conflict. The dry, repetitive, drafted cross-section of both houses, dated October 16

Fig. 96
Study drawing of the section, structure of the columns and the vaults, October 16, 1951. FLC 10310.

Fig. 97
Sketch of the lateral facade, dated October 17, 1951. FLC 10328.

(Fig. 96), reflects the rational expression of a standard system of construction, evoking a factory typology. By contrast, the elevation of both houses dated October 17 (Fig. 97), a multicolored drawing, conveys the expressive warmth of a picturesque, individuated vernacular building. To complete the joviality of the scene, a female figure leans over the balcony, enhancing the idea of a welcoming home. These two visual representations reveal two opposing approaches, imposed from the very beginning of the commission, a contrast between technical modernity and crafted warmth of hearth and home.

This same multicolored elevation drawing (dated October 17, 1951) can also be compared profitably to another section-elevation study of the same facade dated September 18 (Fig. 98). The latter is considerably more

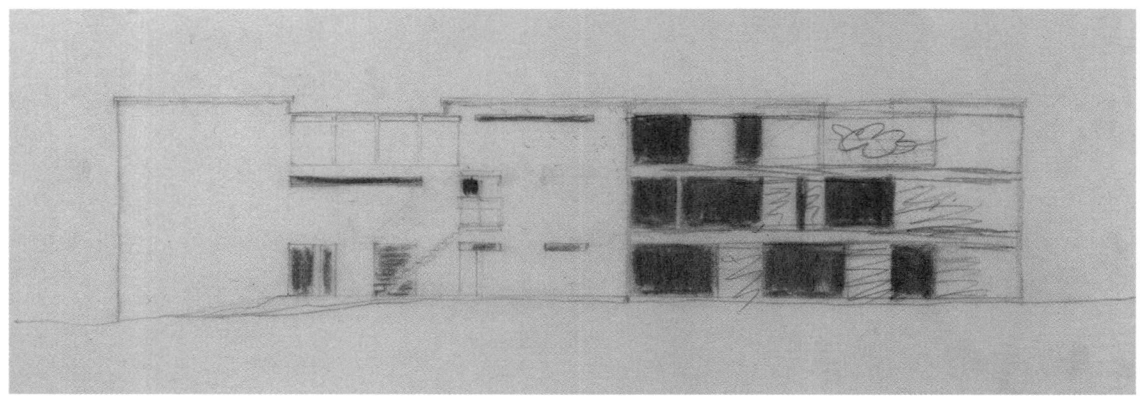

Fig. 98
Sketch of the lateral facade, September 18, 1951. FLC 10363.

Fig. 99
Elevation of the northwest facade drawn by Samper, FLC 10262, August 30, 1951. This document recalls the work of Louis Kahn from the 1950s, infused with Roman references that he admired during his three-month journey to Rome during the winter of 1951.

Fig. 100
Sectional elevation showing staircase, openings, walls, doors, and structural elements, FLC 10365, September 6, 1951.

somber in both its formal and graphic expression. The horizontality of each of the three levels is accentuated by the effect of a lintel or continuous exterior strip banding. The solids and voids alternate. The full glazed bays are deployed from ground to ceiling.

A later northwest elevation drawn by Samper on August 30, 1951 (Fig. 99), offers the image of a monumental building composed of twelve juxtaposed alveoli or hollow cores. The vaults rest on thin concrete beams that assure the chain bonding of the bare brick walls. The plans of the ground floor and upper levels, corresponding to this design option, reveal the axis of the vaults running perpendicular to the street.[78] The treatment of the cores is here resolved by uniform loggias, but still they remain very distant from the geometry elaborated by the *pans de verre* (glass wall sections) and the *pans de bois* (post-and-pane wall sections) in the definitive design.

Samper's plan dated October 15, 1951 (Fig. 103), seems almost alone in corresponding to the facade shown in Le Corbusier's highly expressive drawing produced two days later on October 17 (Fig. 97). These illustrations complete an unrelenting phase of work between September and October devoted to resolving the interior planning of the two houses. Observable details in these plans reveal Le Corbusier's determination to incorporate planted terraces on the second floor level, despite his draftsman's counter-efforts to reduce open spaces to a minimum. In actual fact, Le Corbusier had always been attracted to roof gardens:

> ...the roof of a house is a garden that has been there for over twenty years and that grows all by itself, with its grasses, bushes [and] flowers....I let nature take over to the fullest, through the play of winds, insects, drought and other haphazards.[79]

He preferred to contemplate nature from a safe distance, thus avoiding the earthbound traditional garden that he considered symptomatic of a narrow bourgeois mind. The Virgilian dream of the Villa Savoye here blossoms from the rooftop terrace.

Ultimately the plans from September through October proved that the placement of the garage was to be the most challenging problem to resolve (Figs. 101–103). At first it was slipped under House A (the closest to the street) with the car approach and entry located to the northwest (Fig. 83, dated July 25, 1951). The garage door opening was later reoriented toward the northeast, probably in order to bring the cars closer to the pedestrian entry.

This option was also studied in drawings (Fig. 101), dated September 20, 1951, and FLC 10272, dated four days later. On October 4, the garage was buried under House A along the property dividing line to the southwest (Fig. 102). On the following day, however, this garage was removed from under House A to occupy three bays (b/a/a) at the center of the plot (Fig. 103), with the idea of facilitating access to the entrance hall (still shared by both

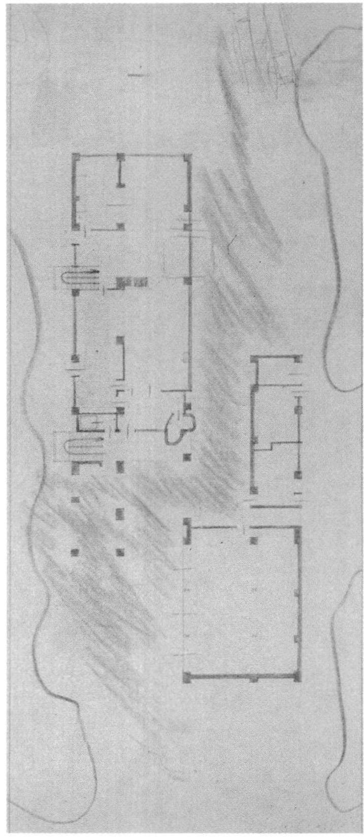

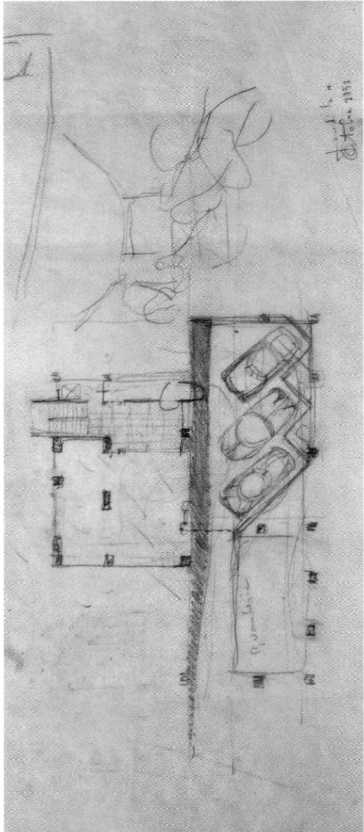

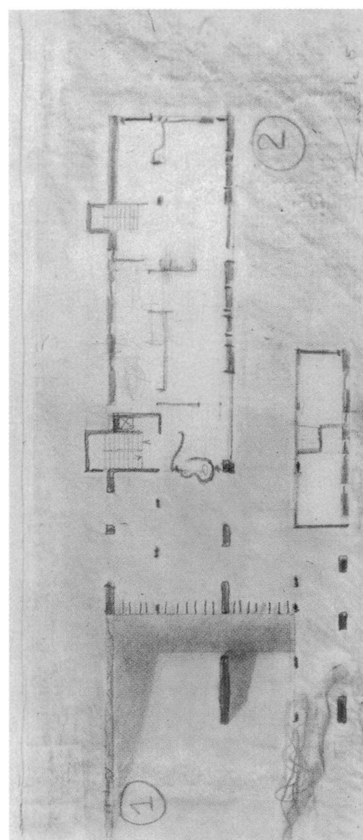

Fig. 101
Ground-level plan. On September 20, 1951, the garage was oriented toward the northeast. FLC 10022.

Fig. 102
Basement plan. On October 4, 1951, the garage was oriented toward the northwest, its definitive position. FLC 10342.

Fig. 103
Ground-level plan. On October 15, 1951, the garage occupied three bays at the center of the site. FLC 10333.

houses) from the garage. The difficulty here arose from having to organize the design along a Modulor-proportioned, alternating bay grid (a/b/b/a). The Neuilly municipal architect also strictly enforced the land-use plan bylaw at this stage, obliging the architect to provide vegetation on at least 80 percent of the area within the restrictive setback margins or within the margins he himself proposed.

Le Corbusier's intervention and care

Torn between technical solutions and poetic aspirations, Le Corbusier complained to the Jaouls on several occasions about the difficulties imposed upon him in order to accomplish his task: "You purchased an impossible, deplorable piece of land, crushed by servitudes and regulations. I myself produced how many plans without a break? In order to reach the stage of being able to achieve a program for the Jaoul family."[80] Le Corbusier here emphasizes his personal investment in the conceptual process. However, in point of fact, only a dozen or so sketches, often executed on Sunday in the tranquility of his deserted atelier, can firmly be attributed to him. On these, he affixed his monogram L. C. along with the date, all underscored by a bold line. Bending over the drafting tables, Le Corbusier left pencil traces of his transient visits. Other rough drafts are clearly the result of a conversation between himself and one of his collaborators (Fig. 104).

Fig. 104
Le Corbusier in his 35, rue de Sèvres atelier, at work on Jacques Michel's drafting board.

Which are the precise details upon which Le Corbusier actually intervened? Where did he leave his identifiable marks? Where are the traces of a dialogue between the draftsman and his master? Several codes have been deciphered. Apparently Le Corbusier alone had the privilege of intervening in color on the plans: his red marks signaled the entrances and his blue-colored pencil shadings indicated the positions of windows.[81] Could one interpret these gestures as concerns over comfort, and the house considered as a crucible of light and well-being? During the 1920s, it was above all Pierre Jeanneret who was responsible for adding a human touch to the drawings, animating the sections with single figures or groups of men and women within the interior or around the exterior of the houses. In the 1950s, illustrated figures animated the sheets to indicate that the houses were designed to a human scale, in response to Modulor proportions. The draftsman thus projected himself into the designed space and verified the validity of his proposal.

Le Corbusier's colored freehand section on tracing paper dated September 11, 1952 (Fig. 105), confirms a major modification to the project, concerning the transformation of the large glazed window on the northeast facade. This longitudinal section of House B indicates openings demarcated and isolated by the wall. In fact, bylaws controlling privacy rights forced the atelier to alter this facade, after the municipal architect had previously refused to issue the building permit to the former design (Fig. 106). Thus the large glazed bay was reconceived as a reversed L-shaped opening (Fig. 107), a design which proved one of the most distinctive features of the houses and eventually attracted the greatest critical acclaim.[82] Research into the most

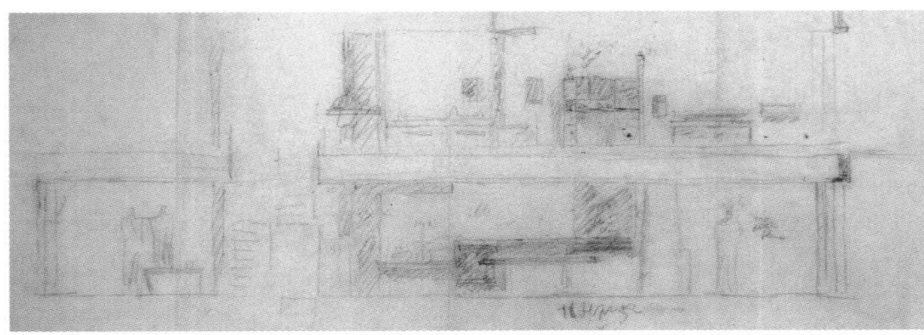

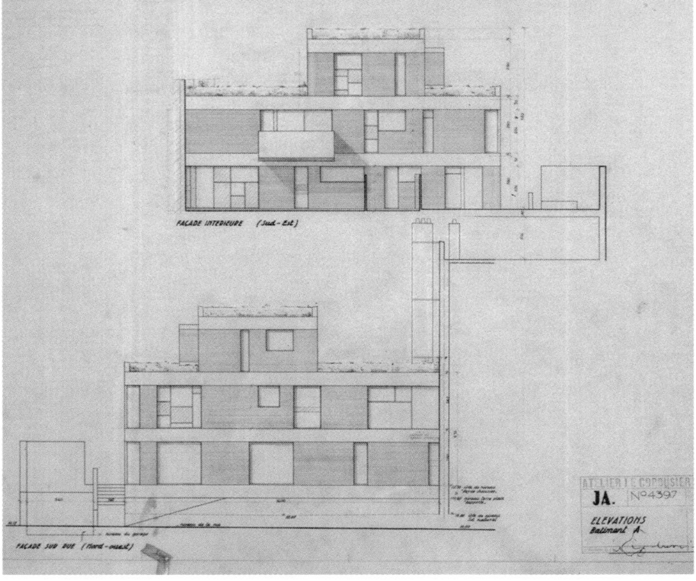

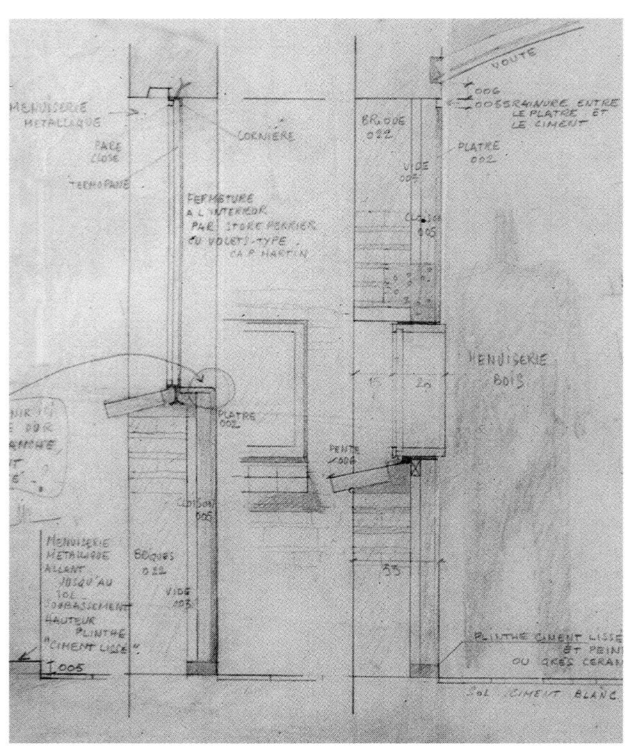

Fig. 105
Sectional sketch (on two levels) signed by Le Corbusier, with dimensions, legends, and profiled figures, dated September 11, 1952. FLC 10083.

Fig. 106
Southeast facade (top) and northwest facade of House A, March 12, 1952. FLC 9901 (detail).

Fig. 107
Northeast wall of House B, modified with the addition of a reversed L-shaped opening.

Fig. 108
Construction detail, lower window section. FLC 30649 (detail).

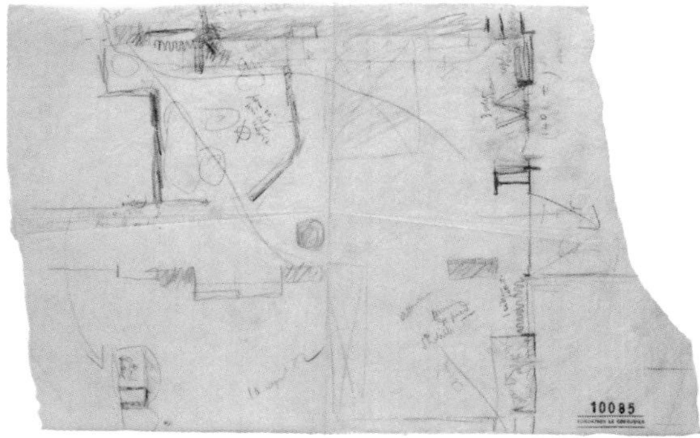

Fig. 109
On September 11, 1952, Le Corbusier decided to shift the position of the entrance to House A, henceforth situated in the extension of the 7.4-foot nave. FLC 10082.

Fig. 110
On September 11, 1952, Le Corbusier concentrated on the vertical openings placed at the corner of the master bedroom of House B and the cross-ventilation there, which allowed the bathroom to be aired out. FLC 10085.

Fig. 111
Sketch by Le Corbusier to study the furnishings in House A. FLC 1 (13) 153.

appropriate solution required even sharper focus on the interior organization as it related to the penetration of natural light. This concern is suggested by the illustrated figures in some of these sheets, either sitting at a table turned back from the window or standing in the salon and entrance hall (Figs. 105 and 108). Such attention would ultimately lead to an asymmetrical design solution for the facades.

The house entrances also prompted a flurry of detailed studies, such as the tracing paper plan study by Le Corbusier, also dated September 11, 1952 (Fig. 109), which indicates a new position for the entrance to House A, corresponding to his undated black-ink perspective section (Fig. 111). Here, he arranges the built-in furniture elements and precisely details window openings with vertical shutters for cross-ventilation and folding shutters in the bays. In this view showing the two bays, he indicates the entry sequence toward the kitchen, on one side, and toward the hallway, on the other side, with a doormat distinctly marking the entrance within the 7.4-foot nave axis. In the hallway, Le Corbusier has drawn a seated figure on a bench, facing inward, along with a low piece of furniture near the staircase,

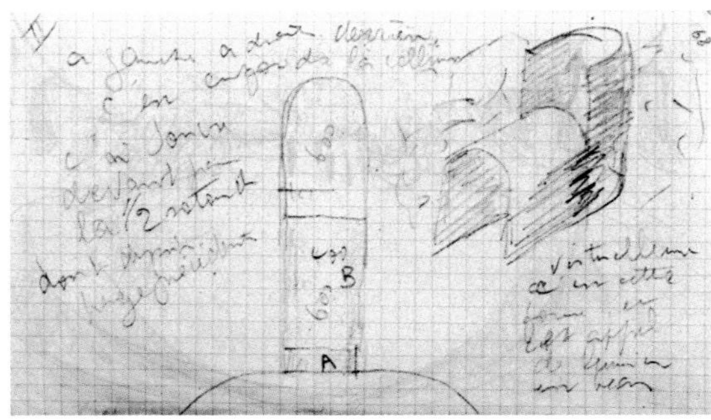

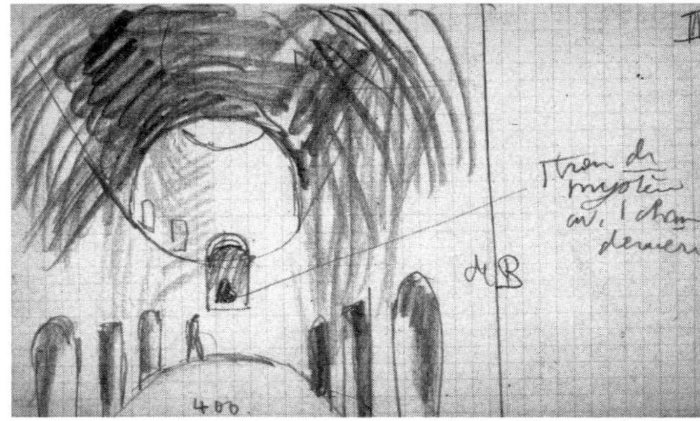

Fig. 112 (left)
In this colored pencil-and-ink study labeled "ma villa (my villa)," Le Corbusier carefully adds personal touches such as a table and stool. Carnet Nivola 187, dated August 12, 1951, Cap-Martin "ma villa (my villa)." FLC W1 (8) 110.

Fig. 113 (top right)
Le Corbusier, annotated pen-and-pencil sketch of natural light effects in the interior of Hadrian's Villa, Rome, 1911. FLC "Voyage en Orient," Sketchbook V, 68.

Fig. 114 (right)
Le Corbusier, analytical sketch of Hadrian's Villa, 1911. FLC "Voyage en Orient," Sketchbook V, 69.

conveying the impression that the architect is tracing, by means of his pencil, a meandering path throughout the interior space.

Le Corbusier's drawing style is recognizable by its fluid, wandering lines, lingering over details, crayoning in colors to indicate natural light sources. A colored plan study (Fig. 110) gives design details of the master bedroom, House B, in which the architect draws vertical openings, that serve as a ventilation device in the corner of the room and two diagonal lines (one with a directional arrow head), that indicates the trajectory of air toward the other ventilation device in the bathroom. This sketch, like FLC 10082 (Fig. 109), is representative of his queries and investigations into various design alternatives, choices, and installation possibilities. He intervenes on an assistant's drawing to test the proposed environment and, through a stumping effect on the paper surface, evaluates the fluctuating light as it penetrates into various rooms. He does not ask the question of how something works, but rather how the prospective user (a projection of himself) will occupy the space with their bench to sit on or to place clothes in the salon, their eye-level window, their shelves, and worktables disposed along the length of windows. On a sheet in his Nivola sketchbook, entitled "ma villa" (Fig. 112), he records the dimensions of what appears to be an abandoned house (a section of the roof seems to have collapsed). Near the window overlooking the sea, Le Corbusier thoughtfully indicates the presence of a table, stool, some loose papers, and an inviting glass of water. The placement of the table in relation to the window is similar to that in House B, which appears in sketch FLC 30652B (Fig. 175). The window embrasure contributes to a sense of comfort. Here, in the context of the Maisons Jaoul,

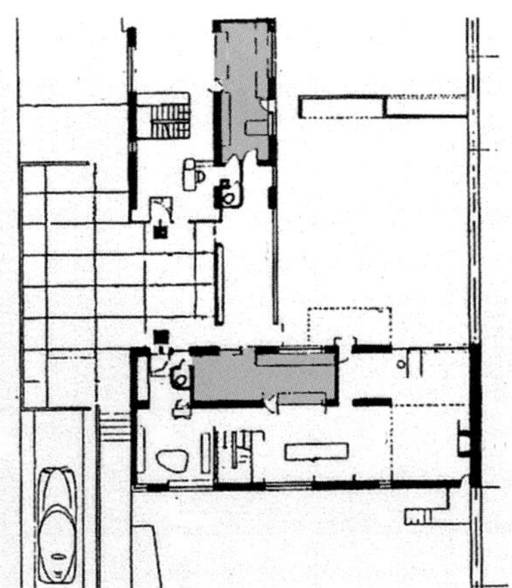

Fig. 115
Detail, ground-level plan, March 7, 1952, showing the relationship between the two kitchens in both houses. FLC 9896, published in *Œuvre complète*, 1946–1952, 29.

Fig. 116
Perspective sketch of the salon in House A, March–April 1953. FLC 10123 B.

the architect develops the conception of the windows, experimenting with the different widths of the window casement detailing.

On Sunday, September 16, 1951, Le Corbusier once again left traces of his interventions on various sketch studies. The next day he had an appointment with André Jaoul and on Thursday of the same week his wife Suzanne.[83] Madame Jaoul had probably encouraged the architect to pursue work on the organization of their House A, specifically as a response to her explicit wish to have a small chapel designed within her home interior. This oratory appears in one of the rough colored pencil plan studies (Fig. 117) and is taken up again in the plans of September 24 (FLC 10274). The private space for prayer, an extension to the master bedroom, occupies the space that Le Corbusier traditionally uses for the library location on the top floor of his other houses (Fig. 118), for example in the Villa La Roche (1923). The proposed system to bring natural light through a double-height ceiling in the living room of House A is yet again a design device that Le Corbusier had observed long ago, notably during a visit to Hadrian's Villa in Rome around 1911, when he produced a survey drawing (Figs. 113 and 114).

The plan dated March 7, 1952 (Fig. 115), shows that the two houses are now linked by a paved passage demarcated by two low stub walls suggesting that the two kitchens harmonize to a certain extent, to form part of the serving space within the same design ensemble. The drawing also indicates that the two kitchens are open to their respective living rooms, conforming to Le Corbusier's black-line freehand perspective sketch (Fig. 116). It was not until April that the open bar in House A would be transformed into a more discreet pass-through in order to reflect the more traditional lifestyle imposed by Suzanne Jaoul. Nevertheless, Le Corbusier had tried to convince André Jaoul that a kitchen open to the living room could be a very agreeable solution, taking as an example the arrangement that José Luis Sert had designed for his own Long Island house, built in 1947.

To this end, in a letter dated October 24, 1951, a few months earlier, addressed to Muncha, Sert's wife, Le Corbusier had written to request a mailing of some drawings of their kitchen design: "We are constructing a

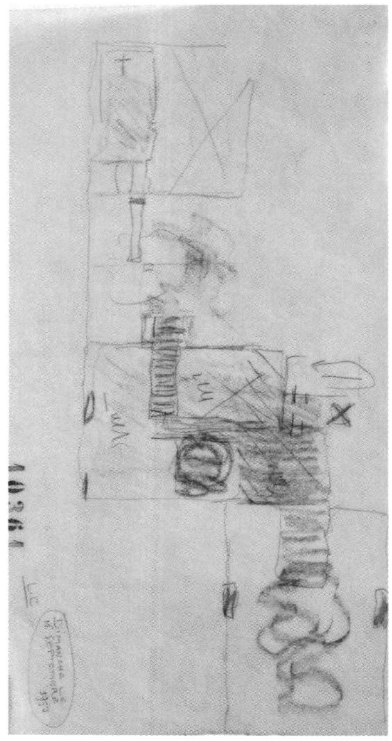

Fig. 117
Colored crayon sketch plan by Le Corbusier, showing the chapel for Suzanne Jaoul indicated by a large cross (left), dated September 16, 1951. Plan FLC 10361.

Fig. 118
The chapel in House A, first floor.

double owner-occupied house for with-it people, and I would like to be able to make use of your personal experiments. I'm really counting on you to ensure that Sert can send the documentation."[84] Le Corbusier was clearly not interested in preassembled American kitchen models, however, but rather the unique solution adopted by Sert:

> Today I received documentation from Crosley, General Electric (*Everything Electrical for the Modern Home*), and St Charles (*Kitchens for Living*). These are only a selection of fascinating or pitiful catalogues to choose from. What actually interests me is how you transformed them to reflect the current life style of people of our standing (simple or complicated, depending on the interpretation). I would appreciate if Sert sent me plans of his kitchen showing its dimensions, hierarchy of appliances, their layout, their continuity, etc. I realize that it's quite a lot to ask to benefit indirectly from the work of others, but I figure that, over these forty years, I have done my fair share in this domain.[85]

Sert responded to his colleague on November 16, 1951:

> Here [are] the plans of my kitchen in L. I. [Long Island]. It really works very well and constitutes the hub of the house, stretching into the room and toward the patio. Muncha is very content with this arrangement, and when we have guests, serving is very easy because the mistress of the house remains with everyone, the preparation of the meal and drinks are of great interest to all, [and] nobody complains about the cooking odors.[86]

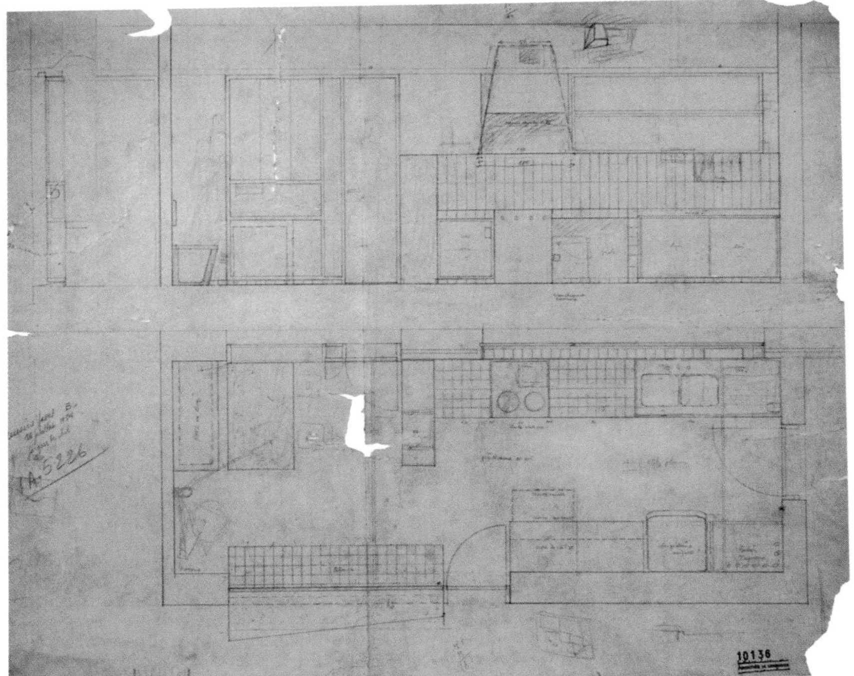

Fig. 119
Kitchen layout, House B, July 10, 1954. FLC 10136.

Fig. 120
The kitchen in House B.

Le Corbusier underlined this passage and noted in the margins "make a copy for Jaoul *père*." In this way, Le Corbusier again searched for references stored in his spatial memory. He loved the atmosphere of the Sert's house, created by the proximity of the kitchen to the living room. He would have liked to recreate the same spirit in Neuilly.[87] Yet, even though the layout of the kitchen in House A does not resemble the Long Island house, Le Corbusier still committed himself to the idea of integrating a number of features here within a relatively narrow 7.38-foot (2.26 m) bay slot.

In House B, by contrast, the integration of the kitchen in the form of a kitchen-bar installed in the living room (Figs. 119 and 120) thus allowed "the housewife the possibility of graciously communicating with her friends [and] her family,"[88] as furniture designer Charlotte Perriand so described the layout and built-in *équipements* of the cellular units at the Unité d'Habitation in Marseilles.[89]

A reference to this type of kitchen installation might also have been based on a more prosaic model, captured in an anonymous interior photograph from 1951 (Fig. 121), discovered among a series of construction site shots of the Unité d'Habitation of Marseilles in the archives of the Fondation Le Corbusier. It shows a view of a café-bar interior. The managers look straight into the camera from their position of command behind the bar.[90] This open-counter arrangement resembles the one that Le Corbusier recreated for the communal living area in House B, between the kitchen and salon.

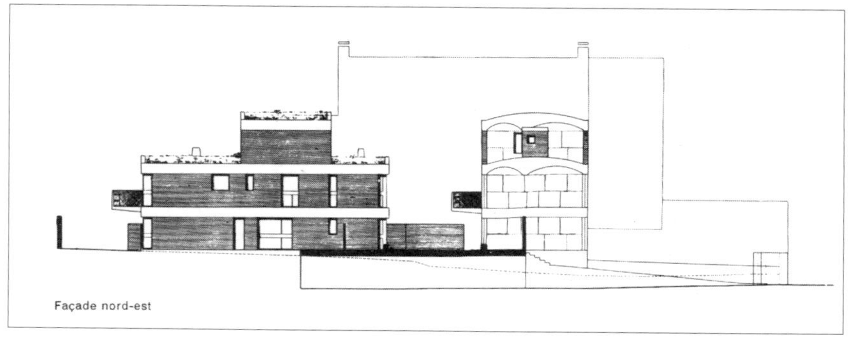

Fig. 121
Interior view of a café bar in Marseilles. Photograph found in the construction file, Unité d'Habitation in Marseilles. FLC L1 (13) 208.

Fig. 122
Elevations of Houses B and A based on plans established on February 12, 1952. Northeast facade before the final modifications.

Financial and administrative difficulties

Germàn Samper prepared a first set of final plans on February 12, 1952 (FLC 4392–4399), which served as the official set of drawings submitted for a building permit on March 3, 1952. A second set of plans was finalized between April 17 and May 4, 1952 (FLC 4407–4435). This time the entry to House A was shifted to the axis of the 7.4-foot nave. These plans were sent to the selected enterprises so that they could establish their estimates to be presented to the various loan organizations solicited by the Jaouls.

A second building permit request was prepared with plans established in May 1952. The permit permission was not delivered until October 23, 1952, after some modifications to the northwest facade openings had been made.[91] A third set of plans was produced on January 8, 1953 (FLC 4534–4560).

The Jaouls had, in fact, hoped to benefit by a bank loan from the Crédit Foncier and a subsidy on the anticipated construction costs within the framework of laws established to encourage postwar construction. In order to obtain such loans, they were obliged to present all the estimates from the various trades, falling within a specific limited budget. The cost per square foot, not counting the structure, was restricted to less than 28,490 French francs, with a fixed ceiling of twenty million French francs for the combined 2,345 square feet of the two houses.[92] Le Corbusier's atelier collaborators therefore recommended to the enterprises that they submit two separate estimates, including one (concerning the woodwork) for simplified carpentry work. In agreement with the client, the carpentry entrepreneur calculated, outside of his official proposal, another estimate for complementary work, covering modifications to the *pans de verre* as well as supplementary quantities.[93] That such practices were adopted in Le Corbusier's atelier is common knowledge, very often leading to unanticipated surprises in terms of construction costs. Tim Benton has demonstrated how infrequently the villa owners of the 1920s were able to keep their architect within the limits of the budget announced at the start of operations.[94] On July 23, 1952, Le Corbusier intervened personally in a meeting with Eugène Claudius-Petit, then minister of reconstruction, to ensure that the Jaouls could benefit from a government loan, arguing specifically that "nowadays for 28,000 F/m^2, one can only construct very modest houses."[95] Claudius-Petit made it clear that the rules for loans from the Crédit Foncier were established "in such a way as to allow for the refusal of loans for luxury buildings... but that the Jaoul case would be examined in the most open-minded manner possible."[96]

On June 24, 1953, costs were estimated at 19,482,511 French francs, but that amount in truth corresponded only to expenses for the full construction of House B and only a partial construction of House A, the Jaouls having envisaged construction in phases.[97] In July 1955, the honorarium fee was fixed at 1,909,585 French francs based on an estimate of work to the sum of 31,287,398 French francs for the two houses.[98]

Yet as early as June 1952, André Jaoul had already informed Le Corbusier's office that he had decided to construct no matter what the outcome over the construction subsidy and loans. He was in a hurry for construction to begin and already showed signs of impatience. André Wogenscky then reminded him of the work already furnished by the entire atelier on his program, without counting Le Corbusier's own time:

> [F]rom the year 1937 when I started to work for him, I never before witnessed Le Corbusier devote so much time and care to a study... he spent his afternoons on your case while setting aside, more than I would have wanted, other studies, such as that for Nantes for example.[99]

A preliminary request for a building permit (dispatch of FLC plan 4362) from the Préfet de la Seine was deposited on December 19, 1951, and a second request on January 22, 1952 (dispatch of FLC plans 4365, 4366, 4367). The full building permit request was deposited on March 3, 1952. Nine days later, on March 12, Le Corbusier's atelier announced that it had received a positive response from the mayor of Neuilly for the preliminary design.

Le Corbusier drew up a résumé of various types of financial aid for construction potentially suitable for his client. Several letters were mailed to obtain the agreement over the common court. In point of fact, the plans of January 22, 1952, necessitated "an agreement with the neighbor to ensure for each neighboring owner the security and advantages of a contract for a common court." Le Corbusier wrote specifically about this issue to Jaoul:

> This contract would authorize the neighbor M[onsieur] X... to eventually construct up to his property line.... Additionally, it would put your window to the east (Michel apartment) at the regulated distance of [thirty feet] from direct view, failing which, the prefecture could exercise his veto on the [twenty feet] only that separate this window from the property line.[100]

By early summer, however, Jaoul had still not obtained the agreement, giving rise to the occasion for Le Corbusier to moralize on the situation. On July 10, 1952, he wrote to Jaoul to announce the end of the first design phase (Fig. 123). His letter testifies to the relationship established over the years between these two principal players, the client and his architect. It affirms the latter's point of view, demonstrates the validity of his proposal, and threatens his withdrawal of interest in the project should Jaoul show "bad faith." Le Corbusier seems to have taken this recourse to unblock the stymied situation. Here, he summarizes items already accomplished to date and requests Jaoul's intervention to obtain legal authorization for the common court agreement, so as to situate his proposal within a real context.[101] He insists on repeating to what point he has been confronted with a terrain "bristling with restrictive bylaws" and affirms that he has done the maximum to ensure that the project comes to fruition, even though he was simultaneously very preoccupied with a number of constructions underway in Chandigarh, Ahmedabad, Nantes-Rezé, and Ronchamp. His letter merits quoting in full:

> Dear Jaoul,
> You are a friend, I am your friend, I write to you as a friend. Your attitude is regrettable, wrong, and would be discouraging if I weren't so strong willed and of so strong a constitution. You lack faith. I did a fantastic job for you. I immersed myself in the project well beyond the normal fees that I should ask for. You purchased an impossible, deplorable piece of land, crushed by servitudes and regulations. I myself, working non-stop, produced how many plans? In order to realize a program for the Jaoul family. You already had the plans of our friend Ent[wistle], plans which appear to have led to a place where I myself would not have led you, and would not let you go. I mobilized my atelier, a veritable team, entering into every detail to ensure that your needs and your financial means would be taken into account. All this work spanned a period of cost inflation. Faced with a project that did not conform to current practices, the contractors covered themselves, again and again,

10 Juillet 1952

Monsieur André JAOUL
26, rue Parmentier
<u>NEUILLY</u>

Cher Jaoul,

Vous êtes un ami, je suis votre ami, je vous écris en ami.

Votre attitude est fâcheuse, mauvaise, et serait décourageante si je n'avais forte tête et coeur solide. Vous n'avez pas confiance. J'ai fait, pour vous, un travail fantastique. J'y ai englouti bien au-delà des honoraires normaux que je vous demanderai. Vous avez acquis un terrain impossible, déplorable, écrasé de servitudes ou de réglementations. J'ai fait <u>moi-même</u>, sans relâche, combien de plans ? Pour arriver à réaliser le programme de la famille Jaoul. Vous aviez des plans de notre ami Ent. plans ayant de l'apparence et qui vous auraient conduit là où je ne pouvais vous laisser aller. J'ai mobilisé à mon atelier un véritable team, entrant dans tous les détails pour être certain de réaliser vos besoins et vos capacités financières. Tout ce travail a chevauché la période d'augmentation des prix. Les entrepreneurs devant un projet qui n'est pas d'usages courants, se couvrent, se recouvrent, arrivant à des prix ridicules. Alors, il faut reprendre pied à pied, redescendre, discuter, gagner les 100 % de trop qu'ils ont annoncé. Ce sont des entreprises sérieuses. Mais les gens désirent travailler sans ennuis, dans la routine, car la main d'oeuvre actuelle est disqualifiée par l'agitation politique ou professionnelle. Je fais des travaux sérieux, je suis un type sérieux, j'ai fait votre travail de <u>mes mains</u>, j'ai délégué les meilleurs de mon atelier pour réaliser votre travail.

Aujourd'hui, fin de semaine, nous sommes arrivés au terme de l'effort : vous aurez une maison admirable à habiter, "à la Jaoul" (votre programme) et au prix fixé.

Mais nous, étant prêts, vous-même vous n'avez pas réalisé votre convention de cour commune qui conditionne tout.

../...

Fig. 123
Letter from Le Corbusier to André Jaoul, July 10, 1952. FLC G2 (13) 43.

ending up with ludicrous prices. Thus, it is essential to review the situation step by step, to come back down, to discuss, to reclaim the 100% excess that they have quoted. They are serious companies. But they are people who want to work without any worries, in a traditional way... I do serious work, I'm a serious type, I carried out your work personally, I delegated the best men in my atelier to execute your work.

Today, at the end of the week, we have concluded our work: you could have an admirable house in which to live, "à la Jaoul" (your brief) and at a fixed price.

But even though we are ready, you yourself have not obtained the agreement for the common court that conditions everything.

You have treated your responsibilities lightly and come down on us heavily. Little matter! It's all part of the game; a client who only builds once in a lifetime naturally gets bogged down. You have the kind of detailed plans that no other architect would [have] ever produced.

Let's get on with it, Jaoul: it is only this week, after a whole year of work, that I have reached the end of the first phase. Be kind enough to show this letter to your wife.[102]

In this letter, the function (house brief), the economic reasons (a budget not exceeding the financial capacities of the families), and the consideration of site conditions constitute Le Corbusier's arguments to convince the Jaouls of the validity of his proposal: to respond to a program with budgetary restraints, on a terrain "crushed by servitudes and regulations."

Yet a sequence of problems slowed down procedures. In fact, one whole year, between the writing of this letter in July 1952 and the start of construction, intervened.[103] To begin, there were the delays imposed by the prefecture to obtain the building permit, then the lateness in taking the necessary steps to obtain the agreement for the common court, and finally the difficulties in proposing a house design with moderate enough costs to fulfill all requisite conditions for the construction loans, all the more necessary at a time when the Jaouls were facing a financial recession in their business affairs. There was even a question in April 1953 of treating House B separately, to be built with prefabricated elements. Only on June 23, 1953, that is eight months after obtaining the building permit, was the order given to start laying the foundations and constructing the basement of the two houses and, finally, the erection of House A.

Bidding was launched from November 1951 onward. Certain companies that were contacted refused to ensure the work on the vaults and masonry. In May 1952, Le Corbusier first accepted a contract with Etablissements Bertrand as the pilot company (handling foundation work, reinforced concrete, and masonry), but the general contractor Allard, selected by Jaoul, ultimately won the contract on June 9, 1953. Meanwhile the architect requested that part of the structural masonry work be given to Salvatore Bertocchi. "Those men in Entreprise Allard do not know how to make this type of vault!...Thus this was how Corbu made the client accept me!" recalled Bertocchi.[104]

Le Corbusier also appointed the remaining building trades: Charles Barberis for carpentry, *pans de verre*, and built-in furniture; Jules Alazard for glazing work; André Missenard for radiating heating panels beneath the floor boards; and Jean Martin for painting and enamel tile work. Delays announced for the start of construction increased to twelve months, counted from the date when the contractors received official notice from the architect to begin work.

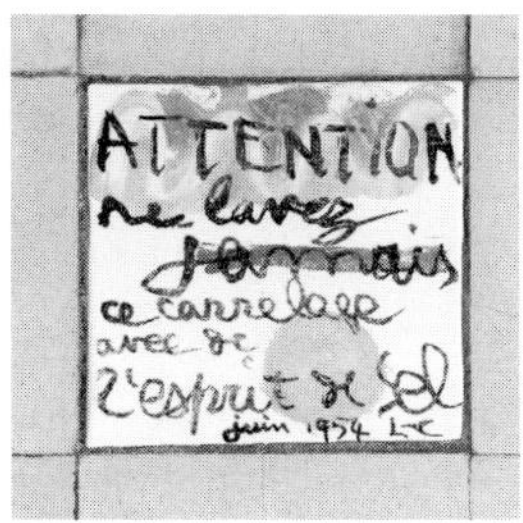

Chapter 2

THE ART OF THE "MAL FOUTU": THE CONSTRUCTION

Fig. 124
The Maisons Jaoul under construction in 1954, showing traces of the timbering of House B. All construction photographs in this book were taken by Lucien Hervé.

Artisan trades and small enterprises

Le Corbusier appreciated craftsmanship. He liked workmanship surface textures. Yet although he enjoyed observing the creative process, he rarely devoted much time to the actual construction site itself.[1] For the most part, he avoided contact with the contractors and all discussions and disputes over prices, delegating such issues to his collaborators.[2] The frequency of his visits to the sites depended largely on their proximity to his atelier and his personal relationships with his clients or contractor-artisans. Among his collaborators, Le Corbusier chose only those in whom "he had total confidence," that is to say, according to a close witness, collaborators who proved "flexible," "with little personal ambition," ready and willing to respect "his own ideas."[3] He expressly assigned such men to the jobsites and to direct contact with the building enterprises. In the case of the Maisons Jaoul, Le Corbusier delegated this role to Jacques Michel who had joined the atelier at the age of 26.[4] It was he who oversaw the construction site from July 1953 through the summer of 1955.

Le Corbusier had need of "loyal" men who could sense intuitively what he wanted without wasting any words. "A spirit of mutual confidence" united, for example, Le Corbusier and Fernand Gardien, who defined himself as a "simple draftsman" without the professional title of architect, "a fan of Le Corbusier" to whom the architect confided several major postwar construction sites. Functioning as a family was essential to the architect.

Whether from the building contractors or the artisans responsible for site work, Le Corbusier looked for this same type of devotion, confidence, and complicity, a capacity to be understood without spelling things out. The

Fig. 125 a, b, c, d
Advertising labels of companies associated with the Maisons Jaoul, reproduced in Jean Petit, ed., *Le Corbusier, Architecture du bonheur* (Le Corbusier, Architecture of Happiness), Les Presses d'Île-de-France, 1955.

Jaoul construction project represents the ideal case study to observe this working method in operation. There Le Corbusier selected his "family" by convincing the Jaouls to hire artisans with whom he had already established sympathetic relations: Bertocchi and Gnuva, Alazard, Barberis, Martin, and Missenard.[5]

Who exactly were these contractor-artisans with whom Le Corbusier collaborated so successfully? What sort of qualities united them? Nothing is particularly unusual in the fact that the architect sought to establish contacts with men who would ensure high standards of work, as any professional would. Nonetheless, it is important to stress the specific nature of this exchange with laborers in the building trades. In his dual quest for "primitivism" and "industrialism," Le Corbusier idealized the role of the artisan who helped to shape his architecture and to whom he conferred a double and paradoxical mission: to apply traditional technical know-how (on the Catalan vault, for example) while renouncing artisan practices (plaster or smooth trowel finishing work) so as to further accentuate the character of the materials (Fig. 124).

Le Corbusier relied upon a solid and homogeneous team, men who were independent and masters of their work, artisans capable and adept in creating an emotive architecture through their attuned sensibilities. In *Architecture du bonheur*,[6] a booklet published in 1955 (Fig. 126), Le Corbusier first introduces the principles that governed the building of the Unité d'Habitation at Nantes-Rezé; he concludes with a directory of all the names of the construction team members (including Barberis, Missenard, and Alazard), their professional addresses, and citations to their built works (Fig. 125 a, b, c, d). An obvious publicity stunt, this publication also corroborates the architect's genuine recognition of the team's contribution.

As early as the 1920s, Le Corbusier had searched for collaborators of Mediterranean descent: the employees of the concrete mason-contractor

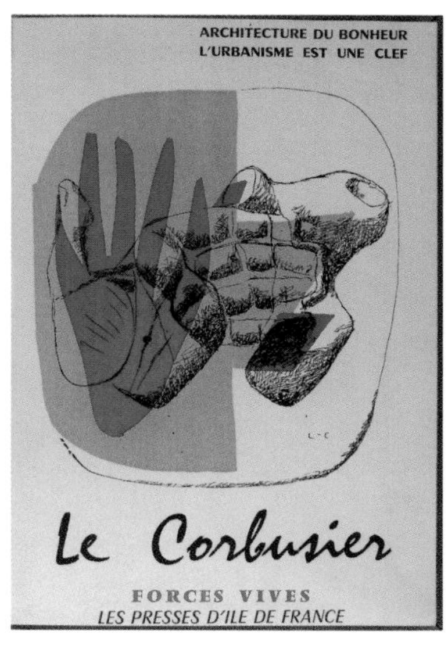

Fig. 126
Book cover, Jean Petit, ed., *Le Corbusier, Architecture du bonheur.*

Georges Summer such as Aimonetti, who worked on the Villa de Mandrot, and A. Celio, the painter and glazier, were recent Italian immigrants. After the Second World War he turned to Salvatore Bertocchi from Sardinia and Charles Barberis from Corsica. For the vaults, he also consulted architects Sert and Escorsa, from Catalonia. Sardinians, Corsicans, Italians, and Spaniards held a privileged place for the architect as "primitive" creative artisans. The rich, coherent details of the 1920s houses are due in large part to this collaborative team, all the more united as projects ofttimes ended in bitter disputes with the clients, reticent to pay additional costs demanded of them for work not clearly specified by either Pierre Jeanneret or Le Corbusier at the start of construction.[7]

Le Corbusier sought to coordinate the different trades, to involve them in the global task of construction. Above all, he tried his best to give the entire team the responsibility to collaborate on a common goal, while at the same time allowing the project to be the occasion for each individual member to test out his own area of expertise. He thereby encouraged these artisan-contractors to contribute intellectually and theoretically, by supporting and even soliciting their research in the form of books, prototypes, and patents. Consequently, he encouraged Barberis to apply for patents, suggested to Jean Martin that he compose a book on polychromy, and congratulated Jules Alazard for his written contribution to the history of window design.[8]

Le Corbusier created partnerships with his artisans in the same way as he cultivated collaborations with various artist-artisans, ceramicists, weavers, and sculptors. With Le Corbusier, to cite a few examples, the sign painter Raoul Simon executed the mural painting for the Swiss Pavilion at the Cité Universitaire in Paris (1947); Joseph Savina carved a series of wood sculptures[9] and Jacques Baudoin produced cartoons for tapestries based, respectively, on the architect's drawings and paintings. Jean Petit often collaborated on publication projects. Over and above the simple relationship

Fig. 127
Le Corbusier designing a concave sculptural form on the beaches of Long Island, following a technique developed by Nivola, accompanied by the latter's children, c. 1950.

Fig. 128
Le Corbusier and the artisan-workers on the roof of the Unité d'Habitation in Marseilles, 1952.

between the architect and the specialists of different techniques and materials, the rapport that Le Corbusier nurtured with these *créateurs-artisans* is proof of his need to find a natural extension to or outlet for his own personal creativity, to express himself fully and, at the same time, to share the artistic process with others. Perhaps a form of creative reserve, this need to collaborate might also reveal a lack of confidence in the architect who was searching for a means to confirm his intuitions through others in whom he had confidence and whose sensibilities accorded with his own. At the same time, such collaborations reveal, in the authority he exercised over the projects, the domineering male temperament of Le Corbusier. His way of securing specific ties with his contractors reiterates this same attitude.

The master mason and the Brutalist aesthetic

Le Corbusier's encounter with the Sardinian mason Salvatore Bertocchi came about through an intermediary, the artist Costantino Nivola, also Sardinian, whom the architect had met in January 1946 in New York during his second visit to the United States.[10] On the several occasions when the architect was attempting to secure his UN project, Nivola put him up at his house. Le Corbusier took the liberty of working in his atelier and found pleasure in experimenting with his friend's technique of executing huge sculptural sand compositions on the shores of Long Island (Fig. 127), as Le Corbusier so describes:[11]

> Nivola ... created sculptures in wet sand at low tide. With knives, spoons and other rudimentary instruments, the sand is formed into a cup-shape which serves as a mould. This mould was then filled with plaster thrown by hand straight on to the sand.[12]

Bertocchi was Nivola's cousin. After immigrating from Sardinia, he set up his own small contracting business in the Île-de-France region during the late 1940s.[13] First starting to work with Pierre Jeanneret (when he was no longer associated with his cousin), he was later hired by Le Corbusier on the Marseilles Unité d'Habitation construction site where he executed the masonry work on the roof terrace and the "artificial mountains," as Salvatore Bertocchi told the author in 1986.

In his *Œuvre complète*, Le Corbusier presents the Sardinian mason as the savior of the Marseilles project, wielding his trowel like an artist, with a sleight of hand capable of transforming the badly executed reinforced concrete formwork that resulted from unfortunate circumstances (according to Le Corbusier): "coordination was lacking, and indifferent workmen, even within the trade, were maladjusted to one another." As Le Corbusier recounts, he called on:

> ...a concretor, a Sardinian who understands his craft.... I designed certain parts of the building in a manner which required them to be modeled with the trowel—the workman is then working like a sculptor, directly shaping the material. By the arrangement of color and the use of the trowel, the contrasts were created and the splendor of bare concrete realized![14]

The Marseilles saga was worthy of Saint George's struggle with the dragon, a combat won in the end with the assistance of the "kind" artisan Bertocchi against the "wicked" entrepreneurs.

Bertocchi himself tells his own version of the Marseilles story:

> On the facade, there were places where the cement work looked dreadful. It was therefore necessary to hide it, but this was impossible to do everywhere because the construction was gigantic. Le Corbusier did not use the word "hide," but he did recommend plastering in the badly made formwork, the poorly poured concrete, the honeycombs.... When plastering over, one fills up those "sorts of things," those malformations, and in doing so, one highlights the imperfections...this was done on purpose...and it was this that interested him! With Le Corbusier, we got along well, we talked to one another... no need to have working drawings or details. We knew straightaway what needed to be done.... We discussed something for five minutes and after that I got on with it on my own and I did what pleased me.[15]

This firsthand witness account conveys an immediate sense of complicity. In this artisan, Le Corbusier had found an unspoken understanding that allowed him to express a certain poetic materiality. He and Bertocchi communicated in the same way on the Jaoul site. Their relationship was consolidated through friendship. It seems that Bertocchi asked Le Corbusier to be a godfather to his son Yves, born in 1951 (Fig. 129); however, it was Le Corbusier's wife Yvonne who would become his godmother. After her death in 1957, Le Corbusier assumed the role by sending Yves a gift, a dedicated book or a money order, two or three times a year.

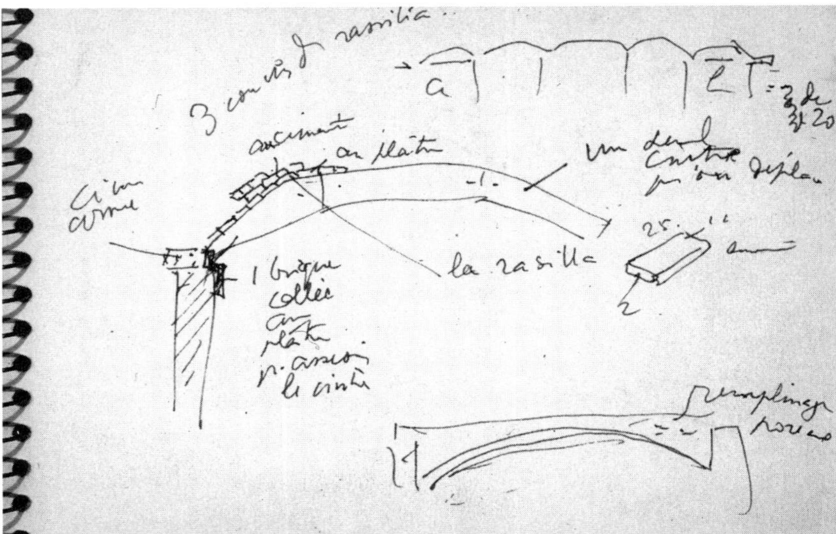

Fig. 129
Bertocchi and his son Yves, the godchild of Yvonne Gallis and Le Corbusier, 1953.

Fig. 130
Vaults in the home of the architect Pizano in Bogotá, September 19, 1950.

Bertocchi's recollections stress the importance of verbal exchanges and the spontaneous complicity between the two men: "We talked to one another...no need to have working drawings or details." His straightforward remark about the lack of need for detailed contract drawings (a conventional communication tool of the architect), due to the expertise of the artisan, reiterates Adolf Loos's critique of the architectural drawing.[16] Le Corbusier closely observed details in vernacular architecture, such as door handle types in Jura farmhouses and battens to close shutters. Not to succumb to the dry rationalism of theoretical architecture, he integrated such details into his own buildings as proof of his attachment to authentic, indigenous craft traditions.

As we have seen, during his trip to Colombia in 1950, Le Corbusier observed the low vaults at the house of the architect Pizano[17] (Fig. 130). On a later trip to Colombia, he took notes in his sketchbook on the system of wooden shutters, with a reminder to develop a similar system for the Jaouls. From Colombia to India, Le Corbusier's observations of the details of vernacular architecture confirmed the soundness of his approach.

The architect met the challenge of exploiting imperfections at the Unité d'Habitation in Marseilles, by acknowledging and endowing them with an aesthetic value, "I have decided to make beauty by contrast. I will find its complement and establish a play between crudity and finesse, between the dull and the intense, between precision and accident."[18] It seems that at Neuilly, too, he deliberately emphasized the play of contrasts. Brick became the medium of this venture, and his voyage to India in 1951 increased his taste for this particular building material (Fig. 131). Repeating the terms he employed in 1949 to specify the type of bricks that he wanted to use for Professor Fueter's house in Switzerland,[19] he asked his good artisan Bertocchi to use "rough brick, with a variety of tints, untreated surfaces, crudely cut edges...some very rough and thick joints."[20] Here he comes

Fig. 131
Indian contractor laying the brick walls of the Villa Sarabhai in Ahmedabad, 1954.

Fig. 132
Le Corbusier with Jacques Lipchitz in Ploumanach, Brittany, 1926. One of the types of photographs that Le Corbusier would have sent to Bertocchi.

close to the aesthetic developed by Jean Dubuffet, sensitive to the latent forces and aspirations expressed by the materials themselves, that, like "the randomness of the hand (its impulses, its tics, its spontaneous reactions) must also appear on stage when the play ends, to greet the audience with the actors."[21]

For the Maisons Jaoul, the architect's approach was similar. Le Corbusier explained to the mason his desire to see a certain number of wall samples made up with different types of joints and sent him a photograph of some Breton masonry as an inspirational model (Fig. 132; appendix):

> My dear Bertocchi,
> I'm sending you an enclosed photo of some Breton masonry; it's in stone, as you can clearly see.
> 1) For Jaoul, I'd like you to make a similar brick wall with joints more or less the same as shown in the photo, respecting all the proportions, as much on the interior as on the exterior. You will discuss this with Jacques Michel.
> 2) The most sensible idea would be to try to reproduce a few small wall sections on site, for example, 75 x 75, oriented in exactly the same way as Jaoul's, with different types of bricks that the general contractor will supply.
> Regards to you.[22]

In the same spirit, the architect had described the party wall of his atelier on the rue Nungesser-et-Coli (Fig. 61):

> Don't you see that this wall over here is beautiful? It's the neighbor's wall. It's the typical rubble stone wall of Paris, there are even two red-brick smoke ducts that traverse it...set between the rubble stones. When I saw this, I said: what an attractive wall. The assemblage is very beautiful. I used a very smooth grout to avoid dust and thus I have the gray of the cement

Fig. 133
The Maisons Jaoul under construction, 1954.

Fig. 134
Detail of the brick wall with its thick, uneven mortar joints.

and the beige of the stone and the pink of the brick, giving off a wonderful overall color.[23]

Bertocchi recalls Le Corbusier's recommendations for the look and texture of the walls of the Maisons Jaoul:

> He wanted the brick walls to be coarse, and that's not easy when you have good masons! It meant that the springers of the vaults were twisted, that the joints varied a little, that the vault took off like a wave along some thirty meters.[24]

There was no question in Le Corbusier's mind of making a tidy little detached brick house in Neuilly as if it belonged in a London suburb, but rather a poetic statement of inexactitude, of prevailing imprecision, a conscious bricolage, a purposefully makeshift, seemingly thrown together execution (Figs. 133 and 134). Le Corbusier's skepticism over the illusion of the suburban house was well known.[25] He detested the individualism derived from a suburbanite mentality (having no place for the suburb within his ideal Radiant City), as Blaise Cendrars, his Swiss compatriot from Chaux-de-Fonds, justly describes:

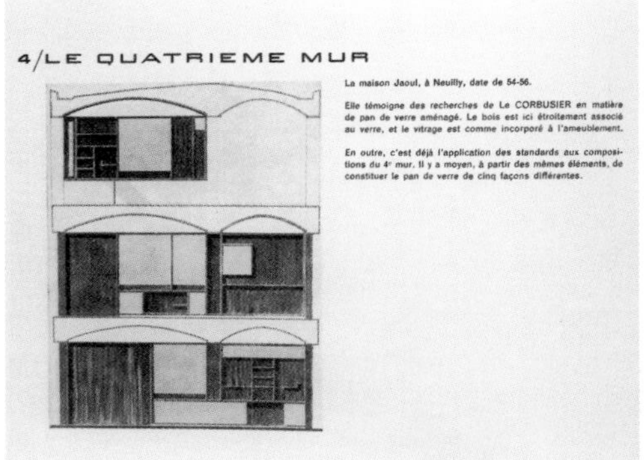

4/LE QUATRIEME MUR

La maison Jaoul, à Neuilly, date de 54-56.

Elle témoigne des recherches de Le CORBUSIER en matière de pan de verre aménagé. Le bois est ici étroitement associé au verre, et le vitrage est comme incorporé à l'ameublement.

En outre, c'est déjà l'application des standards aux compositions du 4e mur. Il y a moyen, à partir des mêmes éléments, de constituer le pan de verre de cinq façons différentes.

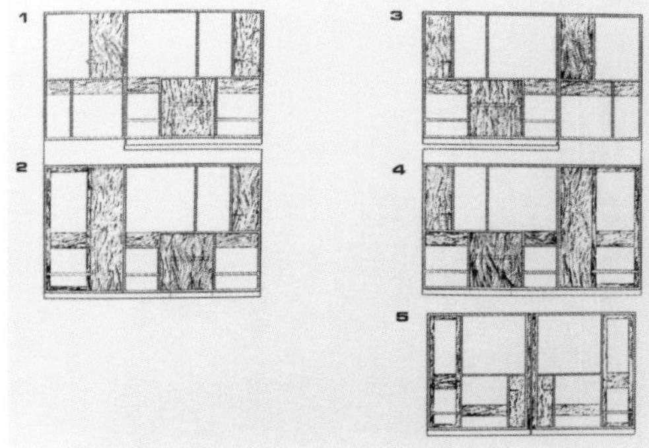

Fig. 135
House B construction site in 1954.

Fig. 136
Typical wall member, House B.

Fig. 137
Page layout, Jules Alazard, *De la fenêtre au pan de verre* (From the Window to the *Pan de Verre*), Paris, Dunod, 1961.

Fig. 138
Page layout, Jules Alazard, *De la fenêtre au pan de verre* (From the Window to the *Pan de Verre*), Paris, Dunod, 1961.

> And how not to be disappointed when one observes the architectural and horticultural extravagances that result from the hysterical love of nature and the desire to be a home owner, and all kinds of privations and petty economies, all for the sake of fulfilling a repressed dream: to possess 'one's own' villa![26]

Le Corbusier chose to expose brick walls whose overall coarse appearance paradoxically demanded a high level of precision in their execution (Figs. 135 and 136). In choosing brick for their variegated color and rough texture, and by playing with the effects of contrasts, he paid tribute to craftsmanship, in a way not unlike Dubuffet, who described its role in the execution of a work of art:

> The more the artist's hand is apparent in the entire work, the more moving, the more human, the more eloquent it will be. Avoid all mechanical and impersonal means. The most meticulous typography and calligraphy are less alluring than a few hand-written, unpremeditated words scrawled by a devoted hand.[27]

The artisan who laid the brick wall, therefore, had to understand and respect nature, the character and the essence of the material itself; he was obliged to do so, in response to Le Corbusier's expectations, not by refining and smoothing out the job, but on the contrary, by accentuating the irregularities intrinsic to it. Again Dubuffet's remarks are relevant:

> One should sense the man with his weaknesses and his clumsiness in all the details of a painting. In a line that's supposed to be straight, shakiness (because his hand is trembling), or interrupted (because of small irregularities or the granular surface of the paper that caused the brush to jump), ultimately trailing off at the end of its course (as the painter's raised arm begins to tire).[28]

In just this way, Le Corbusier celebrated the authenticity of the gesture. However, the very care summoned up to obtain this prosaic and mundane result—thick-jointed bricks—in actual fact called for a renunciation of traditional techniques and standard professionalism, while the "*bricolage*" (that is, the intentionally shoddy work) in reality demanded control, concentration, availability of time and additional work, thereby generating cost overruns and price increases despite the fact that the brick option was originally chosen at the start of the project, so it was argued, as a way of economizing. Untreated concrete formwork, too, required more time than plastered concrete because the former solution required good quality wood planks for this formwork and detailed drawings to specify their layout. In the end, therefore, the Jaouls lost out financially exactly because of their architect's Brutalist aesthetic choices.

Le Corbusier's attitude in all this was hardly new. The premise of a Brutalist aesthetic was already apparent in his work of the 1920s and 1930s, an important example being the rough concrete pillars of the Swiss Pavilion (1929–33), along with his search for materials with perceptible rudeness, specifically millstone grit.

This orientation can be linked to two politico-ideological episodes. In response to one of the clauses in the Loucheur law resulting from a petition of local artisans, the celebrated stone wall or "*mur diplomatique* (diplomatic wall)" of 1928 became a requirement, onto which two prefabricated cells would be attached. This episode captured the spirit of Le Corbusier's attempt to be populist, to demonstrate solidarity with the peasants and the contractors. In the early 1940s, a "return to the land" movement was initiated, with its associated ideology to express the substance or materiality of things, the myth of the "*main qui fabrique*" or the handmade. At this very same moment, in 1940–41, Le Corbusier was proposing that the "*Cercle des jeunes* (youth club)" themselves build the Murondins housing project (Fig. 139):

> It [the building] will be constructed by the users themselves, with their hands, on the site, with raw or practically unfinished materials found on the terrain: earth, sand, wood from the forest (poles), branches, bundles of wood, sod.[29]

Fig. 139
Book jacket designed by Le Corbusier, *Les Constructions "Murondins"* (The "Murondins" Buildings), Paris/Clermont-Ferrand, 1942.

Physical engagement was perceived as a reappropriation of his moral rights:

> Some walls, thrown up any which way, not having any real function as supports, made of pisé [rammed earth], hollow bricks, plots (agglomerates with a little lime), or even stone masonry or brick found in dilapidated abandoned farm outbuildings...walls that can be made by non-professionals.[30]

Mary C. McLeod has argued that formal changes in Le Corbusier's architecture during the 1930s should also be considered in light of his political engagements. Without claiming a direct relationship and clearly defined link between regional syndicalism and rustic forms, she nevertheless suggests that the architect's style and political transformations cannot be dissociated, as they inevitably and mutually influenced each other. In fact, these two aspects reflect his attempts to go beyond the sterility and inhumanity of the capitalist system, challenged during the Great Depression of the 1930s.[31] In the early 1940s, Le Corbusier created a collective called Ascoral (Assemblée de Constructeurs pour une Rénovation Architecturale), oriented toward a new perspective on postwar architectural and urban reconstruction policies in France.

The carpenter-cabinetmaker, the master glazier, and the panels

Two other artisan-contractors particularly appreciated by Le Corbusier were Italia-born Charles Barberis, carpenter-cabinetmaker in Villeneuve-Loubet, who later moved to Ajaccio, Corsica (its geographic location eventually

T 2 7 12

RÉPUBLIQUE FRANÇAISE

MINISTÈRE DE L'INDUSTRIE ET DU COMMERCE

SERVICE de la PROPRIÉTÉ INDUSTRIELLE

BREVET D'INVENTION

Gr. 7. — Cl. 3.

N° 996.664

Perfectionnements apportés aux ensembles à usage humain constitués par la juxtaposition d'éléments.

M. Charles-Édouard JEANNERET-GRIS, dit LE CORBUSIER, résidant en France (Seine).

Demandé le 15 mai 1945, à 16h 32m, à Paris.

Délivré le 5 septembre 1951. — Publié le 24 décembre 1951.

(*Brevet d'invention dont la délivrance a été ajournée en exécution de l'article 11, § 7, de la loi du 5 juillet 1844 modifiée par la loi du 7 avril 1902.*)

L'invention est relative aux ensembles à usage humain, tels que meubles, habitats, logis, immeubles, agglomérations, constitués par la juxtaposition d'éléments, notamment d'éléments standards préfabriqués.

Elle a pour but, surtout, de faciliter l'établissement de tels ensembles présentant une grande diversité dans leurs formes, leurs dimensions et leurs agencements, à partir d'un nombre relativement très limité d'éléments standards appropriés.

Elle consiste principalement à constituer, au moins en partie, les ensembles du genre en question par une pluralité d'éléments présentant chacun un contour en forme de quadrilatère rectangle, certains au moins de ces éléments étant juxtaposés par des côtés dont les longueurs respectives, exprimées en une unité de longueur choisie à volonté, répondent substantiellement à la formule ci-après :

$$L = N(A \times a + B \times b + C \times c + D \times d + E \times e + \ldots\ldots + N \times n)$$

dans laquelle :

N est un coefficient fixé selon les besoins mais constant pour un ensemble donné;

A, B, C, D, E... N sont les termes successifs d'une série telle que chacun de ses termes soit la somme des deux précédents et soit de préférence égal au précédent multiplié par $\frac{1+\sqrt{5}}{2}$,

et *a, b, c, d, e... n* sont des coefficients dont l'un au moins n'est pas nul et présente une valeur égale à l'unité divisée ou multipliée par un nombre entier.

Elle consiste, mise à part cette disposition principale, en certaines autres dispositions qui s'utilisent de préférence en même temps et dont il sera plus explicitement parlé ci-après.

Elle vise plus particulièrement un certain mode d'application, ainsi que certains modes de réalisation, desdites dispositions; et elle vise plus particulièrement encore, et ce à titre de produits industriels nouveaux, les ensembles du genre en question comportant application desdites dispositions, ainsi que les éléments spéciaux préfabriqués propres à leur établissement.

Et elle pourra, de toute façon, être bien comprise à l'aide du complément de description qui suit, ainsi que du dessin ci-annexé, lesquels complément et dessin sont, bien entendu, donnés surtout à titre d'indication.

La figure 1 de ce dessin, réunit six schémas (*a* à *f*) représentant autant de combinaisons d'éléments recouvrant une même surface.

La figure 2, enfin, est une construction géométrique qui sera explicitée ci-après.

Selon l'invention et plus particulièrement selon celui de ses modes d'application, ainsi que selon ceux des modes de réalisation de ses diverses parties, auxquels il semble qu'il y ait lieu d'accorder la préférence, se proposant, par exemple, d'établir un panneau de pièce d'habitation, ce panneau devant être constitué par la juxtaposition d'éléments présentant chacun une forme générale de quadrilatère rectangle et correspondant respectivement à des éléments de mur ou à des plaques de revêtement en matières diverses, à des parties transparentes (fenêtres), à des portes, à des meubles tels que casiers, coffres encastrés dans la paroi ou appliquées sur elle, etc., on s'y prend comme suit ou de façon analogue.

On dimensionne ces éléments de telle façon que au moins certains et de préférence la totalité de leurs côtés présentent respectivement des longueurs

1 - 02026

Prix du fascicule : 25 francs.

B LC

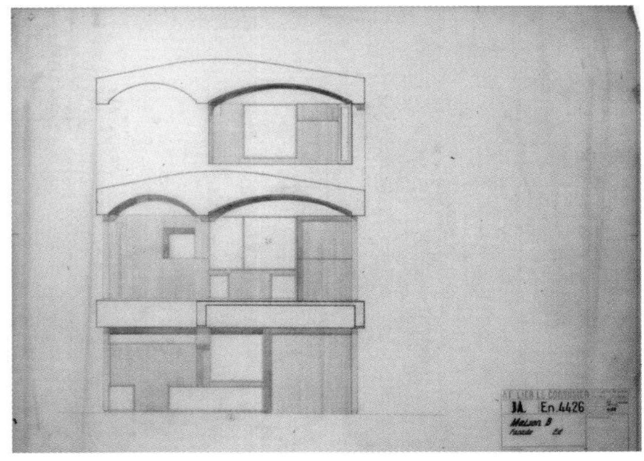

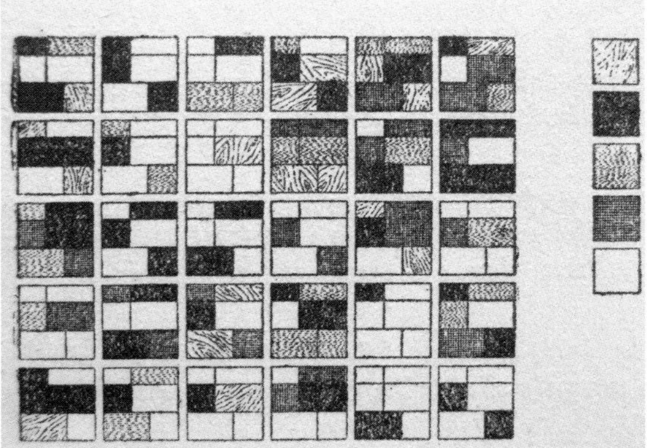

Fig. 140
Le Corbusier, patent certificate issued on September 5, 1951. FLC T2 (7) 12.

Fig. 141
The facade elevation of House B, drawn by G. Samper, showing the rough concrete and *pan de verre* in laminboard, dated April 24, 1952. FLC 9926.

Fig. 142
"Le jeu des panneaux (The play of panels)" [for the composition of the facades]: five different materials are introduced into the design. Extract from Le Corbusier, *Le Modulor*, Éditions de L'Architecture d'aujourd'hui, 1950, 101.

proving problematic, (Figs. 143–145) and Jules Alazard, master glazier, situated in the 19th arrondissement of Paris. These two artisan-contractors were closely associated with installing the "built-in *pans de verre*," alternating with the wooden panels and glazing, all based on the Modulor system.

Le Corbusier was interested in interchangeable combinations to allow a juxtaposition of rectangular elements (Fig. 142). He filed a patent application on May 15, 1945, delivered on September 5, 1951, and published on December 24, under the following designation: "Improvements to design units for human use composed with juxtaposed elements" (Fig. 140). This patent defined a panel wall for a domestic room, made up of diverse, contrasting elements (rectangular or square), corresponding either to wall elements or to revetment panels in various materials (aluminum, plywood) or transparent elements (windows), doors, furniture, shelving units and storage compartments, built into the wall or attached to it.[32] Assembled in a workshop and installed in-situ, these panels required careful calculation to integrate them into an already existing structure. With Barberis and Alazard, Le Corbusier considered prefabricating these building parts in a factory. He certainly would have harbored memories of the painful setbacks caused by the prefabricated metal-frame windows for the Cité Frugès housing complex at Pessac (1928), which turned out to be ill-adapted to the preexisting openings in the concrete walls.[33]

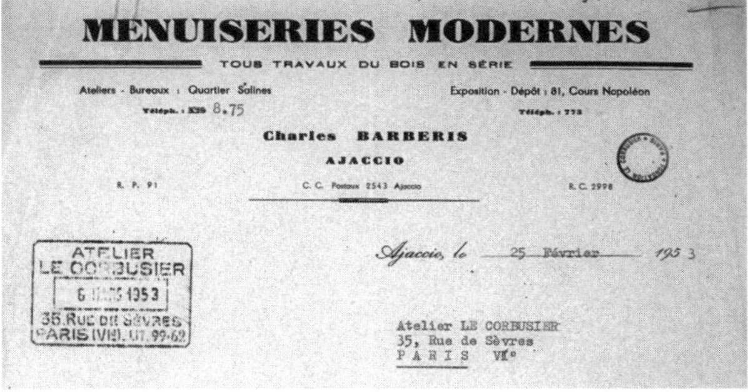

MENUISERIES MODERNES

TOUS TRAVAUX DU BOIS EN SÉRIE

Ateliers - Bureaux : Quartier Salines
Téléph. : 8.75

Exposition - Dépôt : 81, Cours Napoléon
Téléph. : 773

Charles BARBERIS

AJACCIO

R. P. 91 — C. C. Postaux 2543 Ajaccio — R. C. 2998

ATELIER LE CORBUSIER 6 MARS 1953 35, RUE DE SÈVRES PARIS (VII). LIT. 99-62

Ajaccio, le 25 Février 1953

Atelier LE CORBUSIER
35, Rue de Sèvres
PARIS VIe

Fig. 143
Le Corbusier at a meeting in Barberis's workshop in Ajaccio, 1952.

Fig. 144
Barberis's letterhead stationery, "Menuiseries Modernes (Modern Woodwork)."

Fig. 145
Le Corbusier during a visit to Barberis's workshop in Ajaccio, 1952.

The letterhead stationery of the two contractors displayed their industrial ambitions: Barberis's carpentry company advertises the execution of "all industrial and specialized work" (Fig. 144); Alazard's glazing company proclaims its "glass for industrial use" using manufactured products from the Saint-Gobain and Boussois factories (Fig. 152).

From the days of the Marseilles Unité d'Habitation construction onward, when the Barberis artisan-industrial firm was responsible for furnishing the *pans de verre* required for the 350 apartments units, Le Corbusier regularly associated with the Corsican carpenter in his research of wood as a major design component. The architect established two guiding principles for the fabrication process: a rough piece of wood was worked from a single timber block, unevenly squared off, or an industrial treatment where the detailing was simplified. The same effect, as Le Corbusier observed, was realized at the Chapel at Ronchamp, without "[a]ny décor, any sculpture, any molding, all hand-made, agreeable to the touch, crafted... worked with the chisel, moving, pared down, yet with a smooth, nuanced exterior."[34]

Barberis applied these two methods when he worked on the Cabanon at Cap-Martin (1951–52) and the five Unités d'Habitation de Vacances (1952–55) in Meaux.[35] He was also in charge of the woodwork for the *pans de verre* at Nantes-Rezé Unité d'Habitation (1948–55).[36] Each case study provided the occasion to reflect on the appropriate type of wood and the

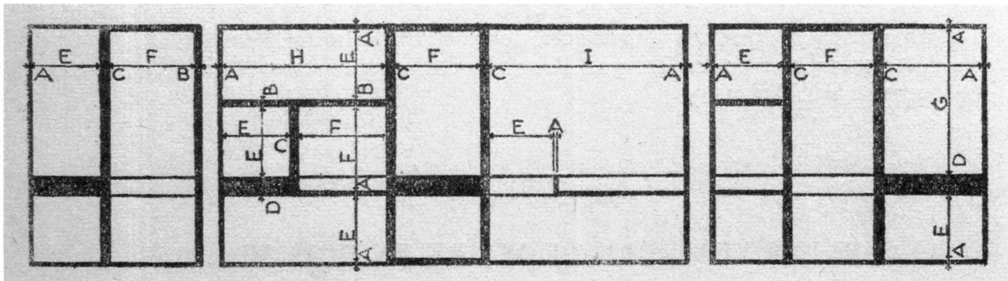

Fig. 146
"A new *pan de verre* in wood." Extract from Le Corbusier, *Le Modulor*, Éditions de l'Architecture d'aujourd'hui, 1950.

Fig. 147
Entrance to House A.

Fig. 148
The "*pans de verre* fitted-in" to House B in alternating patterns with the wood panels and the windows based on Modulor proportions.

Fig. 149
Book cover, *Claviers de couleurs, Salubra* (Keyboards of Colors, Salubra), Basel, Salubra, 1959, after a drawing by Le Corbusier.

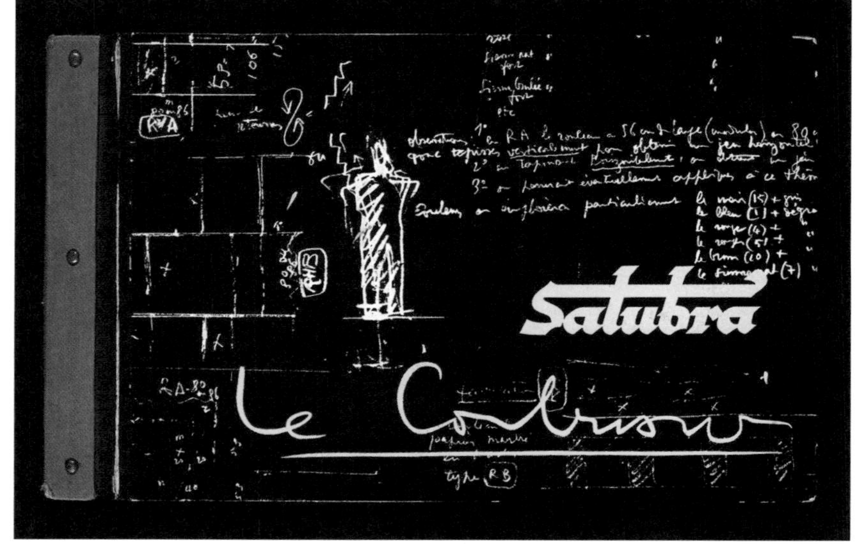

system of assembly and prefabrication, testing the close collaboration between the atelier and the contractor. Both teams devised alternative wood joints and shared their discoveries. Le Corbusier encouraged Barberis to present these prototypes at various trade fairs. Here again Le Corbusier evokes the teachings of Loos:

> I entered the workshop timidly, like an apprentice. I looked up at the man with the blue apron respectfully, and begged: let me share your secret. Because many a secret of the workshop lay modestly hidden from the architect's sight. And when they understood my intentions, when they recognized that I was not one of those who wanted to deform that beloved wood by drawing-board fantasies, when they saw that I did not want to desecrate that reverentially venerated material with green or violet staining, their own proudness came to the surface, their carefully concealed tradition was brought to light and their hatred of their oppressors was vented.[37]

The same creative dialogue characterized the relationship between Le Corbusier and Alazard, one which led to the latter's writing a book called *De la fenêtre au pan de verre dans l'œuvre de Le Corbusier*.[38] Before becoming a master glazier, Alazard had studied architecture and worked in the rue de Sèvres atelier during the 1930s. However, upon the death of his father, he took over his mirror-and-glazing company. Following the family tradition, he became interested in participating in the architect's research on the evolution of window design (from the *fenêtres en longueur* and neutralizing *pan de verre* to the *brise soleil* and *quatrième mur*) and on the diverse and distinct functions of the window, from illumination to ventilation[39] (Figs. 137, 138, and 141). Le Corbusier appreciated his competence: "M[onsieur] Jules Alazard has been a precious collaborator: he was a man born of the trade (from a dynasty of glassmakers) and, as for me, I was Le Corbusier discoverer of... among other things: the architecture of reinforced concrete."[40]

In *Modulor 2*, Le Corbusier took up Alazard's remarks about his research on windows:

> What a thorough, meticulous, continuous evolution the window [has undergone] since your articles in the *Esprit Nouveau* of 1920 until now! The windows "*en longueur*" [strip window] developed out of industrial wood, metal or reinforced concrete construction and dimensions of the human body. Then the "*pan de verre*" [window section]... gets rid of the costly "lintel" under the ceiling and alleviates weight on the floor; it brings considerable resources to one of the principle functions of the façade: to illuminate. Then over the years the *pan de verre* becomes "the fourth wall" of the bedroom; it is not made entirely of glass; some panels are opaque; book shelves can be attached to it; tables can lean against it; it plays a role in bringing light to strategic places, the lateral walls, the ceiling and the floor. Then came the "brise soleil"

[sun breaker] that quells the sun's intensity, this enemy suddenly appearing through the *pan de verre*.... From then on, the glazing being protected from the rain, wood can replace metal. At this point, the wood window frame is no longer made as a flat sash, but as a recessed frame. This is a new aesthetic for the window. The window rises to the rank of furniture, it can be an architectural statement in and of itself, inside and out.[41]

Allard executed the glazing-and-mirror work for the Unités d'Habitation of Nantes-Rezé (1948–55) and Briey-en-Forêt (1956–63), as well as for the Maison du Brésil (1953–59) where double-glazed "thermopanes" were installed on a cement rebate. This great flurry of commissions allowed the Allard Enterprise to evolve into a medium-size enterprise with more than ten salaried workers.

Bertocchi, Barberis, and Alazard were not the only artisans whom Le Corbusier valued. He also appreciated the glazier and enamelist Jean Martin who ran a paint factory in Luynes. Le Corbusier enjoyed going there to work with him when executing the glazing, enamel, and ceramic decorations in the National Assembly Building at Chandigarh and the Chapel at Ronchamp. It was here in Martin's atelier, during the year 1954, that the architect completed a series of tiles carrying the warning "Be careful never to clean this tile with bleach [*esprit de sel*]!" Jean Martin executed the paint work on the interior walls, ceilings, exterior panels (one coat of varnish) and interior panels (one coat of oil to two coats of matt varnish) and furnished the glazing, enamel, and ceramic sheet-iron tiles that were fixed to the kitchen worktable.[42] The paints used on the Jaoul job were called "Matroil" and "Matone" from Berger Etablissements, a brand highly regarded by the architect, according to his letter addressed to Marcel Levaillant in 1956:

The point of my letter is to say that if you want to be in a harmoniously painted environment, you cannot and must not use anything but Matroil paints from the company 'Peinture Berger'.... There is no other color to compare with them, and if your painter objects, get rid of him.[43]

As for André Missenard, a graduate engineer from the Ecole Polytechnique in Paris and heating engineer by profession, Le Corbusier met him in the circle of Alexis Carrel in the late 1930s. Professor at the Conservatoire national des arts et métiers, he published several texts on home heating and air conditioning, in particular *L'Homme et le climat* in 1937 (Fig. 150).[44] In 1950, he contributed to an issue of *Techniques et Architecture* devoted to thermal equipment, with an article on the effects of temperature on human beings:

The social consequences arising from the possibility of heating all rooms in a house are considerable: no longer constrained during ever-increasing leisure hours to gather round the single family hearth, members of the same family

Fig. 150
Paperback cover, André Missenard, *L'Homme et le climat* (Man and Climate), Paris, Plon, 1937.

Fig. 151
Metal latches on the wood shutters in the kitchen of House B.

> could spread themselves out, reflect on their own, read, educate themselves, separated from the noise and idle chatter of the family circle. Given that a sound education would have instilled a taste for instructive reading in them, the spiritual life of all family members would be enhanced. And democracy which, generally speaking, the all-powerful masses are still incapable of using intelligently, would be more than a beautiful dream.[45]

Missenard not only practiced as a heating engineer, but also understood the importance of the role of the acclimatized environment as an essential feature of architecture.

Le Corbusier was also very attached to the locksmith Dujourdy who invented the metal latches that became a characteristic feature of the ventilation shutters in the Maisons Jaoul (Fig. 151), the Maison du Brésil, and ultimately in the Cabanon at Cap-Martin.

Adventures on the site

A frank description of relations with these artisan-contractors cannot, however, be summed up as altogether idyllic and non-conflictual. If Le Corbusier strove above all to collaborate with his carefully selected artisans, this tactic did not prevent a long drawn-out period of construction at the Jaoul site (July 1953 to October 1955) from becoming a theatre of adventures: defects; delays in the delivery of materials; budget overruns; financial difficulties for the owners; and late payments to suppliers, workers, and architects. This was hardly an unusual scenario for Le Corbusier.

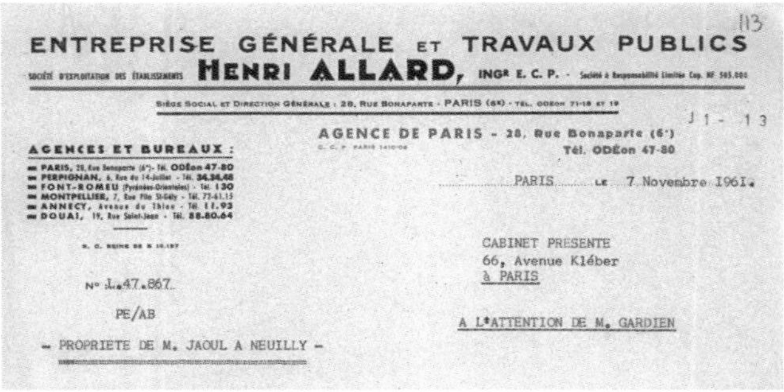
ENTREPRISE GÉNÉRALE ET TRAVAUX PUBLICS
HENRI ALLARD, INGR E. C. P.
AGENCE DE PARIS - 28, Rue Bonaparte (6e)
Tél. ODÉon 47-80
AGENCES ET BUREAUX :
PARIS
PERPIGNAN
FONT-ROMEU
MONTPELLIER
ANNECY
DOUAI
PARIS le 7 Novembre 1961.
CABINET PRESENTE
66, Avenue Kléber
à PARIS
No L.47.867
PE/AB
A L'ATTENTION DE M. GARDIEN
- PROPRIETE DE M. JAOUL A NEUILLY -

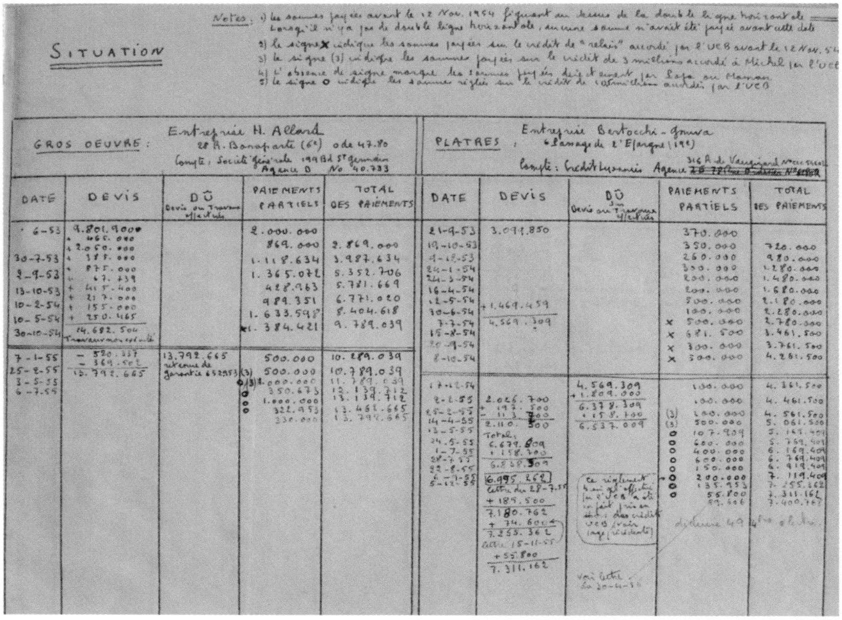
SITUATION
GROS OEUVRE :
Entreprise H. Allard
PLATRES :
DATE
DEVIS
DÛ
PAIEMENTS PARTIELS
TOTAL DES PAIEMENTS

Fig. 152
Letterhead stationery, Entreprise Allard.

Fig. 153
Michel Jaoul's account book, 1954. Jaoul archives.

However, the Jaouls too played a part in the unforeseen turn of events on the building site. It turned out that they were not able to borrow as much money as they needed. During the year 1953, they encountered difficulties, and Michel Jaoul alerted Le Corbusier on December 1, 1953, by referring to the "CMB business," the loan organization on which they had depended:

> This forced us to reconsider the sequence of work at least until such time as I can discuss with my father alternative financial solutions that one might envisage. The contractors and your collaborators have taken the necessary steps so that we can provisionally limit the structural work and the damp proofing.[46]

Activity progressed slowly. On June 17, 1954, Le Corbusier left a note for Wogenscky regarding delays caused by the Jaouls' difficulties: "Despite the Jaoul payment delays, we must press on with the building work and insist that the contractors make an effort to terminate this thundering good jobsite before winter."[47] The death of André Jaoul in November 1954 again

Fig. 154
The construction site in 1953, showing traces of the timbering on House B.

threatened the financing of the project. During a three-month period, Michel Jaoul halted the work. He needed a clearer picture of the family's financial situation and demanded an up-to-date statement of expenses already incurred by the contractors, becoming very fastidious over all cost outlays (Fig. 153).

From this difficult period, only a few of the most memorable moments of this adventure (fortunate or unfortunate) are here evoked. They include the havoc surrounding the pouring-in of the rough concrete; the saga of the vaults; the delays over the delivery of the woodwork; and the difficulties encountered by Allard Enterprise, responsible for the structural work, including foundations, basement, and ground-level floor, as well as the lintels crowning the brick walls.

Havoc over the installation of the rough concrete

From the very start of the building process, a stormy correspondence ensued between Jacques Michel and Monsieur Espinasse from Allard (Fig. 152). This company (which André Jaoul himself had originally insisted on hiring) encountered difficulties in installing the reinforced concrete beams (2.29 feet in height and 1.08 feet in width), forming both the continuous chaining band along the entire construction and the lintels above the bays. These beams required special formwork, timbering with planks laid either vertically or horizontally, or in a herringbone pattern based on Modulor proportions (Figs. 133 and 154). On October 12, 1953, Jacques Michel notified Allard that the formwork had not been executed in conformity with the plans:

> In agreement with M[onsieur] Le Corbusier, I am informing you that the high concrete beams at the ground-floor level of House B are unacceptable. You have poured these beams using the most outmoded methods possible, for example: to carry the concrete from the ground to the height of the beams, that is 3m[eters], you used an intermediary platform and poured the concrete in two castings up to the formwork, which caused the cement slurry to harden on the floor; it is possible that the intensive reinforcing bar in the beams

> prevented the cement from spreading evenly, or as the vibrator was broken, you compressed the cement into the formwork poorly; perhaps it was also a question of the measured quantities. Faced with this *fait accompli*, we hope that the high beams on the first story will be executed according to correct procedures and that you will kindly remedy this deficiency in the future.[48]

Allard indeed tried to remedy this less than satisfactory work. However, on October 29, 1953, Jacques Michel once again wrote to give precise directions for redoing the faulty work:

> I hope that the formworks that you are reconstituting will give the impression of a beam poured in one casting. Under no circumstances can we accept variations in materials and colors. I advise you not to lapse into decoration. This morning I noticed that some formwork that you executed are cantilevered past the brick wall by 0,33. If the wall measures less, it will be necessary to cheat and reestablish the unity of the beam. But you made an academic statement out of it by creating beautiful formwork compared with the others. . . . Let me remind you that the architecture of this building is utterly simple: rough concrete, large bare walls of exposed brick, etc. The final result resides in good execution with certain precautions taken at the opportune moment.[49]

Faced with defects in execution, Le Corbusier reacted by looking to justify the imperfections and by defending the aesthetic of the accidental, as Bertocchi emphasizes in recalling the following incident:

> Sometimes things were badly made, he was reluctantly obliged to retain them; but later, he played with the contrasts. For example, in House B, the central line of pillars in the concrete staircase was badly poured, it was awful. There were honeycombs everywhere. The company wanted to plaster them over. Then Corbu said: "No, this is the way it is and this is the way it will remain!" By contrast, on the exterior of House A, the workmen had poorly executed the band molding, the design of the rough concrete had come out badly. There, Le Corbusier had it regrinded![50]

Difficulties with Allard did not stop in 1955 when the Jaouls finally moved into their houses. In January 1961, they notified Le Corbusier's office of the subsidence of the balcony on House A and, to the right of the balcony, vertical fissures (running from below ground to the second floor) affecting the lintels on the upper floor. An expert appraiser concluded, on April 22, that the cause of the problem was due to "a settlement of the ground underneath the footing of the post. . . . We have agreed that the balcony should be raised by an hydraulic jack and that the underpinning of the post should be redone from its foundation."[51] Several months later, both architect and Allard were declared equally responsible for the

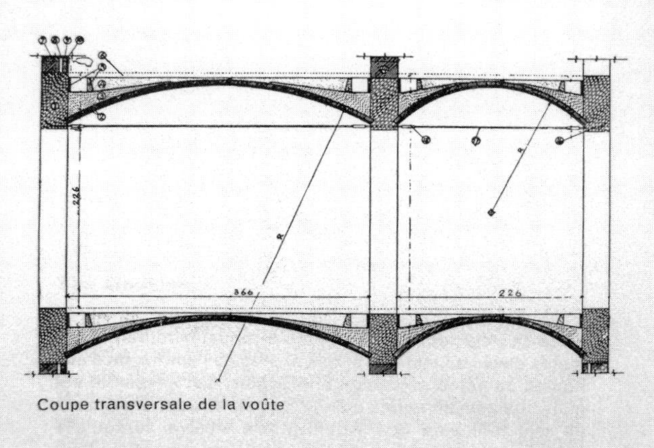

Fig. 155
Erection of the Catalan vault in House B, 1953.

Fig. 156
Section through the vaults, House B. *Œuvre complète*, vol. 5, 177.

damage incurred. The expert identified the cause of the accident: "In any case, if precautions were not taken to keep away the rain waters, the post should not have been supported on the surface of the topsoil, but lower down on more solid ground."[52] On November 7, 1961, after being given notice by the Jaouls, Allard informed Fernand Gardien (one of the collaborators in the rue de Sèvres office responsible for estimates and contacts with the contractors) that "to satisfy M[onsieur] Jaoul, we confirm that we have decided to redo... the foundations of the balcony post without waiting for a decision from the insurance company."[53] From that point, it took almost one year to resolve the problem.

Installation of the vaults

In contrast to these difficulties, Bertocchi's installation of the Catalan vault was a moment of great satisfaction on the jobsite, mobilizing the entire team—Le Corbusier, his atelier collaborators, the Jaouls, and the mason—in this "successful achievement." Domènec Escorsa, specialist in this domain, was also present to oversee this full-scale demonstration.[54]

During July of 1951, Le Corbusier had sketched out the basic construction principle for a low-slung Catalan vault, one made without centering (Fig. 77), giving precise dimensions of the brick (11.4 in x 5.5 in x 0.59 in). The total thickness of the layer of terra-cotta tiles had to be 5.9 inches. A lightweight form could be moved on after each row was laid. For the first non-plastered row, some *plafonnette* bricks, also called fire guard bricks or *barcelonines* were used, either mounted longitudinally or in a herringbone pattern. Once the first row of terra-cotta tiles was laid, it produced both the formwork to the other rows and the visible face of the vault (Fig. 130).[55]

Bertocchi initially explained the role of the portable arch center: it was mounted on the wooden wedges cotters resting on cantilevered bricks, the line of bricks forming a sort of rail at the springing of the vaults. This light formwork, made of soft wood, took on the desired shape in order to serve as a support for the first row of 0.78-inch hollow *briquettes*, joined with plaster on the underside. A screed of 0.4-inch cement mortar was laid, on top of which a second row of cement-jointed solid bricks of 1.9 inches reinforced the entire structure. After having executed a section of the vault few meters long, Bertocchi himself climbed on top of the vault, already a few meters long, to reassure the onlookers (who feared that the whole structure would cave in): "If you understand how vaulting works, you know that it can't collapse. The more weight you put on the vault, the more it can withstand!"[56]

Afterwards, the groins of the vault were filled with concrete and slag to prevent any deformations (Fig. 156). A screed of 1.5-inch cement concrete enclosed the floor-heating tubes that slid into the intrados. The concrete culverts, placed into the groins of each vault, contained the water pipes and electrical canalization. In the interior, the floor covering was laid directly on the heating slab. On the roof garden, the concrete cement screed was replaced by a sloping concrete vermiculite form to improve thermal insulation. A thick asphalt layer of 0.78 or 1.18 inches, poured while hot, covered by a layer of topsoil seeded with grass, guaranteed waterproofing.

Inside, on the ground and first floors of the two houses, the vaulted ceilings in *barcelonines* were left exposed. Elsewhere they were plastered over. In the main rooms, the flat tiles of the vaults were waxed; in the rooms prone to humidity, they were treated with waxed varnish.[57]

The vaults rest on continuous reinforced concrete beams, 13 inches wide and 27.55 inches deep. Situated 7.4 feet from the ground, these beams are an integral part of the longitudinal walls. They create a continuous chain bond, at each floor level, forming the lintel over the bays. The 8.66-inch-thick solid brick exterior walls are laid and jointed with cement mortar. The interior walls are doubled with a 2.36-inch-thick brick wall, covered with a 0.75-inch-thick plaster finish. A space of 2.36 inches is left between the two walls. The 13-inch-wide interior spine wall is made of solid bricks.

The transverse tie-rods

An unexpected problem cropped up during the course of construction in September 1953. On the advice of the engineer Escorsa, some transverse metal tie-rods (0.62 inches in diameter) were anchored into the lintels.[58] This requirement would not have been necessary had a decision been made to incorporate a wider beam section, extending past the Modulor unit, which would have allowed a construction free of such stiffeners, judged unsightly by Le Corbusier. This issue gave rise to a correspondence between the engineer in Béziers and Jacques Michel at the rue de Sèvres atelier who expressed his dissatisfaction: "This morning I saw the tie-rods installed with their stretching devices, they really aren't very attractive. They're enormous."[59] Escorsa responded:

> I never advised making the vaults without tie-rods as it is obvious that the natural thrust of the vaults must be absorbed, but in the case of your space, a wider beam section would have allowed the vaults to be made without any tie rod. If you had three or more bays of vaults, you could, if need be, eliminate

> the tie rods in the bay or the intermediate bays, but it would always be necessary to 'tie rod' the end vaults.[60]

Given the necessity for these stiffeners, the construction of the Catalan vault at Neuilly was slightly different from the traditional model, where the natural thrust of the vaults is absorbed by the thickness of the supporting walls.

In these discussions, an obvious contradiction emerged between the customary techniques of the artisan, on the one hand, associating a vault with thick walls and the aesthetic choice of the architect, on the other hand, seduced by the association of thin vaults with thin walls. What resulted was an unanticipated technical concession that forced the introduction of the metal tie bars.

Installation of the finishing carpentry and furniture

Delays in fabrication and delivery caused by the Corsican artisan woodworker Charles Barberis greatly upset the Jaouls. Le Corbusier's letters addressed to him on the subject convey a good idea of his tactical approach, a subtle balance between firmness of tone and demonstration of feeling.

Barberis accumulated endless delays in the delivery of the wood panels, originally ordered on June 15, 1954 (Figs. 154, 157, 158). Tension mounted between the architect's office, the client, and the contractor, the latter adopting the tone of a scolded child in his letter to Le Corbusier dated September 20 of the same year:

> You sent me one complimentary letter, you sent me another full of reproaches. Both of them as you know affected me deeply. The first came as a surprise to me; I awaited the second with growing anguish as the days went by.[61]

Le Corbusier did not let himself be softened by Barberis's confession. He responded firmly on October 1: "I hardly think that you're someone who has bad intentions. Unfortunately, though, facts are facts and I ask that you immediately perform the impossible in order to make up for the terrible delay."[62] Despite this unequivocal firmness, he did however defend his artisan in the eyes of the Jaouls: "I have every confidence in Barberis as a man of extreme seriousness whose professional qualities are indispensable to our work."[63] Irritated by the long delay in construction, however, Michel Jaoul wrote to Barberis on October 19. He pointed out that the delivery of eight crates (which ought to have been assured early that month) had been delayed until October 16, that is seventeen days after the notice of their arrival in Marseilles, and then, adding insult to injury, only six of the expected eight crates had arrived safely:

> I am taking this opportunity to express my total dissatisfaction over the unacceptable delay incurred over fulfilling the order that I agreed you should

Fig. 157
View of House B pending the overdue delivery of the woodwork inserts, 1954.

Fig. 158
View of House A pending Barberis's overdue delivery of the woodwork inserts, 1954.

> make with the Atelier Le Corbusier. I should also like to remind you that the sum of 660,000 francs was transferred to your account on 31 March, and it was only during the month of July that I received one part of the order for the interior door and window frames for my house, [and] then in October, a small portion of the exterior woodwork. Moreover, the installment of these interior frames was not carried out in the presence of your company representative, so that another contractor was obliged to assume the responsibility for this operation.
>
> In agreement with Le Corbusier's office, we had established the construction schedule to allow my moving into the house by October. In spite of a lamentable late delivery, I had by then accepted the commitment that you had made with Le Corbusier's office to deliver the wainscoting that I had ordered at the end of the month of August. The end of August arrived and I was informed that this delivery would be made only in the month of September. Here now the 2nd or 3rd of the month of October has gone by and once again the deliveries are incomplete.[64]

A change of circumstances brought about by the death of André Jaoul on November 12, 1954, obliged Michel Jaoul to inform Le Corbusier's atelier by mail that he did not want to take on:

> ...any new engagements for expenses before having had the chance of working out the exact amount owed for the work already completed as well as the possibilities of other sources of financing. As soon as these two sums have been established, together we shall review the exact estimate of the remaining work necessary to complete the construction and then we shall consider how the work could be organized.[65]

In this letter, he also sought to clarify this seemingly confused situation. In the meantime Le Corbusier's atelier relayed information to Michel Jaoul that there was urgency in protecting House B from the rain (despite the interim decision to interrupt all construction work)[66] and added that a

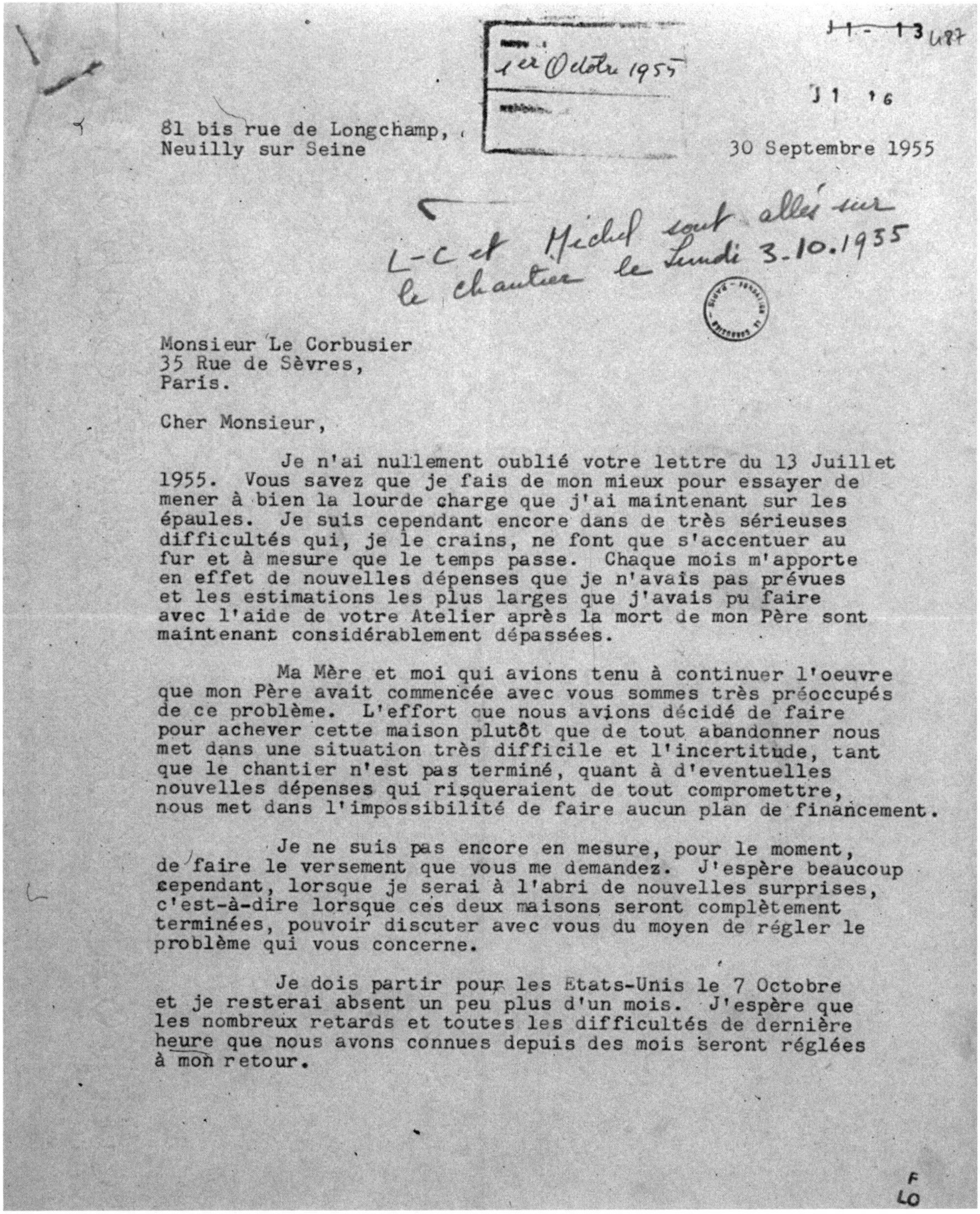

81 bis rue de Longchamp,
Neuilly sur Seine

1er Octobre 1955

J1 16

487

30 Septembre 1955

L-C et Michel sont allés sur le chantier le Lundi 3.10.1955

Monsieur Le Corbusier
35 Rue de Sèvres,
Paris.

Cher Monsieur,

Je n'ai nullement oublié votre lettre du 13 Juillet 1955. Vous savez que je fais de mon mieux pour essayer de mener à bien la lourde charge que j'ai maintenant sur les épaules. Je suis cependant encore dans de très sérieuses difficultés qui, je le crains, ne font que s'accentuer au fur et à mesure que le temps passe. Chaque mois m'apporte en effet de nouvelles dépenses que je n'avais pas prévues et les estimations les plus larges que j'avais pu faire avec l'aide de votre Atelier après la mort de mon Père sont maintenant considérablement dépassées.

Ma Mère et moi qui avions tenu à continuer l'oeuvre que mon Père avait commencée avec vous sommes très préoccupés de ce problème. L'effort que nous avions décidé de faire pour achever cette maison plutôt que de tout abandonner nous met dans une situation très difficile et l'incertitude, tant que le chantier n'est pas terminé, quant à d'eventuelles nouvelles dépenses qui risqueraient de tout compromettre, nous met dans l'impossibilité de faire aucun plan de financement.

Je ne suis pas encore en mesure, pour le moment, de faire le versement que vous me demandez. J'espère beaucoup cependant, lorsque je serai à l'abri de nouvelles surprises, c'est-à-dire lorsque ces deux maisons seront complètement terminées, pouvoir discuter avec vous du moyen de régler le problème qui vous concerne.

Je dois partir pour les Etats-Unis le 7 Octobre et je resterai absent un peu plus d'un mois. J'espère que les nombreux retards et toutes les difficultés de dernière heure que nous avons connues depuis des mois seront réglées à mon retour.

F
LO

Fig. 159
Letter from Michel Jaoul to Le Corbusier, September 30, 1955. FLC J1 (16) 487.

financial statement of work carried out up to November 15 would be sent from the office by December 31.[67] Despite all this, the jobsite was interrupted for a considerable period,[68] as the Jaouls' financial predicament was dire. Loans had been stopped. The financial burden imposed by the construction of the two houses was a constant preoccupation of Michel Jaoul, who put off until a later date—when the construction was actually terminated—a transfer of payment due to the architect's office, as he explains in a letter to Le Corbusier (Fig. 159):

> In fact, each month brings news of additional and unforeseen expenses, and the ever greater estimates, which I could have met with the help of your Atelier after the death of my father, are now considerably beyond my means.... The effort that [my mother and I] have decided to expend to achieve this house, rather than abandoning it all, has landed us in a very difficult and uncertain situation, as long as the construction is not finished, [and] as for eventual new expenses that risk compromising everything, they put us in the impossible situation of not being able to establish any financial planning.[69]

After the winter of 1955, the settling of André Jaoul's estate finally permitted his son to resume the construction work. In April, he drew up an order with Barberis for the remaining furniture to be provided. Unfortunately, this last commission would not be fulfilled on time because complete delivery only took place at the end of October 1955, after the Jaouls had finally taken up residence in their houses.

Modifications during construction

Le Corbusier supported his artisans and intervened personally in conflicts with his clients. When he found out that Bertocchi had still not been paid for work already done, but that the Jaouls had deemed unsatisfactory, Le Corbusier resorted to writing a letter in his defense: "This man has proven his extraordinary devotion to the construction of your house. It is he who was responsible for executing much very good work in the midst of all the other questionable things carried out by the entrepreneur whom your father imposed upon us."[70]

Le Corbusier also intervened during the course of construction work to obtain certain desired effects in the materials, textures, and colors. Sought-after contrasts in the materials—sanded-down or rough wood, granular or smooth plasterwork—were controlled by him with great precision, with critical decisions taken directly on the site. Jacques Michel describes such practices in a letter to Monsieur Espinasse from Entreprise Allard:

> I shall communicate with you at an appropriate moment concerning the placement of the tie rods on the specific floor levels, the modifications and all the necessary details that we want. I reserve the right to make

Fig. 160
Rainwater spouts, House A.

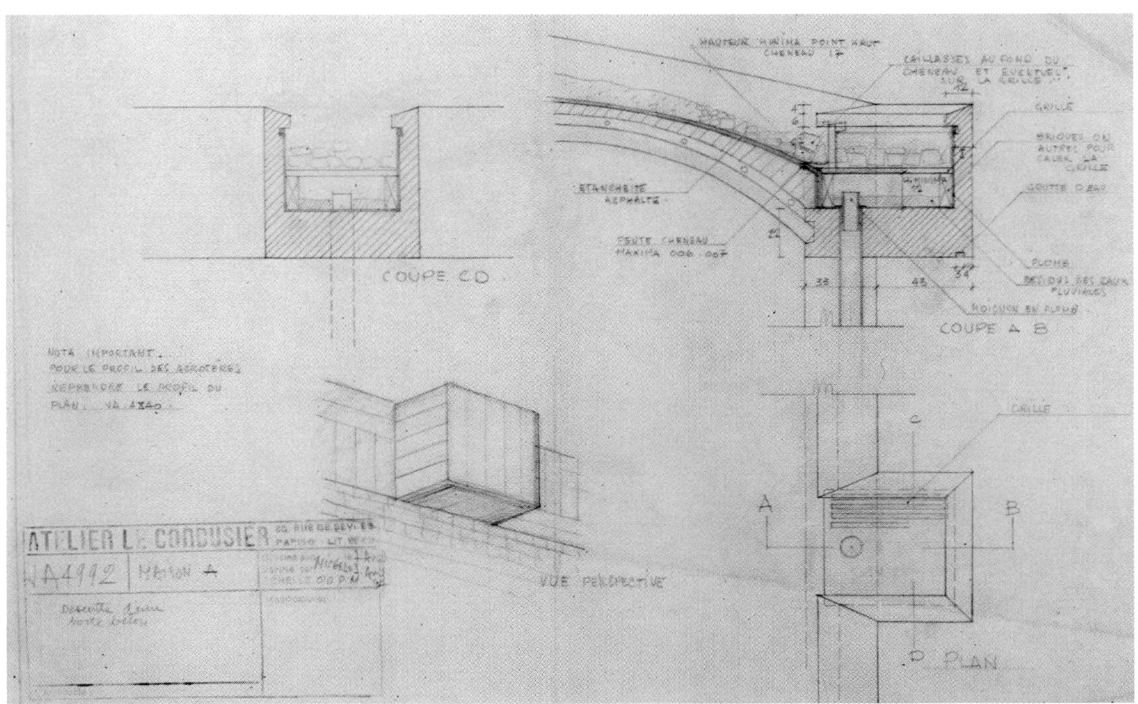

Fig. 161
Working drawing of the rainwater downpipe details, House A. FLC 9994.

> modificationsonyourplansandonthejobsiteaccordingtothedesiresof M[onsieur] Le Corbusier.[71]

On the spot, he spontaneously viewed and judged the situation, adapting his ideas and making alterations. The building was conceived as a full-scale model and experimentation site.

During one of his construction site visits in early November 1953, Le Corbusier suggested adding some exterior projecting concrete boxes as rainwater spouts for the downpipes. Jacques Michel retorted that it was too late to introduce this idea: "It is not possible to adopt your idea for the downpipes on House B. The ironwork has already been mounted and cannot be further modified. I'll reserve this idea for House A."[72] Thus House A profited from this earlier experimental idea. The addition of these modern rainwater heads not only provided a better technical resolution for drainage, but also accentuated the monumental character of the house (Figs. 160 and 161). This was a typical example of the manner in which Le Corbusier worked, never hesitating to set aside technical considerations in favor of an innovative design concept. The trials and tribulations on the building construction site, in fact, elicited his contribution. Pushed to resolve a technical problem for the evacuation of rainwater a posteriori, he continued to improvise on the architecture by adding an aesthetic dimension in the form of a sculptural device, thereby reinforcing the corner motif.

Such unforeseen or spontaneous modifications during the course of construction also played an intrinsic role in Le Corbusier's strategy with his clients, allowing him to submit lower estimates in the first instance in order to gain their initial approval. This classic ploy of misrepresenting costs, typical of his atelier practices, can be recognized throughout the 1920s, with well-tested arguments to convince the client of the substantiated extra expenditures: "A fine gentleman setting out for a ball would never wear a paper collar with his dinner jacket."[73] Le Corbusier and Pierre Jeanneret "seem to have deliberately allowed the painter-glazier Celio to underestimate the costs in all their houses, leaving the quality of the glass to be used (wired, frosted, rolled, or plate glass) open to later negotiations. Yet, invariably, they specified the most expensive plate glass for all visible windows later on in the proceedings."[74] For the Jaoul site, to the contrary, Le Corbusier suggested that his contractors not inflate their prices, as reflected in his letter addressed to Bertocchi on February 25, 1953:

> The Jaoul transaction might be sorted out in your favor: vaults, brick walls and tiles, to be handled with Allard.... Instructions: make the most reasonable offer. I'm not saying that you should lose money on the job, rather that you shouldn't overcharge. Success or failure in this transaction is in your hands.[75]

On the site, purposefully circumventing all intermediaries, Le Corbusier believed in dealing directly with the person in charge, someone "reliable" at the technical level, no matter what the hierarchy or status of the enterprise. This direct communication on a one-to-one level, as people personally engaged in a mission, was perceived by Le Corbusier as the only effective means to achieve the desired effects. Affective ties and amicable relations he accorded to some of his contractors (as well as to his atelier collaborators) allowed these persons to find a deeper meaning and pleasure in their joint work, thereby investing more of their time and effort on his experimental projects than they would ordinarily expend on less demanding jobs.

Le Corbusier's quest on these Paris building sites during the 1950s was out of step with the reality of construction sites directed by major enterprises. Often difficult to control, made up by the *corps de métiers* (trades) who were unfamiliar with one another, it was one of the issues that Le Corbusier had already dreaded and found hard to accept on the Marseilles site. In the 1920s, the Corbusian strategy had taken another tack because work by a single trade team had detrimental effects (according to the architect), that is, the elimination of craftsmanship, giving all the power to the builder. In the 1950s, he searched for an ideal team, a corps of unified trades, committed to the same spiritual objectives, to the shared execution of an "*objet-sculpture*," enriched and deeply imbued with handcrafted qualities. Whatever he turned his hand to, Le Corbusier was no doubt influenced by the apprenticeship training he received in his native Swiss village of La Chaux-de-Fonds.

The young 1960s generation was alert to Le Corbusier's type of quest, finding there an alternative to the monotony and anonymity of vast contemporary construction sites and to rationalist building procedures, essentially making way for heavy industrialization dependent on prefabricated elements. To compensate for this loss of identity, architects took pleasure in the exaltation of the visual and the tactile characteristics of materials as signs of the tangible dimension of their architectural work. In this quest for substance, they began to play with contrasts and assemblages, thereby making a considerable contribution to aspects of comfort and a sense of well-being.

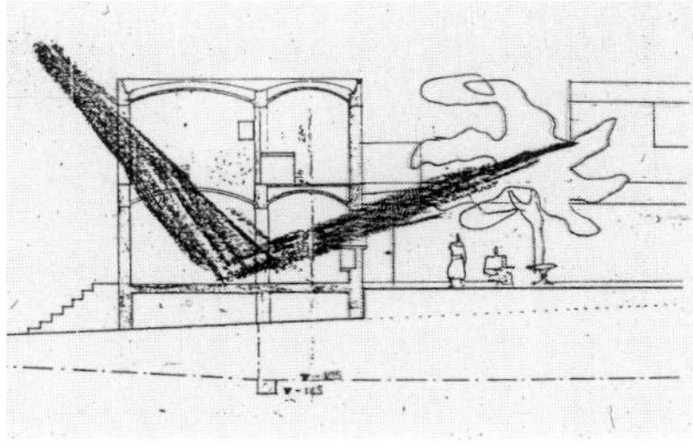

Chapter 3

THE ART OF LIVING: ADJUSTING TO LE CORBUSIER

Fig. 162
Termination of the Maisons Jaoul construction, 1955.

Fig. 163
Michel and Nadine Jaoul in front of their house, 1956.

The question of intimacy

In June 1953, Le Corbusier was in Chandigarh. Sitting by a window to capture the evening breeze, he wrote to his friends and colleagues of the CIAM (Congrès internationaux d'architecture moderne) in preparation for their conference at Aix-en-Provence. He stated: "To pose the question of the modern dwelling is to pose the problem of the art of living today: does this art exist?"[1] Why ask such a fundamental question? Was Le Corbusier perhaps concerned about the orthodoxy of his "brothers in arms" in the modern movement, or was he questioning his own attitudes?[2]

Several recent works have focused attention on the difficulties encountered by twentieth-century architects in responding simultaneously to the modern aesthetic and to the dweller's desire for comfort. Witold Rybczynski has traced the history of domestic comfort from the Middle Ages to the present day.[3] He posited that the idea of comfort developed in seventeenth-century Holland, only to be interrupted by the aesthetic of modernism. For this author, the modern movement was particularly damaging to the sense of well-being of inhabitants, since architects were too focused on making the modern house respond visually to the aesthetic of the industrial era. For him, Le Corbusier's houses were more like cubist, cold, storage warehouses than cozy nests. For the architect, however, the house was more than a *machine à habiter* (machine for living); it was also *la coquille de l'escargot* (the snail's shell).[4] He had always been personally attracted to the idea of an intimate house, full of memories, stimulated by the objects in his private collection: sea shells, stones, ceramic pots, works of art. His reputation, however, created by the impact of his Purist villas of the 1920s, has nourished the image of a Le Corbusier who is functionalist, cold, and abstract—inhuman. Christopher Reed, in his introduction to *Not at Home* (1995)—evocatively subtitled *The Suppression of Domesticity in Modern Art and Architecture*—emphasizes the extent to which modern art and architecture have insisted on suppressing feelings of well-being in the home. He holds Le Corbusier to be at the head of this anti-domesticity, citing as evidence his criticism of the "sentimental hysteria" surrounding the "cult of the house."[5]

Modern architects have often been accused of overdesigning their clients' houses. The fact that Le Corbusier liked to inscribe himself personally and metonymically into the photographic and graphic representation of his modernist interiors, by strategically placing his glasses, his hat, or perhaps a book on a table in the foreground, has been seen as proof of this.[6] In a similar vein, criticizing the authority of the architect, Alice Friedman studied the case of the house designed by Ludwig Mies van der Rohe for Edith Farnsworth, a well-known doctor, and the legal action that she brought against him once the building was complete. She documents precisely the incompatibility between the aims of the architect—an architectural minimalism—and the desire of his client for a place of refuge and physical comfort. In practice, the elegance and formal simplicity of the house proved difficult to adapt to.[7]

To consider Le Corbusier's domestic architecture requires a response to these harsh criticisms of modern architecture. Was the architect, the spokesman for this modernity, capable of building a sensible and comfortable home? Could he be attentive to the needs of its inhabitants? Le Corbusier was at least aware of the problem. He declared, "You can say that a house is an act of love."[8] (Fig. 164)

Fig. 164
Back cover, Jean Petit, ed., *Le Corbusier, Architecture du bonheur* (Le Corbusier. Architecture of Happiness), 1955.

Old furniture or new equipment?

Always sensitive to the problem of furnishing the home, Le Corbusier once again raises the question of comfort in the text presenting the Maisons Jaoul in his *Œuvre Complète 1952–1957*, but also in referring to the Unité d'Habitation (his housing block in Marseilles, 1947–52), he wrote:

> Modern man has become a nomad, a nomad living in apartment blocks with communal services, various dwellings adapted to the crucial stages of his life. The war and aerial bombardment have destroyed furniture and houses. The next generations can set up home without the burden of inherited "family furniture." From now on they can enter their apartment with their suitcase in their hand, their box of books, their bedding, and their clothes. All that remains is to provide themselves with beds (and what simplified beds!), tables (and what kind of tables, what size, combinations, and possible juxtapositions?), and finally some chairs (what kind of chairs?).[9]

For Le Corbusier, then, the post–World War II home owner was a nomad free of possessions to clutter up the space. In 1929, he had represented the arrival of the new occupants of his houses in idyllic terms: "I draw the modern arrangement in plan and in section: windows, walls and built-ins. I have created a large empty space; you can move around easily; your gestures are rapid and precise; tidying up is automatic. Minutes are saved every day."[10] Further on he added:

> When the house is finished, when the painters are applying the last coat, the day before the inhabitant brings his books and his suitcases, we will insert the built-in cupboards, the necessary fittings to meet the needs of the inhabitants. We will fix the doors to these cupboards—sliding panels in sheet metal, in plywood, in marble, mirror glass, in aluminum, etc.[11]

One of the first examples of this type of installation, influenced by Charlotte Perriand, was the music pavilion of the Villa Church of 1928–29, designed by Le Corbusier and Pierre Jeanneret, in the Parisian suburb of Ville d'Avray.

It has to be said, however, that the architect never really did resolve the problem of the furnishing of his houses. "The problem of furniture has not been tackled,"[12] he said in 1957, with regard to the Maisons Jaoul. There are several groups of Jaoul perspective drawings in the hand of Le Corbusier or his collaborators, however, that demonstrate that the question of furnishing was discussed at length. If Madame André Jaoul was determined to keep her old furniture, Michel and Nadine Jaoul were ready, at least in part, to embark on "the furniture adventure" and to furnish the children's rooms from scratch. In reply to the set of plans (FLC 4392 to 4399) and estimates provided by Le Corbusier on March 3, 1952, Michel Jaoul wrote:

> I should like to use some spaces in the living room and the parent's bedroom (for my wife and me) to put a few pieces of furniture that constitute my only heirlooms. On the other hand, the children's rooms definitely could be furnished, I mean to say, newly designed and built-in by you.[13]

Le Corbusier adds a note to this letter as a concession to the client's need for economy: "N.B.: Remove our tables." In the end, financial constraints put a stop to these ambitions as Michel Jaoul explained to Le Corbusier eighteen months later, on December 1, 1953:

> Michel [Jacques Michel, Le Corbusier's assistant] shared with us your ideas for the internal organization of the ground floor, and I must say that, apart from a few details, we are very enthusiastic. We particularly like the table. Unfortunately, I am afraid that I absolutely cannot countenance the cost of realizing it. I think that, although we may come back to this eventually, we can only consider furnishing our house with what we already own. Your ideas permeate us, my wife and I, like water through sand, but we regret that there are sordid and anti-progressive imperatives at play.[14]

It was only later that Michel Jaoul was able to have some pieces of furniture made by a carpenter to his own designs.[15]

Fig. 165
View of the salon furnishings, House A, 1956.

When Madame André Jaoul set her family up in House A in 1955, the dining room and living room were equipped with a Louis XV chest of drawers in dark oak, a green leather divan and armchair suite in the *retour d'Egypte* style, a round Louis XVI dining table with a marquetry rose in a geometric design, and some straw-seated chairs in the *jardin du Palais Royal* style (nineteenth century) (Fig. 165).[16] The effect is elegant, and Le Corbusier was encouraging, assuring the Jaouls that he was not hostile to this arrangement. He confirmed this in a comment to Françoise Choay, who had noted in her book *Le Corbusier* (1960) that the architect appeared to be exasperated by the fact that his clients did not live in his houses in a way he would have wished but had committed the "error" of installing the antique furniture that they loved.[17] He wrote to her: "I just spent an evening in the Jaoul house. It was a beautiful moment for me because of the Jaouls, because of their interiors and because of the way they have settled in here."[18]

Choay stressed the contradiction of the Jaouls' highly personal choice of furniture and the completely integrated equipment of the Cabanon, the small wooden cabin Le Corbusier built in 1952 as a summer house at Cap-Martin on

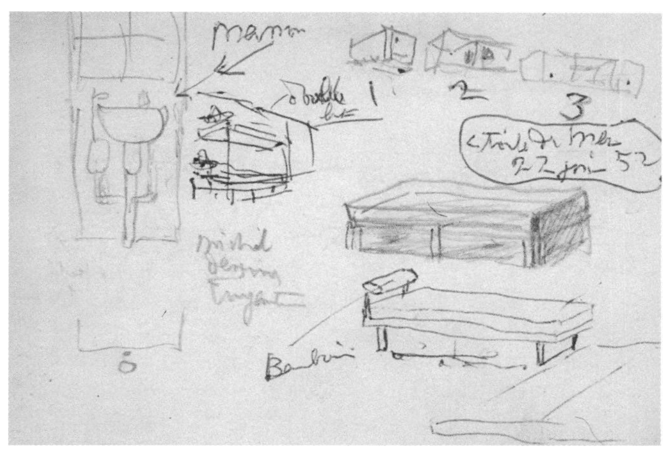

Fig. 166 (top left)
Fireplace and surrounds, House A, 1956.

Fig. 167 (top right)
Le Corbusier, pen, pencil, and colored pencil sketch with detailing of the furniture in the Cabanon at Cap-Martin, June 22, 1952. Sketchbook 2, sheet 584.

Figs. 168 and 169 (bottom left and right)
The "*équipement*" designed by Le Corbusier for his Cabanon at Cap Martin, constructed in 1952.

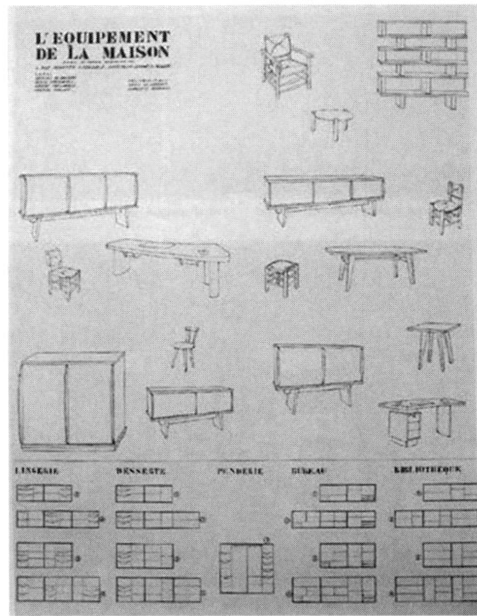

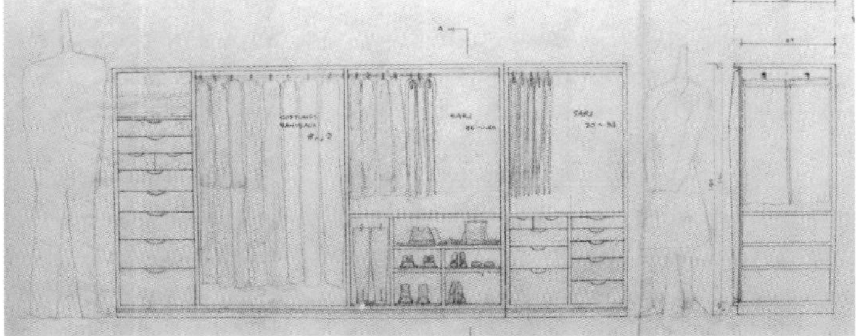

Fig. 170 (top left)
Double photographic spread showing options for storage units, in Charlotte Perriand, "L'art d'habiter," *Techniques et architecture*, vol. 9, n° 9–10, 1950, 34–35.

Fig. 171 (top right)
Advertising brochure for "L'équipement de la maison," utilitarian house furniture designed by Charlotte Perriand and Pierre Jeanneret, April 1948.

Fig. 172 (bottom left)
Charlotte Perriand, "*Placard/ Unité de rangement*," a cupboard and storage unit system manufactured by the Société de construction aéronavale (Scan), displayed in the first exhibition called *Formes utiles* (Functional Forms) at the Musée des Arts Décoratifs, Paris, 1949.

Fig. 173 (bottom right)
Studies of furniture arrangements for the Villa Sarabhai, Ahmedabad, drawn by Kim Chung-Up, an assistant in the rue de Sèvres atelier, dated April 7, 1954.

the Côte d'Azur (Figs. 168 and 169). She interpreted Le Corbusier's attitude to the Jaouls as a denial of human individualism and diversity. Only clients possessing a particular frame of mind would be capable of putting up with a space rigorously ordered according to Le Corbusier's principles.[19] This line of criticism later became common in Anglo-Saxon literature. It should be remembered, however, that in the case of the Cabanon, Le Corbusier had precisely adjusted the furniture to his everyday needs, creating a space that was both intimate and functional.

Architect and client define the domestic

For the younger Jaouls, Le Corbusier proposed an interior with integrated and built-in furniture (Fig. 177). To help them consider the question of such furniture, the office provided a folder containing an article by Charlotte Perriand entitled "Les pionniers du rangement" (pioneers of storage) published in *Maison Française* in 1952 and some professional leaflets that she also produced (Figs. 170–172).[20] From the 1940s, Perriand had been developing systems of modular shelving, sometimes in collaboration with Pierre Jeanneret and Jean Prouvé, with whom she had worked on furniture sold by the Steph Simon Gallery.[21] Indeed, her designs for cupboards based on modular shelving had been shown in the exhibitions of the group Formes Utiles, the first of which took place at the Musée des Arts Décoratifs in 1949. The designs presented to the Jaouls illustrated the different storage solutions deployed in this exhibition. A standard element in the system consisted of brightly colored plastic drawers (yellow, red, black, white), fitted with handles on both sides. Inspired by reading this material, Michel and Nadine Jaoul asked that the partition dividing their bedroom from that of their daughter should be fitted with shelves, and this eventually housed Perriand's plastic drawers.[22]

In a set of perspective drawings of October 20, 1954 (Figs. 174 and 175), Jacques Michel worked out the storage details in a series of perspective sketches for House B. The basic principle was to eliminate pieces of furniture in order to incorporate all their functions in architectural units. This is an example of the application of the slogan "a single building trade," which Le Corbusier had described in 1930 in "L'aventure du Mobilier," in his *Précisions*. Apart from the table and bench for the living room, the built-in units represented in these drawings were carried out. The fixed concrete-topped table was eventually turned into an extension of the fireplace and moved from the glazed bay facing the fireplace.

Having accepted the big decisions concerning the articulated window walls, the wooden cupboards, the sideboards, and the concrete shelves, the Jaouls nevertheless resisted a more complete furniture installation. The order placed on March 2, 1955, by Michel Jaoul with the office in the rue de Sèvres makes clear the ambition of the decisions taken.[23] Far from bowing to the architect's taste for internal equipment, Jaoul understood the advantages of built-in furniture and helped determine the arrangement, specifying precisely the space required for each member of the family group. Some pieces of

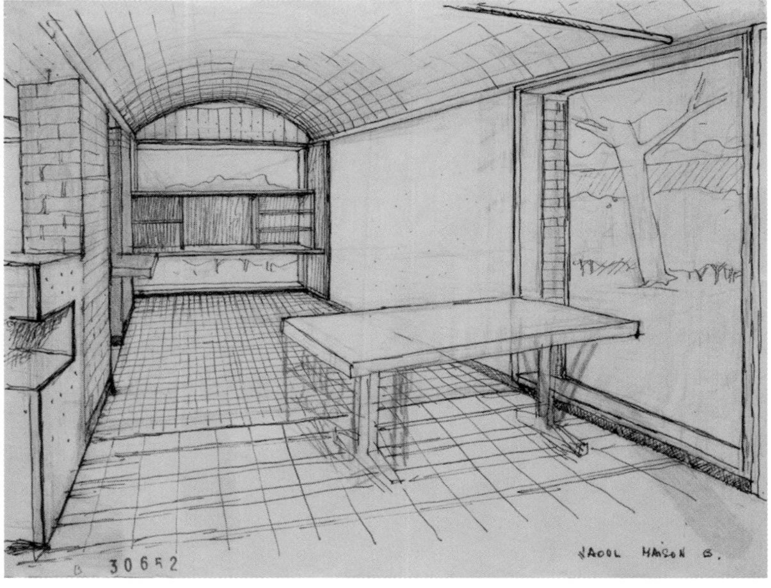

Figs. 174 and 175
Jacques Michel, perspective studies showing variant proposals for the built-in furniture in House B, dated October 20, 1954. FLC 30652.

J1 14 421

- 2 -

5) Grand meuble de rangement avec aménagement suivant :

voir emplacement exacte Tuyaux.

- du côté des tuyaux, placard à balais,
- emplacement suffisant pour frigidaire comme pour la Maison B, à prévoir à l'extrémité opposée au placard à balais,
- arrangement général du meuble suivant même principe que la Maison B.

Salle à Manger 6) Plancher sous emplacement table fixe

Bibliothèque 7) Casiers à livres suivant plan
8) Petite table à écrire suivant plan
9) Casiers sous tablette béton suivant plan
9 bis) Plancher suivant plan

ler étage

Couloir 10) Grand meuble divisé en penderie sur une largeur de lm,20 et placard à linge sur une largeur de lm,50; penderie organisée suivant principe habituel, c'est-à-dire, chaussures au sol, penderie sur lm,70 environ et rangement à la partie supérieure; placard à linge divisé en rayonnage mobile.

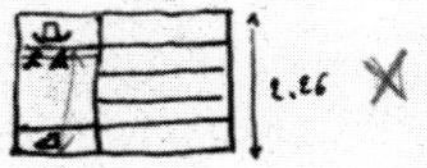

non 126

2.26

Chambre Madame 11) Meuble rangement sur 2m,26 de haut (voir croquis ci-joint), comportant 2 penderies, l'une accessible de la chambre, l'autre accessible de la salle de bains. Pour penderie salle de bains, porte ouvrant dans passage entre chambre et salle de bains pour permettre pose miroir.

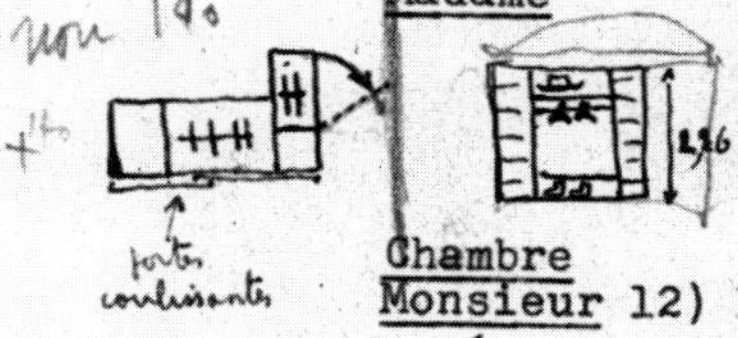

non 140

portes coulissantes

2.26

Chambre Monsieur 12) Meuble rangement sur 2m,26, chaussures en bas, penderie au milieu et rangement au-dessus de la penderie; penderie sur une partie seulement du meuble, le reste étant destiné à casiers à linge (voir croquis), le tout accessible du côté de la salle de bains.

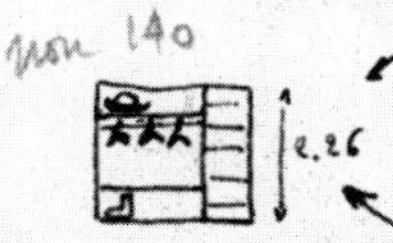

non 140

2.26

Chambre Fils 13) Penderie sur 2m,26 de haut et pas sur toute la largeur laissant la place de casiers à linge personnel (voir croquis)

140 ou 226

170

140

Fig. 176
Letter from Michel Jaoul addressed to the Atelier Le Corbusier, indicating his preferences for the furniture arrangements in House A, April 7, 1955. The thumbnail diagrams were drawn by Michel Jaoul. FLC J1(14) 421.

Fig. 177
Built-in furniture and wood panels on the first floor of House A. The shadow along the horizontal ceiling plane articulates the curved volume of the vault.

built-in furniture used in House B were also employed in House A, such as the sideboard at the foot of the staircase in the living room. This piece, the carcass of which was cast in smoke-blackened concrete waxed to provide a smooth finish, was fitted with sliding doors stiffened by vertical wooden fins in the profile, a device used by Charlotte Perriand. On the other hand, Michel Jaoul was careful to specify, on April 7, 1955, that he did not propose to commission the fixed table in the hallway, the two screens on either side of the staircase on the ground floor, and other pieces of furniture.[24]

The summary of the joinery sent to Le Corbusier's carpenter, Charles Barberis, in April 1955, indicates that the kitchens required, among other things, two sliding doors with slotted frames underneath the concrete bar; a 4.6 by 3.7-foot storage space for glasses, plates, table linen, and cutlery; a partition to close off the work space of the sink that would also serve to divide the kitchen and the breakfast area, and a large storage element against the wall facing the sink.[25]

All the bedrooms are furnished with cupboards with hanging space, adjustable shelves, and plastic storage drawers. The furniture on the first floor was described as follows:

> In front of the staircase, a storage cupboard with hanging space, clothing, and bookshelves. This piece separates the bedroom from the wash area (opening cupboard with clothing and hanging space on the washroom side; bookshelves on the bedroom side).... In the girl's bedroom, at the end on the left, a divider element placed in a space left in the wall.[26]

The divider forms a partition with Michel Jaoul's bedroom. On the side facing the bedroom are storage with shelves and plastic drawers, a socket for a light, and an insulated sliding panel; on the side of the girl's bedroom, the space becomes a niche in natural wood.

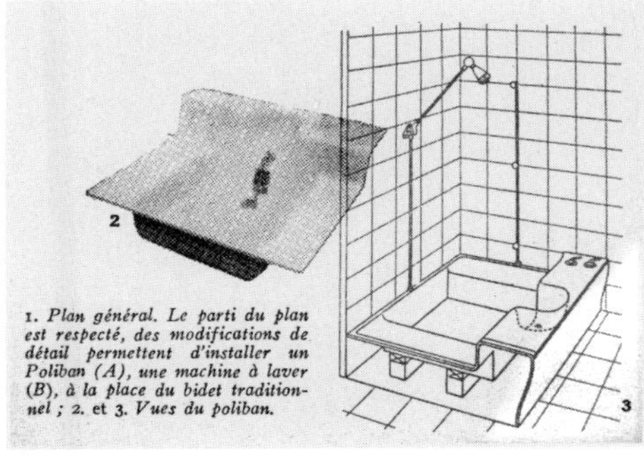

1. Plan général. Le parti du plan est respecté, des modifications de détail permettent d'installer un Poliban (A), une machine à laver (B), à la place du bidet traditionnel ; 2. et 3. Vues du poliban.

Fig. 178
"Poliban," *L'Architecture d'aujourd'hui*, n° 34, March 1951.

Fig. 179
The Tokyo-type wood-frame *banquettes* designed by Charlotte Perriand for the salon in House B, 1957.

For the bathrooms, Le Corbusier was very enthusiastic about the use of the "Poliban,"[27] described in the supplier's advertisement as: "The modern hydrotherapeutic solution assuring daily hygiene of the body in a minimal space—half that required by a regular bath—and providing maximum economy in installation, water consumption, power, and time."[28] (Fig. 178) Based on "bathing by aspersion, completely different from bathing by immersion, where the water is stagnant, as in the case of the traditional bath," the "Poliban" claimed to eliminate the bath, "that old bulky object that has changed neither in form nor in practice for centuries, which is still used despite the fact that it has been denounced as unhygienic by medical science."[29]

In 1957, Michel and Nadine Jaoul decided to furnish their living room with "Tokyo" benches designed by Perriand (Fig. 179). These were displayed in the Steph Simon Gallery in the boulevard St.-Germain. This gallery had specialized in the furniture of Charlotte Perriand and Jean Prouvé since 1956.[30]

The architect's hand and the inhabitants

Were the Maisons Jaoul built to celebrate an architectural idea or for the benefit of their occupants or both? Modern architects have often been accused of deprecating the intimate bric-à-brac that expresses the individuality of the inhabitant. The writings of Adolf Loos in the 1910s, Le Corbusier in the 1920s,

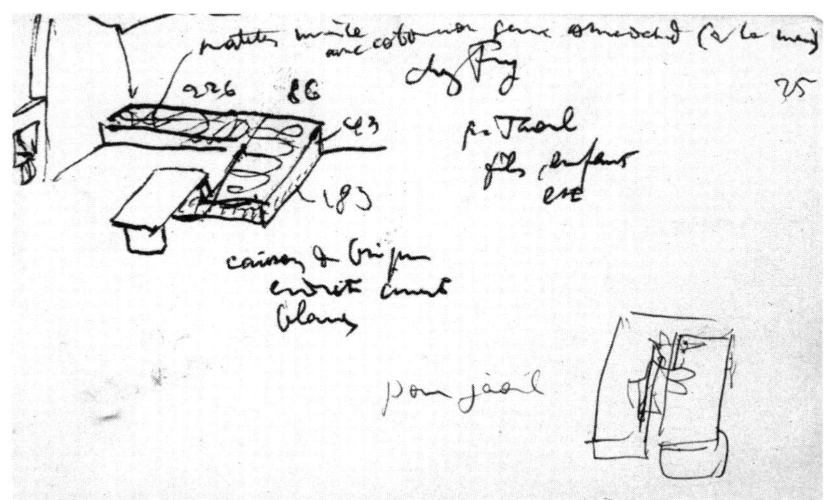

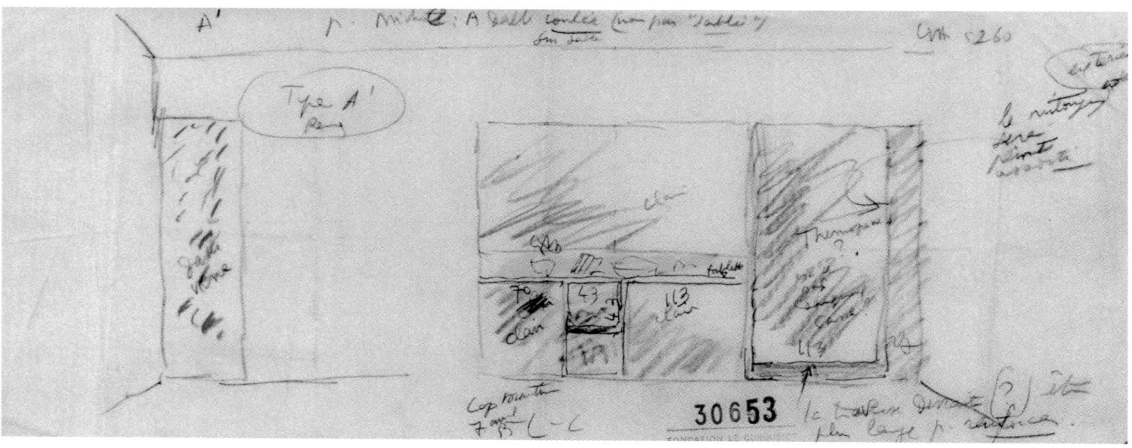

Fig. 180
Le Corbusier, Sketchbooks, vol. 2, 1950–1954, sketchbook G 28, sheet 945: sketch studies of the *banquettes* at Jane Fry's house in Chandigarh, May–June 1953, with indications of possibilities for the Jaouls (bottom right).

Fig. 181
Le Corbusier, annotated color pencil perspective study of a *pan de verre*, fitted with a built-in *tablette* holding a plate and books, initialed and dated "Cap Martin/7 avril 55/L.C." FLC 30653.

and Walter Benjamin in the 1930s, had established the idea of a modern space which was markedly superior to the conventional ways of organizing the interior, the latter often described in terms of degeneracy, dirt, and sickness. Ideas like these had a marked influence on avant-garde thinking.[31]

At Maisons Jaoul, as he attended to the treatment of flooring, the arrangement of shelves, and the judicious placing of windows to suit the internal arrangements, Le Corbusier showed that he was capable of designing provocative spaces that were also pleasant for the inhabitants (Figs. 180 and 181).

Floor surfaces

The floors in House B are finished in white cement tiles. Le Corbusier had a particular affinity for such tiles, which he also used in his apartment at rue Nungesser-et-Coli and in the Salvation Army Hostel.[32] In discussing them, he stated,

> This is the poorest material in the whole of France. It consists of white cement squares 20 cm x 20 cm; you can't find anything cheaper. I didn't use them to

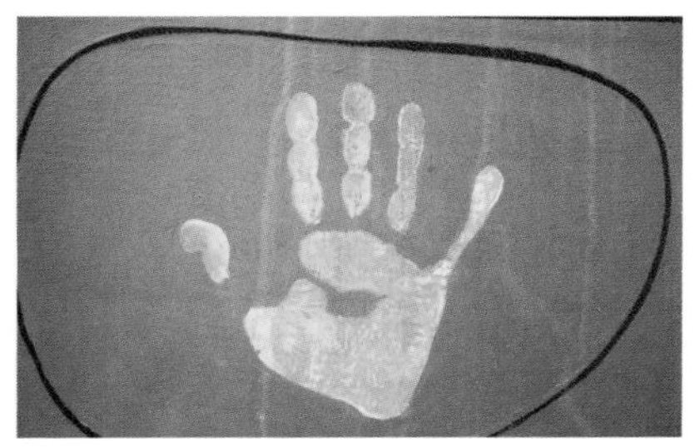

Fig. 182
Colored ceramic tiles above the kitchen countertop, House B.

Fig. 183
Low-relief silhouette of the Modulor man set in the concrete wall, Unité d'Habitation in Marseilles.

Fig. 184
Imprint of Le Corbusier's hand on the wall fresco at the Étoile de Mer restaurant, Roquebrune-Cap-Martin.

> save money but because I love this poverty. I find that it dignifies everything else; I don't like ostentatious materials. I like rich ideas expressed by simple means, intense, compressed, and condensed; I don't want to be attracted to a parquet in an exaggerated way. These white tiles create an agreeable little grid and cover the whole apartment from one end to the other.[33]

Le Corbusier's wife, Yvonne Gallis, on the other hand, knew that these tiles were difficult to maintain, and she advised Madame Jaoul not to accept them. Le Corbusier insisted, but agreed to compromise, only specifying this kind of tiling for House B where, on Yvonne's recommendation, he noted that the tiles should not be washed with *esprit de sel* (bleach).[34]

By contrast, the floor of House A was finished in cream earthenware tiles. The floors had worried Michel Jaoul, who wrote, "We very much like the combination of tiles and wood blocks that you propose, but it assumes a layout that we do not at the moment foresee."[35] The rest of his letter shows how attentive he was to the detailed organization of his house, to the choice of materials, and above all to their financial implications:

> I think that it would be better to limit ourselves to a single surface finish, yet to be determined. It's a question of finding something that is easy to maintain and whose color and durability are acceptable. The ceramic tiles possess these qualities but we do not find them very exciting. The types of wooden flooring that I am aware of are not satisfactory. The cement tiles are very difficult to maintain and stain easily. This leaves various kinds of more or less durable stone among which we should be able to find the solution to our

problem. For the first floor we are hesitating between wood or ceramic tiling with a preference for wood.[36]

Le Corbusier conceded the drawbacks of hard floor surfaces, and for the living room, he added a "carpet" of wooden blocks in the area where the dining table would be placed. This wooden surface provides a greater sense of warmth than cold ceramic tiles could have done. Compared to ceramic tiles, the wooden flooring also absorbs the sounds of furniture moving.

Le Corbusier's mark

When Le Corbusier directed photographs of his houses, he liked to leave traces of his presence in the photographs. He also left physical marks: he molded the profile of "Modulor man" (a man with an upstretched arm indicating the dimensions of Le Corbusier's modular scale) in a wall of the Unité d'Habitation at Marseilles (1952) (Fig. 183), printed his hands in paint on the wall of the Étoile de Mer restaurant next to his cabin at Cap-Martin (1951–52) (Fig. 184), and signed the stained glass in the chapel at Ronchamp (1950–55) with his emblems.

At Neuilly, the architect continually made his presence felt through little details. We have already discussed the enamelled tiles warning against cleaning with *l'esprit de sel* (bleach). He also personally fixed heat resistant tiles (11.8 x 3.9 in each) in the kitchen around the sink (Fig. 182), ordering twenty-four light blue, thirty-four white, eighteen yellow, and seventeen light purple tiles from Jean Martin on May 27, 1955.[37]

Objects: witnesses of private life

The design historian Gillian Naylor has noted that if, in "modernist interiors, personal objects and furniture in a different style, have been more or less ostracized, works of art and craftwork have always been readily accepted."[38] The example she gives is of the objects assembled from the end of the 1930s to the 1970s by the architect and the artist Ernö and Ursula Goldfinger in their house in London. These works of art and craft personalized their home. In the same spirit, careful to find places for the Jaoul family's decorative and personal objects, Le Corbusier provided waxed, smoke-blackened concrete ledges and shelves in the sideboards and cupboards. The fireplace of House A, for example, is composed of a series of niches for the display of works of art, crafts, and travel mementos to give a personal touch (Figs. 166 and 185). The same arrangement is continued on the first floor in the space reserved for Suzanne Jaoul's chapel (Fig. 186).[39]

The objects present in the Maisons Jaoul helped to create a lived-in space that bears the marks of its inhabitants. They included paintings and engravings, suspended gourds, Indian sculptures, wooden animals, and earthenware from Greece or Egypt (Figs. 187–197).[40] The collection of André and Suzanne Jaoul included engravings by Jacques Villon, paintings by Suzanne Duchamp, Dada works by Jean Crotti, some paintings by Le Corbusier, and several works

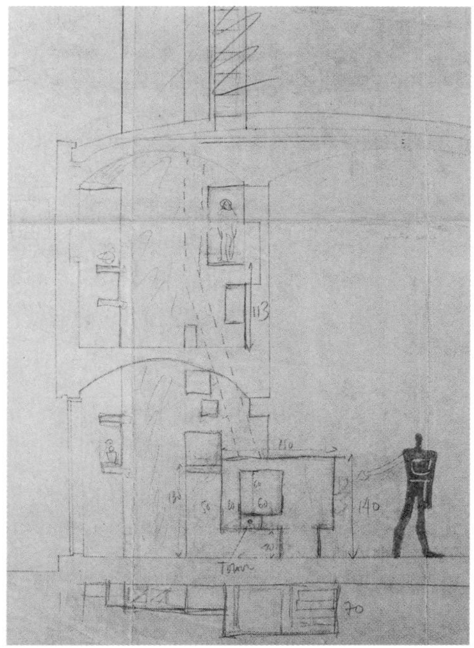

Fig. 185
Perspective view of the fireplace, House A.

Fig. 186
Elevation study (with Modulor man) of the fireplace, showing its vertical extension into the first-floor chapel, House A, undated. LC 10055 (detail).

by Jean Dubuffet.[41] The house of Michel and Nadine Jaoul included works by Jean Crotti, Jacques Villon, Jean Dubuffet, Pierre Soulages, and Le Corbusier. As witness to Michel's business trips in the 1960s and 1970s, Aboriginal, Pre-Columbian, and Indian sculptures accumulated over the course of time on the wooden shelves that form part of the window walls: they testify to his interest in "primitive" and non-Western art.

Every personal collection is unique. Naylor makes the point that exhibiting works of this kind constitutes not only a mirror of the personal experiences of the inhabitants but also a gauge to their aesthetic values. Thus they help to represent a lifestyle characteristic of a time and place: "This is an artist's and a designer's selection, and it also says as much about the time it was accumulated as it does about its accumulators."[42] This observation applies perfectly to the Jaouls. The works of art and objects with which they surrounded themselves make it possible to imagine their network of friends and to understand their artistic taste. In fact their taste and that of Le Corbusier were in harmony to such an extent that the architecture of the houses was influenced by their taste. These personal objects effectively mediate between the abstraction of the architectural form and the particularity of the daily lives led in the interiors; the collections both personalized the spaces and gave them historical and cultural specificity.

Discussion of this intimate landscape prompts a reflection on Le Corbusier's own "personal collection" of objects and his attitude toward them. In 1951, in his penthouse apartment at rue Nungesser-et-Coli, he gave an interview to Robert Mallet—a writer and radio journalist who specialized in interviewing writers and intellectuals—to discuss architecture and urbanism. The latter commented on some of the objects distributed around the apartment.

Fig. 187 (top left)
House A. Jean Dubuffet, *Bouquet de fleurs aux gants* (Bouquet of Flowers with Gloves), oil on canvas, 1943. Private collection.

Fig. 188 (top right)
House A. André Bauchant, *Sous-bois* (Scene of a Forest Interior), oil on wood panel, c. 1935. M. and N. Jaoul collection.

Fig. 189 (bottom left)
View of the library and office in House A, 1986.

Fig. 190 (bottom right)
House A. Le Corbusier, *Tête* (Head), oil on canvas, 1938. Private collection.

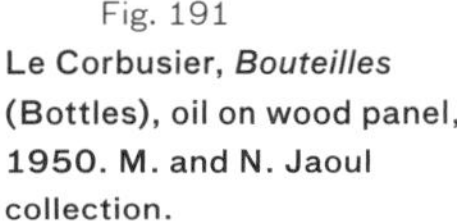

Fig. 191
Le Corbusier, *Bouteilles* (Bottles), oil on wood panel, 1950. M. and N. Jaoul collection.

Fig. 192
Stones arranged on a bench in the hallway of House A.

Fig. 193
Paintings and objects in the office of House B.

Fig. 194
House B. Nadine Jaoul, *Spirale* (Spiral), oil on canvas, 1950. M. and N. Jaoul collection.

Fig. 195
Pre-Columbian statue. M. and N. Jaoul collection.

Fig. 196
House B. Pierre Soulages, Untitled (4.26 f. x 3.18 f.), oil on canvas, 1949. M. and N. Jaoul collection.

The ensuing discussion is particularly revealing about the place of material culture in the construction of a personalized domestic identity. Imagine the visitor looking around the room: "All these walls, bare as they are, are populated by a crowd of objects. Would you like to talk about these things, all these things which surround us and which create such a sense of intimacy?" Le Corbusier began with some remarks about the vase of flowers, which for him belonged to the feminine world: "In the studio that we have just left, I will not have any flowers, I won't, because they disturb me. I am a man. But on the other hand, in the shared part of the apartment, flowers add a living touch."[43] He consciously distinguished between feminine and masculine zones in his own apartment. He went on:

> As for the rest, there are some paintings—not laid out like a stamp collection, but carefully placed in a good light. And there are some sculptures by friends of mine, such as Henri Laurens, Jacques Lipchitz, etc., and some antiquities, some very modest vernacular antiquities, especially some Greek works perfectly proportioned, so clear and moving. There are some Byzantine things that I picked up here and there in the Balkans and that perfectly expressed the style of their age. There are all sorts of things. There is what I call my "personal collection"—these are bits of wood, knapped [dressed] flints, pine cones, buildings bricks that I use as a base for a statue; there are seashells, either whole or broken by the waves, which are fascinating. I could even point out butcher's bones . . . thrown up by the sea. These are extraordinary tools of material meditation, demonstrating the properties of materials, of the harmony and beauty of natural forms. I am not ashamed to call this my PC, that is to say my personal collection, and I take great pleasure from it.[44]

Fig. 197
Le Corbusier on his terrace at the rue Nungesser-et-Coli apartment, Paris, holding a terra-cotta pitcher in the shape of a goose.

Each object prompts memories that humanize the environment. Le Corbusier remembered precisely where he found every object, every statue, and every stone during his travels in Greece and Turkey, or simply by the seaside. Talking about these emotionally resonant objects, Le Corbusier is far from his reductive and dogmatic sloganeering.

When the two Jaoul families took possession of their houses at the beginning of October 1955, they were pleased to invite the architect to dinner. Michel Jaoul sent him a note of thanks: "I hope that you will be able to spare us a few more hours when I return. It would be good for the architect to have the chance to participate in the life of the houses he has built."[45] Despite the twists and turns of the building process, the relationship between the Jaouls and their architect remained cordial and respectful, a relatively rare case in his

Maison & Jardin

la première
résidence créée par
LE CORBUSIER depuis 1935
et cinq autres maisons nouvelles

350 F

FÉVRIER 1956 · N° 34

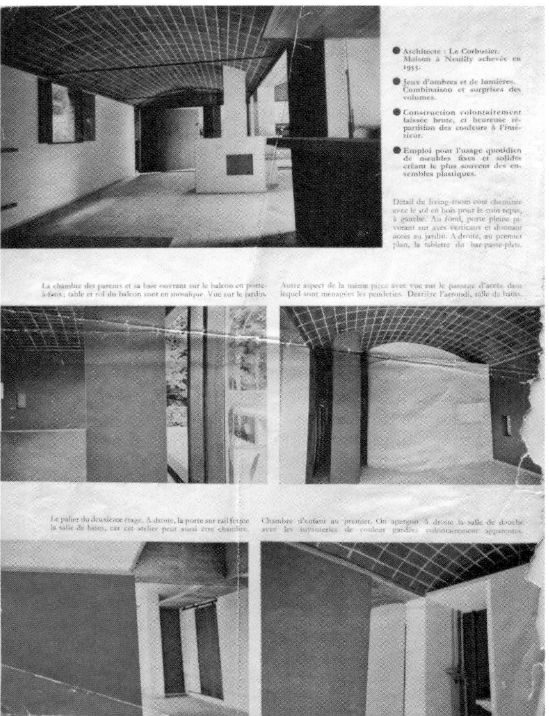

● Architecte : Le Corbusier. Maison à Neuilly achevée en 1955.

● Jeux d'ombres et de lumières. Combinaison et surprises des volumes.

● Construction volontairement laissée brute, et heureuse répartition des couleurs à l'intérieur.

● Emploi pour l'usage quotidien de meubles fixes et solides créant le plus souvent des ensembles plastiques.

Détail du living-room côté cheminée avec le sol en bois pour le coin repas, à gauche. Au fond, porte pleine pivotant sur axes verticaux et donnant accès au jardin. A droite, au premier plan, la tablette du bar-passe-plats.

La chambre des parents et sa baie ouvrant sur le balcon en porte-à-faux; table et sol du balcon sont en mosaïque. Vue sur le jardin.

Autre aspect de la même pièce avec vue sur le passage d'accès dans lequel sont ménagées les penderies. Derrière l'arrondi, salle de bains.

Le palier du deuxième étage. A droite, la porte sur rail ferme la salle de bains, car cet atelier peut aussi être chambre.

Chambre d'enfant au premier. On aperçoit à droite la salle de douche avec les tuyauteries de couleur gardées volontairement apparentes.

Figs. 198 and 199
Extracts from "La première résidence créée par Le Corbusier depuis 1935 [The first private residence created by Le Corbusier since 1935]," the first coverage of his houses in *Maison & Jardin* (House and Garden), n° 34, February 1956, front cover and 37. Jaoul archives.

career. There was no animosity, not one dramatic row. The sharing of responsibilities in the studio, delegating the difficult task of completing the building to specific assistants, was beneficial for Le Corbusier, who could keep his distance and preserve his identity as a friend of the family.

The childhood home

There is a case for the prosecution regarding the Maisons Jaoul, however. The principal witness is Michel Jaoul's daughter, Marie, who was interviewed in 1984 and whose criticisms have been gleefully taken up by architects and critics ever since. "Did Le Corbusier ever really think about the family?" wondered Marie Jaoul, the daughter of Michel and Nadine Jaoul, reflecting on her life in House B between the ages of six and nineteen,

> because I could hear everything. The partitions are wood or brick, but I could hear everything my parents did because I was only separated from them by a cupboard.... What's more, there were lighting problems in that house; it was very dark. This natural light was beautiful but depressing. The subdivision of panels and windows allowed the sun to enter in places but the rest was rather dark, especially downstairs.[46]

These remarks, recorded by François Barré, add to the long list of criticisms of modern houses. The Brutalist exterior of the houses, built of rough brick walls and apparently massive concrete arches, also attracted unwelcome attention. As a young girl, Marie suffered from the peculiarity of the house:

> My school friends would say: "Why do you live in a factory? Don't your parents have any money?" They thought that it was a factory because it was not finished off like the others.... What I liked were the houses that used to be in the rue de Longchamp. They have all been demolished. Houses hidden behind wisteria and Virginia creeper, buried away in overgrown and half-abandoned gardens with balconies in painted wood or cement worked to look like wood.... I would have liked a house like that, a little cottage full of tenderness. In Corbu's house, I had no secret life.[47]

Fig. 200
Le Corbusier, *Femme écrivant* (Woman Writing), metal-point drawing on dark-varnished brown paint, 1955. Greeting card sent to the Jaoul family. M. and N. Jaoul collection.

Marie complained that the interior slit window in her room allowed her parents to know whether she had the light on at night. This is surely not the only house to raise the issue of parental surveillance and the liberty of teenage children. These observations testify to the conflict between the avant-garde ideas of their parents and the child's desire to conform to the conventions of her circle of friends.

The opinion of the mayor of Neuilly

Avant-garde ideas did not play a significant role in the development of the housing stock in Neuilly. "Houses hidden behind wisteria and Virginia creeper," gave way to large modern apartments in stone clad concrete, compared to which the Brutalism of the Maisons Jaoul seemed shocking.

In 1970, Achille Peretti, the mayor responsible for building permissions, authorized the construction, in the wooded park of the Lopez Villa, of a seven storey apartment block. This was right in front of the Maisons Jaoul, which had just been listed at the request of the Minister of Cultural Affairs André Malraux as a landmark building (Inventaire supplémentaire des monuments historiques). A local protest group, with the support of Malraux, made a complaint to the Council, and the newspaper *Le Figaro* denounced "the outrageous abuse of building permits."[48] Peretti replied by accusing the author of the article of "not perhaps having had the time to see the villa in question..." and added, "we, and all those who know the city, will certainly consider that the Lopez Villa has greater architectural value than the Maisons Jaoul."[49] And this was a point of view shared by the school friends of Marie Jaoul.

Chapter 4

FORTUNA CRITICA OF THE MAISONS JAOUL

The significance of a work of art, whether literary or architectural, is transformed ad infinitum by the variety of readings and critical theories surrounding it, provoking Roland Barthes to make the following observation: "[These] facts at least bear witness to the truth that the work has several meanings. Each age can indeed believe that it holds the canonical meaning of the work, but it suffices to have a slightly broader historical perspective in order for this singular meaning to be transformed into a plural meaning and the closed work to be transformed into an open work."[1] Le Corbusier' s œuvre, its reception, and impact are particularly susceptible to such a pluralist interpretation, especially in the case of the Maisons Jaoul. Without claiming to be exhaustive, this critical assessment nevertheless demonstrates the influence exerted by these houses during the 1950s and 1960s, particularly in England, while being relatively overlooked in France and the United States. That they attracted special attention in Britain was partly due to propitious conditions, enhanced by the growing influence of Brutalist tendencies, as Reyner Banham highlights.[2] In effect, the "New Brutalism" movement was both a reaction against the rigid dogmas of modern architecture and, more importantly, a call for a more radical artistic approach to the search for authenticity.

Due to their massive brick vaults configured as arched naves, the Maisons Jaoul design was viewed as an error of judgment, a volte-face, a throwback, and a change in perception that represented, according to James Stirling's strongly worded critique, an affront to all those nurtured on the myth of Modern architecture. This was founded on an architectural ideal of smooth, standard, machine-wrought surfaces and skeleton frame, in which the relation of plan to elevation must be strictly harmonized. Distancing himself from his own highly venerated white architecture of the 1920s, here Le Corbusier proposed an alternative repertoire of forms: rough surfaces, hand-built, expressed brick cross-walls, and longitudinal bays anchored into the floor. The quasirural location of this habitation, within the chic rue de Longchamp neighborhood, was in itself a provocation, a house as "*brute*" as an industrial brick factory from the Paris outskirts transported into a refined enclave of private ownership.

Originally provoking a negative reaction, condemning them to a sort of purgatory, these houses ultimately attained cult status—as models of a new aesthetic expression and social responsibility—within the British New Brutalism movement and for a whole generation of French architects.[3] Some observers recognized the Maisons Jaoul as an innovative departure from and a critical response to contemporary architecture,[4] sparking off a debate on the fundamental precepts of Modern architecture, manifested in both written and built form. Did these houses contribute to the transmission of a norm, the creation of a norm, or did they provoke a rupture with the norm? It would seem that, in turn, they played out all three of these roles.[5]

James Stirling

GARCHES TO JAOUL

LE CORBUSIER AS DOMESTIC ARCHITECT IN 1927 AND 1953

Villa Garches, recently reoccupied, and the two houses for Mr. Jaoul and his son, now nearing completion, are possibly the most significant buildings by Le Corbusier to be seen in Paris to-day, for they represent the extremes of his vocabulary: the former, rational, urbane, programmatic, the latter, personal and anti-mechanistic. If style is the crystallization of an attitude, then these buildings, so different even at the most superficial level of comparison, may, on examination, reveal something of a philosophical change of attitude on the part of their author.

Garches, built at the culmination of Cubism and canonizing the theories in "Towards a New Architecture", has since its inception been a standard by which Le Corbusier's genius is measured against that of the other great architects of this century. Inhabited, again by Americans, after 15 years' splendid isolation, it has been painted in a manner more "de Stijl" than the original; walls white inside and out, all structural members black and single planes of primary colour on areas of lesser consequence. It is never possible to see more than one coloured plane from any single viewpoint. On the principal façade, the underside of the entrance canopy is painted sky-blue as the underside of the slab over the terrace. Inside, one wall of the living area is painted yellow, etc.

As with the still deserted Poissy, the deterioration at Garches was only skin-deep; paint decay, broken glass and slight cracks in the rendering; there has been no deterioration to the structure nor any waterproofing failures. Though the landscape has thickened considerably to the rear of the house, trees have not yet grown close against the main façades; where this has happened, at La Roche, Cook and Pleinex, the balanced asymmetry of the elevations, as total compositions, has been grossly disfigured. The one instance among the Paris buildings where trees are sympathetic is the Pavilion Suisse where they have grown the full height of the south elevation, significantly one of the most repetitive façades that Le Corbusier has produced. In more

Garches: *The triangulated balance of the projecting elements appearing in front of the wall, is similar to the rear where the complete elevation is divided into three asymmetrically-balanced features: the plinth, the recess and the wall.*
Jaoul: *The adjoining private garden is the only place from which a conventional examination of any façade can be made.*

Garches: *Metal saucers to throw water clear and avoid staining are pressed into the rendering under the lower canopy supports. The entire building is detailed with similar foresight.*
Jaoul: *The projecting balcony is an extension of the structure, whereas at Garches the external elements have the appearance of being applied.*

Garches: *The plinth, on a line with e structural columns, is painted black as re all other principal structural members.*
Jaoul: *The relationships of the façade elements follow no visually apparent geometry.*

GARCHES TO JAOUL

149

Figs. 201 and 202
Pages from an article by James Stirling, "Garches to Jaoul: Le Corbusier as Domestic Architect in 1927 and 1953," ***The Architectural Review,*** **n° 118, September 1955, 145–151.**

Anglo-American critical reception

From 1955 onward, critical Anglo-American commentators posed tacit questions on the language of Modern architecture, reconsidering the use of "traditional" materials (such as exposed brick and wood) and the return to load-bearing walls as valid expressions within its established lexicon.[6] Certain critics even speculated on the possible risk that might be incurred as a result of circulating images of the Maisons Jaoul through the *Œuvre complète*, whether in plan and section (volume 5, 1946–1952) or in photographs (volume 6, 1952–1957) because they deviated from the Rationalist idiom. Nikolaus Pevsner was preoccupied by what he considered a downward spiral into Expressionism.[7] Consistent with the opinion of the narrow world of functionalists who attended the CIAM meetings at Hoddesdon in 1951 or Aix-en-Provence in 1953, he saw Le Corbusier' s Unité d'Habitation at Marseilles, his Chapel at Ronchamp, and his Maisons Jaoul in Neuilly as sending nothing less than an electric shock through the architectural world. The quasi-exclusive attention focused on the materiality of these works thus relegated Le Corbusier's entire principle of composition, rationality of plan, and regulating lines to a secondary role.

Garches: *'The key to aesthetic emotion is a function of space.'*
Jaoul: *View of the first floor, showing the nine-inch brick cross walls from which the vaults spring.*

Fig. 203
Page from James Stirling, "Garches to Jaoul," on the free plan and load-bearing walls.

Fig. 204
House B, detail of the brick wall with its extruding exterior plug corresponding to the end of the tie-rod.

James Stirling's reaction was more subtle. In 1955, he launched the first real debate by dedicating an article to a comparative analysis between the Villa Stein de Monzie at Garches (or Villa Garches, 1927) and the Maisons Jaoul (Figs. 201–203),[8] and a second article in the following year on the Chapel at Ronchamp and the "crisis of Rationalism." [9] Stirling' s critique is doubly interesting because it bears witness to his own development as architect and critic, which occurred during the course of his writing. At the very moment he was criticizing aspects of Le Corbusier's architecture, he was simultaneously in the process of absorbing and assimilating the very essence of it, and thereby altering his own architectural output. In his 1955 article, he classifies the Villa Garches and the Maisons Jaoul according to one sole criterion, their adherence or not to modernity, and constantly oscillates between conformity to the established norms of modernity, represented by the Villa Garches, and rejection of those norms, deliberately exaggerated by the Maisons Jaoul. Such issues come to the fore because in these houses (visited in 1954 while still under construction), Stirling sees revealed "a philosophical change in attitude" in comparison to the Villa Garches. He bases his interpretation on a summary of fundamental principles: the structural system, the harmonic proportions, the formal references to the machine aesthetic, the construction process, and, lastly, the social objectives of the work.

"Differing from the point structure and therefore free plan of Garches, the structure of Jaoul is of load-bearing, brick cross-walls, cellular in planning by implication."[10] Among the definitions that Le Corbusier himself gave to his architectural vocabulary, Stirling extracts those that strike him as characteristically modern, for example the free plan. In contrast to this free plan, he evokes the cellular plan, even though, it should be stressed, the biological cell metaphor had already entered into the Corbusian lexicon before the Jaoul project. At Neuilly, the consideration of serial elements and the Modulor grid constitutes the clearest expression of a rationalist approach to design, and hence its modernity.

Fig. 205
View of the thin Catalan vault installed in the Maisons Jaoul.

Fig. 206
Southeast facade of House B.

According to Stirling, "while Garches is not the product of any high-powered mechanization, the whole spirit of the building expresses the essence of machine power."[11] He draws on comparisons to industrial, railroad, and steamship fabrication, arguing that the villa crystallizes the symbol of modernity (the basic element of the Pavillon de l'Esprit Nouveau) and the Machine Age. By contrast, he argues that at Neuilly, "There is no reference to any aspect of the machine... either in construction or aesthetic."[12] Perhaps not overtly drawing an analogy to the machine, nonetheless, the vault motif could be interpreted as making an oblique reference, in a less recognizable form, to the low barrel-vaulted railway freight car. The spatial discipline of the bay had long fascinated Le Corbusier. In the Maisons Jaoul, the 7.4-foot and 12-foot naves serve as the modular components of the composition.

On the subject of these vaults, Stirling made several misleading remarks on their structural composition (errors later reiterated by Reyner Banham), ones that need clarification. Where he perceived only "massive, concrete, Catalan vaults [with] the ceiling or underside of the vaults... frequently finished in a dark clay tile,"[13] was, in fact, an integral tectonic structure composed of three layers of flat *briquette* plates of which the first, or outer layer constitutes the ceiling texture (as described in Chapter 2). In his reference to the "massive, concrete Catalan vaults," one wonders if Stirling is not associating or confusing the depth of the concrete feature masking the vault in elevation with the vault structure itself. Construction site photographs taken by Lucien Hervé, which capture an overview of the exposed brick arch vault (before the upper floor has been laid over it) and an oblique side view of the extrados, confirm, to the contrary, the actual thinness of the Catalan vault (Figs. 155 and 205).

The Maisons Jaoul are examples of the architect's desire to synthesize two different technological procedures. Yet the dialectical rapport between industry and craftsmanship completely escapes Stirling's attention. It seems an exaggeration on his part to claim that "technologically, they make no advance on medieval building,"[14] when one recognizes the effort that Le Corbusier invested in the design of the wood panels, the installation of what he called "the fourth wall," the incorporation of shelving and opaque materials into the window opening, the study of the distinction between various window functions, the natural illumination, and the ventilation. Stirling's remark all but reduces weight-bearing wall architecture to an architecture of the past.

Kenneth Frampton's point of view on Le Corbusier's attitude toward mechanization is more nuanced, contending that his work is characterized by two distinct phases. The first, up to the 1930s, is dominated by a wholly confident approach toward the positive contribution of industry. The second is forged upon a system of double references "to combine primitive and industrial techniques, according to... needs and resources,"[15] best illustrated by the Petite Maison de Weekend in La Celle-Saint-Cloud, completed in 1935 (Fig. 63).

Following his comparative analysis in the 1955 article, Stirling concludes by evoking possible affinities between the Maisons Jaoul and Provençal farmhouses or vernacular Indian architecture, qualifying Le Corbusier as "the most regional of architects."[16] He also notes that the quality of the Jaoul brickwork is poor in comparison to English standards. Reyner Banham emphasizes that Stirling and his contemporaries were unsparingly critical of the fact that the Maisons Jaoul were not "Utopian" and "did not anticipate and participate in the progress of Twentieth-century emancipation."[17] Stirling also recognized that they had been "built by and intended for the status quo."[18] This judgment is based on the myth of an avant-garde architecture founded, by definition, on technical innovations and intended to promote social change. If, in effect, the Maisons Jaoul are not as radical as Jean Prouvé's Maison Tropicale (1951), they hardly constitute a technical regression or any sort of "halt to the reforms." If Banham shares Stirling's opinion of the Maisons Jaoul as "status quo" architecture, he nevertheless identifies the polysemy of the Corbusian debate, noting that the Jaoul project represents for Le Corbusier the rejection of the "diagrammatic, formalistic and legalistic categories of the Athens Charter" and his preoccupation with "trying to create the ideal habitat for a particular place (Neuilly) at that particular time (the mid-fifties)."[19]

If the expressive materiality of the work (brick walls with thick joints) initially acted as a deterrent to Stirling, Le Corbusier' s proposed innovative architectural and formal aesthetic directions ultimately served as a stimulant for him. Regarding this phenomenon, Michel Thévoz has observed the following:

> [I]n the artistic domain as in the general psychic sphere, resistance or denial can be more telling than immediate alliance, the subject thereby absolving himself of all responsibility. One takes more liberties with objects categorized as shoddy, decadent, crude or ignoble than with those that one reveres. One dares to observe them at a closer range and one takes pleasure in dismantling them.... If one resists, denies or rationalizes [the object], it is precisely because one has sensed the danger in all its implications and has foreseen the consequences of the ideological stakes.[20]

In retrospect, Stirling recalls the advantages he derived from his ventures:

> My own ambivalence was evident in the articles I published at the time. Since I had been drawing on Le Corbusier' s work of the 1920s and 1930s... I was disoriented by his new direction, though it soon became important in my work. To most of us, Le Corbusier seemed richer and more interesting than Mies, who had been the key figure slightly earlier. Le Corbusier could be tied in with popular culture more easily, and even his Modulor system, which was widely discussed after his book was translated, seemed to have an integrative potential that was lacking in Miesian grids.[21]

During the very same period in which he was strongly criticizing Le Corbusier' s Jaoul design concepts, Stirling was simultaneously borrowing and readapting them within the framework of his own architectural work, most notably in his low-cost Langham House development, Ham Common, near Richmond in Surrey (Fig. 207).

In effect, these apartment blocks built between 1955 and 1958, in partnership with James Gowan, along with his 1956 proposal for an unbuilt private house in the Chilterns are clearly indebted to Le Corbusier's Neuilly scheme, in their use of rough concrete lintels and exposed brick (even though the English brickwork is highly refined). Stirling also adopted another characteristic feature, the reversed L-shaped window module. However, in contrast to the Neuilly window, whose shape was dictated by local bylaw restrictions applied to party wall conditions, Stirling's irregular

Fig. 207
James Stirling and James Gowan, Langham House development, Ham Common, Surrey, 1955–58.

window openings became part of an arbitrary, autonomous design vocabulary (Figs. 206 and 207).

As an example of the ways in which a work of art comprises numerous detours and complexities, Stirling reevaluated a posteriori the Corbusian influences on his own work. Adrian Forty pointed out that his critical reading differed from his practice as an architect. If Ham Common can be understood as a transposition of Corbusian propositions, here the student corrected the "errors" of his master by modifying certain features: the messy brickwork in Neuilly is, at Ham Common, decidedly neater, as is the poured concrete detailing; the geometric scheme is clearly expressed. Some spatial effects are created in the entrance halls and staircases, even though Stirling had noted the absence of a modernist treatment of space in the Jaoul [houses]: "There is certainly no question of being able to stand inside and comprehend the limits of the house."[22] This last remark on the lack of a comprehensive overview, due to a certain spatial complexity, is, however, paradoxical because here Stirling criticizes the very quality that eventually came to be considered a sign of modernity.

While the English architect-critic shed light on the innovative motifs of Le Corbusier' s œuvre, he appropriated the very work he criticized. It was precisely in recognition of the great gulf that this work produced in relation to the established modern idiom that allowed Stirling to meditate on the master's lesson, at first from a critical distance and later from a profitable position of reconciliation, no longer only as pure architectural criticism. Robert Maxwell explains this discrepancy: "Le Corbusier's volte-face at the Maisons Jaoul was obviously the origin of Stirling's freedom in his architectural practice. It gave legitimacy to the Ham Common project and his ensuing experiments in the vernacular use of brick.... One searched instead for the means to extract from recalcitrant materials the abstract, immaterial qualities of a pure architecture. Form and variations thus became the source of infinite possiblities."[23] Here Maxwell takes great care to emphasize the continuity of architectural lessons.

In his article entitled "Regionalism and Modern Architecture" published in the *Architects' Year Book 8* (1957) and illustrated by a series of vernacular buildings (lime kilns, beer distilleries, among others) and industrial types (Liverpool warehouses), Stirling notes that the picturesque aspects of these indigenous, often anonymous buildings gradually became more appreciated. Then he added: "Today Stonehenge is more significant than the architecture of Sir Christopher Wren."[24]

In comparison to Stirling, Banham delves much further into an appreciation of Le Corbusier's work and motivations.[25] He describes the perspectives, expectations, and cultural framework out of which his search for primitivism emerged. On the one hand, he evokes temporal overlaps between the artistic attitudes and sensibilities of Dubuffet, Fautrier, Pollock, and other "anti-artists" who mark this period, and their search for authenticity in association with the Art Brut movement. On the other hand, he analyzes the role of the exhibition "Parallel of Life and Art" organized in 1953 by Alison and Peter Smithson, Nigel Henderson, and Eduardo Paolozzi.

This show was organized around a selection of bizarre, destructive, and antiaesthetic images (highly reduced and grossly over-enlarged photographs of structures, materials, and human figures). Chosen for their emotional value, the taste for coarse, grainy, textured blow-ups already characterized this period. Artists and architects were thus open to works emphasizing found objects and the expressive power of an image. According to Banham, a two-way exchange was established between the Brutalist movement and the Maisons Jaoul. If, on the one hand, the theoretical elaboration of the movement had already existed by the early 1950s, on the other hand, a built work to serve as a paradigm was missing. This role was to be filled by the Unité d'Habitation at Marseilles and the Maisons Jaoul.

Architectural and urban lessons

Banham also stressed that the Smithsons attached great importance to the urban and social aims implicit in the Jaoul design: "The relationship of the two houses to their underground car parking was [perceived as] a fair example of a building as a prototype of a new urban order"[26] (Fig. 208). This

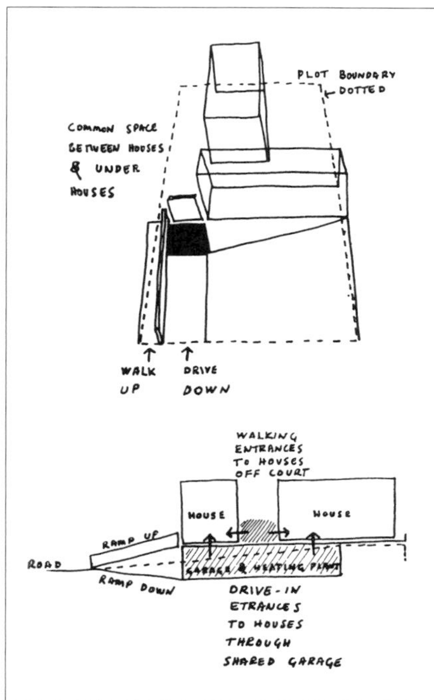

prototype became one of the underlying components in the Smithsons' "Cluster City" proposal, formulating a new social structure, the question of the architect's social responsibility being a crucial dimension of English modernism, equal to that of the role of technology. Team X members[27] had begun to protest against this social responsibility that they believed paralyzed creativity and produced nothing but dull, brick buildings (out of an obligation to design "popular" architecture). Le Corbusier's expressive alternative had, therefore, been received with enthusiasm, as a means of regeneration. The New Brutalism endeavored to reclaim the artistic commitment of an avant-garde, freed from the obligation of social engagement. Their stance was not so very different from Jean Dubuffet's defiant claim, "What one expects from art is that it certainly not be normal. One expects just the opposite from it... that it be as original and unanticipated as possible. One also expects that it be highly imaginative."[28]

Fig. 208
Alison and Peter Smithson, axonometric drawing of the two Maisons Jaoul (reproduced in Reyner Banham, *The New Brutalism*, 96). The Smithsons were seduced by the emplacement of the garage beneath the two houses, a strategy they considered as the start of a new urban order.

Fig. 209
Alan Colquhoun visiting the Maisons Jaoul in 1956.

Reyner Banham pursues his commentary by insisting that Brutalism was, in large part, an issue of surfaces derived from the Maisons Jaoul, Stirling had suggested that the Jaoul walls had to be "considered as surface and not as structure" as opposed to Garches. For Banham, "the numerous emulations and derivatives of Jaoul to be called Brutalist has nothing to do with prototypes of a new community structure, and a great deal to do with raw concrete and exposed brickwork."[29] It is valid, however, to cite a number of architectural works whose schematic urban organization does resemble, to a certain extent, both Corbusian studies for the "Roq" project (a vast seaside land development at Cap-Martin, 1948–50) and the Jaoul proposal. They include the Djenan el-Hasan housing development

Fig. 210
Merlier vacation village, Cap Camarat, France, designed by Atelier de Montrouge (Jean Renaudie, Pierre Riboulet, Gérard Thurnauer, and Jean-Louis Véret), 1958–65.

Fig. 211
Falmer House, University of Sussex, Brighton, England, designed by Sir Basil Spence and Associates, 1962–63.

Fig. 212
The extension of the Cambridge School of Architecture, England, designed by Alex Hardy and Colin A. St John Wilson, 1957–58.

in Algeria designed by Roland Simounet; the Merlier vacation village at Cap Camarat (1958–65) by the Atelier de Montrouge (Jean Renaudie, Pierre Riboulet, Gérard Thurnauer, and Jean-Louis Vére) (Fig. 210); and the Halen housing ensemble (1961), near Berne, by the Atelier 5. Considered by this postwar generation of architects, the "Roq" project and its partial adaptation in Neuilly seemed capable not only of resolving the dichotomy between the individual and the collective, but also of diminishing social divisions in the inner city. From the Maisons Jaoul, architects borrowed the Modular theme (suggested by the vaulted bay) and adapted it to their sites. Construction features resembling those used for the Maisons Jaoul can be seen in other examples, such as the 273 housing units at Vigneux (1960–64) by Paul Chemetov and the La Courneuve Senior Citizens home (1961–65) by Paul Chemetov and Jean Deroche.[30]

In England, the Corbusian model is strikingly evident in Alex Hardy and Colin A. St John Wilson's extension to the School of Architecture building in Cambridge (1957–58) (Fig. 212). Sir Basil Spence and Associates' Sussex University in Brighton (1962–63) also manifests recognizable elements of the Maisons Jaoul, such as the vault, concrete lintels, and exposed brick walls.[31] (Fig. 211).

Le Corbusier's continued involvement

Le Corbusier had advised the proprietors of the Villa Savoye (1928–1929) to keep a guest book in order to collect their visitors' signatures. The Jaouls did the same. From 1955 to 1987, they received a number of architects and architectural historians, for the most part foreigners from Latin America, India, the United States, and England (architectural historian and architect Alan Colquhoun visited the site in 1955) (Fig. 209). On these pages can be deciphered various well-known signatures, among them: Nino Dardi, Richard and Susan Rogers, Norman Foster, Roberto Burle Marx, Peter Eisenman, Colin Rowe, Frank Gehry, Paul Rudolph, Shadrach Woods, Neave Brown, Christian de Portzamparc, Roland Simounet, and Bernard Wauthier (Fig. 213).

During the sixties, at a time when a fierce battle was being waged against the glass curtain wall, Le Corbusier's "primitive technology" was being replicated throughout the world. Faced with all these imitations, he once again altered his strategy. His sketch proposal for a roof extension for the Jaouls in 1962, although never executed, illustrates his return to industrial technology, in the form of a metal structure intended for the roof at the fourth level of House A. Le Corbusier described the design in his written response to Madame Jaoul's request for an extension to their habitable space:

> While waiting for M[onsieur] Michel Jaoul to return from Australia, here is a sketch that I myself studied of a possible installation for a new family on the roof of your house. The study is drawn up with accurate dimensions, but needs updating. As I am leaving for India soon, we could resume discussions during the month of May, upon M[onsieur] Michel Jaoul's return. My impression is that the thing could be built very conventionally, on the condition that a sort of square airplane cabin space with soldered tubes be installed on the roof, a very light-weight and fully resistant construction.[32]

This airplane cabin anchored to the brick-and-concrete structure was interpreted as the ultimate provocation. After designing a vernacular building type for the Jaouls, Le Corbusier now proposed a "technological" adjustment,[33] documented by two sketches, a plan, and an elevation (Figs. 214 and 215).[34] A model of the two houses and the extension was developed by Jacques Michel and Jean Prouvé in the 1970s (Fig. 216).

This proposition appears at a timely moment, confirming a constant trait in Le Corbusier's conceptual process, which consists in thinking of a building as having a dual personality or an ability to divide itself in two, in order to expand. In the case of the Maisons Jaoul, one could have speculated that the reference to a Monol type would eventually lead to a proposal to extend horizontally. The lack of ground space on the Jaoul site undoubtedly forced a superimposed scheme.

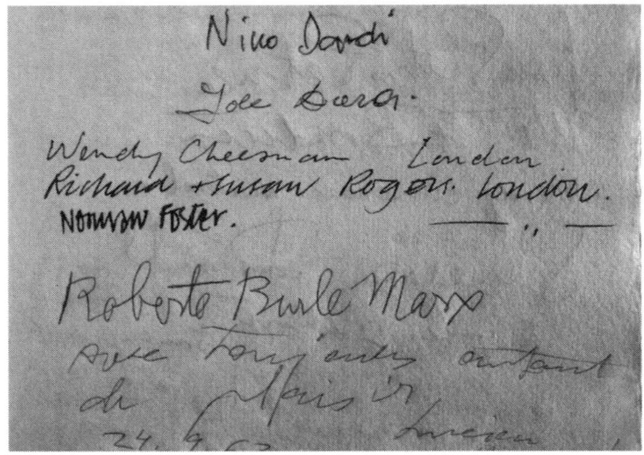

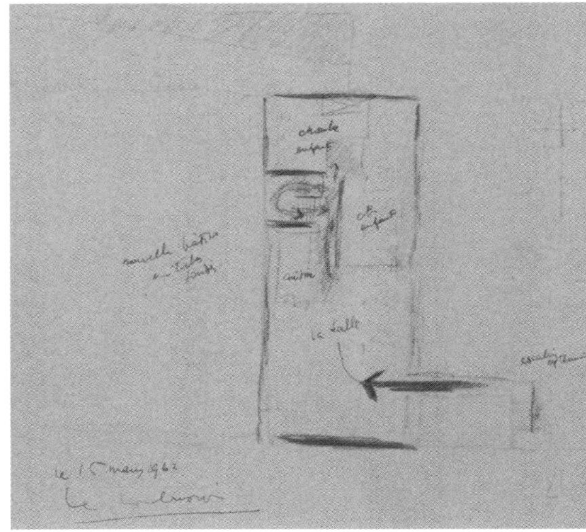

Fig. 213 (top left)
A page from the Jaoul family guest book, 1967. M. and N. Jaoul archives.

Fig. 214 (bottom left)
In an elevation study of House A, initialed and dated March 15, 1962, Le Corbusier proposes to install "a sort of square airplane cabin space with soldered tubes" on the roof. FLC 10052.

Fig. 215 (top right)
Le Corbusier, colored pencil plan study of the proposed roof extension, dated 12/15 March 1962. FLC 10051.

Fig. 216 (bottom right)
Cardboard model of the two Maisons Jaoul with the proposed roof addition, as developed by Jacques Michel and Jean Prouvé after Le Corbusier's sketches.

Epilogue

On March 11, 1965, Michel Jaoul warned the Enterprise Allard that the glazed sections—the Thermopane windows and the double glazing or "Nantes" types furnished by Maison Boussois (Fig. 217)—showed traces of condensation and ordered replacements under the 10-year guarantee:

> For the past four or five years, we have observed the progressive deterioration of some of the double-glazed windows that, in certain cases, are extremely spotted by the humidity.... You are aware of the fact that, on an almost daily basis, architects and designers, etc. from the world over pay visits to our houses... considered as one of Le Corbusier's works that merit a visit. What's more, we recently came across a catalogue with a Boussois advertisement that cites [our houses] as references. I therefore think that Boussois ought to take the necessary steps as rapidly as possible to restore the high quality of these houses.[35]

Apart from a few malfunctions, the balcony collapse and defective double glazing, the Jaouls lived contentedly in their dwellings for thirty-two years. But in 1987, the centennial year of Le Corbusier's birth, the Jaoul families consigned the sale of the two houses to Sotheby's auction house. Peter Palumbo, a collector and amateur of art and architecture, acquired

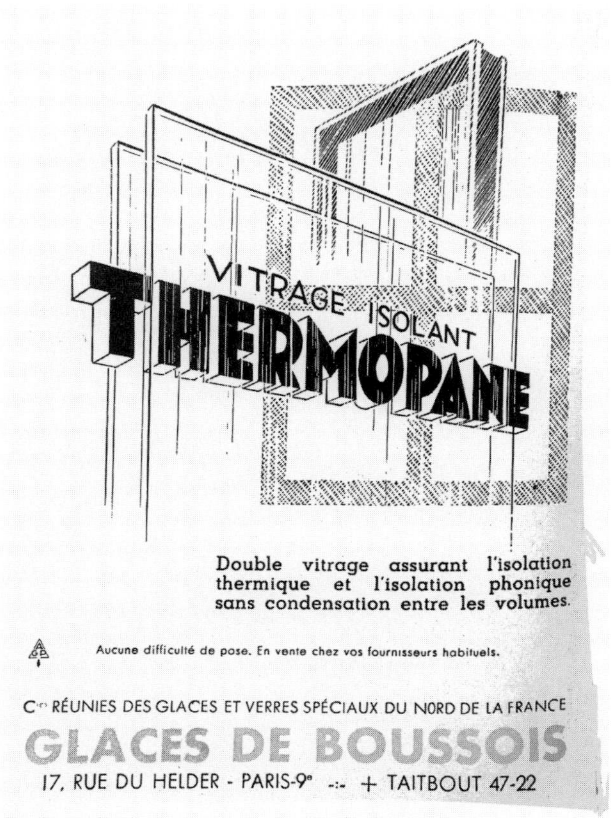

Fig. 217
Advertisement for Thermopanes, a brand of insulated windows, *Techniques & Architecture*, n° 5–6, 1952, 16.

the properties, adding them to his other architectural possessions: the Mies van der Rohe-designed Farnsworth house (1950) in Plano, about sixty miles from Chicago, Illinois, and the Frank Lloyd Wright-designed Kentuck Knob house in Chalk Hill, Pennsylvania (1954).[36]

Palumbo contributed to the popularization of the Maisons Jaoul, restoring them with great care and encouraging public accessibility. As a result, entire busloads of architecture students arrived at 81 *bis*, rue de Longchamp, seduced not only by the contrasts between the interior and exterior of the houses, but also by the owner's exceptional contemporary collection of art and furniture. All this, however, detracted from the domestic atmosphere of the original Jaoul family homes.

In contrast to the Purist works of the 1920s, whose image of machine perfection was, in large part, their raison d'être, despite their technical failings, the Maisons Jaoul, in 1988, appeared, after more than thirty years, in relatively sound condition. The visible natural aging of the materials conformed by and large to the original architectural concept. Iron laid bare, spalling concrete, rusting metal millwork, cracked exterior varnish, and the like were part of the general deterioration that, in the end, did not dramatically affect the overall design aesthetic (Figs. 218–220). Palumbo, as the new owner, nevertheless wanted to improve the overall level of comfort and security, and restore the buildings to their original

Fig. 218
House B. Repointing the exterior concrete bands during the restoration campaign, 1991.

Fig. 219
Restoration of the *pans de verre* and movable sashes, 1991.

Fig. 220
House B. Detail of the "bird-nesting" boxes.

state, in conformity with national heritage protection regulations following the listing of their facades on the supplementary inventory of Monuments historiques on June 29, 1966.[37]

The restoration campaign was conferred to Jacques Michel, then practicing architect in Neuilly. Salvatore Bertocchi was also consulted in an advisory capacity, with Marie-Jeanne Dumont, architectural historian, preparing a descriptive inventory of executed work: "The deteriorated concrete on the continuous exterior bands was repointed along several centimeters and redone with formwork of the same pattern and the same dimensions as the original. Waterproofing on the terraces was entirely redone. The exterior woodwork was repaired or replaced."[38]

The *pans de verre* and some moveable sashes were completely restored by conserving their original oak structure. The brick walls were cleaned with jet-propelled water. All the interior plumbing, heating, electricity, and alarm systems were redone. Some shutters were added in the gridded window openings. Jacques Michel decided on adding closing plugs on the distribution pipes, indicated by wood screens, which nevertheless damaged the colored panels. All the original polychromy was respected: red, yellow, green, blue, grey, black, and white.

Twelve years later, in 2000, the houses were once again placed on the market. The sales board described them as twin houses. Two sisters and their respective husbands purchased them within the year and have lived there ever since.

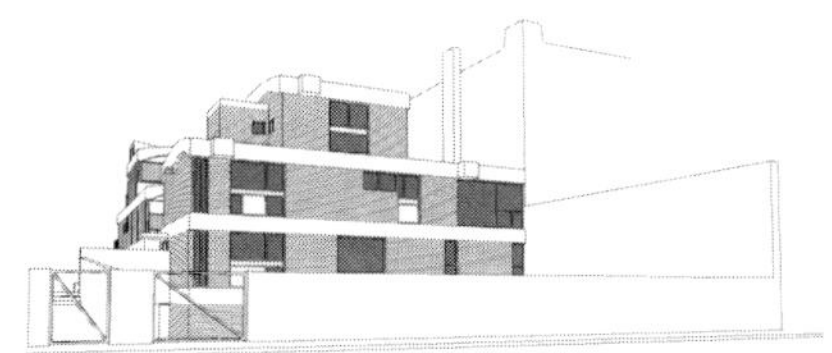

Conclusion

RETURNING THE SNAIL TO ITS SHELL

"The snail is in a snail's shell: true enough. As for us, when mechanization drastically disrupted our society, we tried to put the snail in, for example, a pillbox. Mechanization should return the snail to its shell. A wise dream."[1]

And so, it was in this spirit that Le Corbusier decided to put an iron-and-steel industrialist into a brick-vaulted house, as a way of "returning the snail to its shell."

The Maisons Jaoul represent a type of architecture particularly open to various readings at multiple levels because here, in this project, Le Corbusier himself reevaluated his entire architectural output to date and put into question the larger issue of modernity itself, a subject of fierce debate throughout the 1950s. In fact, all the architect's postwar buildings may be interpreted as reflections on the difficulty of being modern. In the Jaoul houses, Le Corbusier played with contrasts, paradoxes, and simultaneous readings. His intention was two-fold: first, to demonstrate his mastery over craftsmanship by specifying unconventional or unexpected design choices and, second, to convey the myth of the simple peasant who constructs his home with his own hands. If, for certain critics and visitors, the "*mal foutue* (messed-up)" brickwork of the Maisons Jaoul evokes a romantic primitivism, for others the installation of machine materials conveys an industrial brutality. This expressive plurality extends to every detail of the houses, through the juxtaposition of diverse materials (brick, concrete, metal), through the ways in which such materials are faceted to various degrees of precision (wood roughly squared off or artfully jointed), and through the contrast of distinct technologies (partition walls machine-assembled in the workshop and brick walls laid by masons on the site). Le Corbusier designed a modular house system whose execution could be achieved by any handyman-client (simplified by an architecture of ready-made parts), yet at the same time and, to the contrary, an end product whose fabrication required exacting supervision and expert craftsmanship.

Above all, however, in conceiving these buildings, Le Corbusier gave great consideration to the house itself. He created small oases of physical comfort for his clients in the same way as he did for himself in his Cabanon at Cap-Martin in 1952. There he designed a variety of spaces, modulated by their dimensions and multicolored harmonies, reserving special niches for an assortment of personal objects, such as paintings, sculpture, and pottery.

Alternatively perceived as an architecture of rupture and as an architecture of consent, the Maisons Jaoul ultimately succeeded, through inciting debate, in transforming the controversy and, thereby, bringing about a reversal of opinion.

The modern architect's ambition involved not only raising questions on the nature of the art of living but also on the means of representing it, on proposing possible solutions. During his participation at the CIAM meeting in Aix-en-Provence during June 1953, Le Corbusier directly confronted the certitudes of this organization, as well as his own convictions. He no longer knew how to proceed, as Manfred Tafuri suggests: "[I]t seems as though Le Corbusier understood what Heidegger was to perceive only later: the essence of technique is *poietica*; production and *poiesis* share common roots. The myth returns when production serves as an attempt to master the future."[2] To resist the myth, which consists in believing that architecture foresees the future, and to grapple with practicalities: such were the aims of Le Corbusier during the course of the Jaoul adventure.

Four years after the houses were completed, Jean-Jacques Duval (director of the textile factory in Saint-Dié designed by Le Corbusier in 1946–50) sent a letter to the architect in which he describes his visit to the Maisons Jaoul, paying homage to these living spaces:

> I had the good fortune... to be able to visit the two Jaoul houses, which were already well advanced at the time, and I believe that never before have I sensed such an impression of accomplishment in a contemporary work of art. This mixture of intimacy and grandeur, very difficult to explain, but constantly felt in every step through these houses, affected me in a way that I had not experienced except in certain 18th-century houses in Strasbourg. How fortunate are these Jaouls, who will have the chance to inhabit such a house in which one would love to live, even before it has even been furnished![3]

The Grosvenor
35 Fifth Avenue
New York
NEW YORK, N.Y.
MAY 29
7:30 PM
MADISON
STATION
3 CENTS 3
UNITED STATES POSTAGE
M. André JAOUL
Hotel Barclay
46 Lexington Av
New York
1224

LETTERS

Letter from Le Corbusier to Professor Fueter
March 17, 1950

—

Dispatch from Le Corbusier to Salvatore Bertocchi
February 25, 1953

—

Letter from Le Corbusier to Salvatore Bertocchi
May 7, 1953

—

Letter from Michel Jaoul to Le Corbusier
April 20, 1953

—

Letter from Le Corbusier to André Jaoul
May 14, 1953

—

Letter from Michel Jaoul to Le Corbusier
December 1, 1953

—

Letter from Michel Jaoul to Charles Barberis
October 19, 1954

—

Letter from Le Corbusier to Charles Barberis
October 21, 1954

Letter from Le Corbusier to Professor Fueter, March 17, 1950. FLC I2 (7) 14.

—

My dear friend,

Upon my return from South America, I found your letter of 27 February. I cannot emphasize enough how much those damned Swiss irritate me with their exaggerated notions of architectural finish. You are an intelligent person and so am I. We're not bourgeois; we appreciate the rough texture of exposed brick, joints coarsely mortared by the mason, whitewash laid over the brickwork, etc. I'm convinced that your house will be much better in its rude state, and you'll economize at least 20% on expenses, well worth your while. I repeat that the extravagant and finicky architectural finish of the Swiss really puts me off.

With many regrets,

Yours,

Le Corbusier

Dispatch from Le Corbusier to Salvatore Bertocchi, February 25, 1953. FLC J1 (16) 65.

—

My dear Bertocchi,

You will probably get the Jaoul job: vaults, brick walls and tiles, to be handled with Allard. Allard will only take a small cut from your overall price. I will find out the two costs: yours and Allard's eventual surcharge.

Instructions: make the most reasonable offer. I'm not saying that you should lose money on the job, rather that you shouldn't overcharge. Success or failure in this transaction is in your hands.

Regards to you,

Le Corbusier

Letter from Le Corbusier to Salvatore Bertocchi, May 7, 1953. FLC J1 (16) 71.

—

My dear Bertocchi,

I'm sending you an enclosed photo of Breton masonry; it's stone, as you can clearly see.

1) For Jaoul, I'd like you to make a similar brick wall with joints more or less the same as shown in the photo, respecting all the proportions, as much on the interior as on the exterior. You will discuss this with Jacques Michel.

2) The most sensible idea would be to try to reproduce a few small wall sections on site, for example, 75 x 75 [2 feet 6 in], oriented in exactly the same way as Jaoul's, with different types of bricks that the general contractor will supply.

Regards to you,

Le Corbusier

Letter from Michel Jaoul to Le Corbusier, April 20, 1953. FLC J1 (16) 468.

—

I am returning the enclosed plan and estimate that you gave me last Monday. I couldn't telephone you today, but can confirm in writing our conversation of the other day.

1) I would like to have a larger living room than the one shown in your plan, perhaps the equivalent of two 3.66 bays.

2) I need a maid's room. It is perfectly possible to envisage one adjoining the kitchen.

3) I should like to use some spaces in the living room and the parent's bedroom (for my wife and me) to put a few pieces of furniture that constitute my only heirlooms.

4) On the other hand, the children's rooms definitely could be furnished, I mean to say, newly designed and built-in by you.

5) The sanitary fittings must, in my opinion, include one shower and one sink for the parents, one shower and one or two sinks for the children. Only one toilet accessible to everyone. I prefer that the placement of these plumbing installations be isolated from the bedrooms.

6) A certain number of closets, at least one wardrobe per person seems indispensable, along with places to store the so-called family linen.

7) I still don't know if the house [temporary prefabricated house] should be built on the site of house B site or located elsewhere. Nonetheless the position of house B seems perfectly suitable if one cannot find another spot for it in the garden that would neither interfere with house A or house B during the completion of construction of the latter, nor obviously have too adverse an effect on our temporary habitation.

8) The general idea of a prefabricated house only makes sense if it is available by September, otherwise I prefer to buy an apartment in which I could live immediately.

9) I forgot to say that in the living room I should like to have, at the least, some large glazed bays openings (French windows?) giving direct access to the garden.

10) The exterior character of the house is not important to me as long as one avoids the look of a military barrack or a house for a "grade-crossing keeper."

I have expressed my tastes to you frankly because I am sure that you prefer to act in the full knowledge of the facts. We are very much counting on you.

Ever yours,

M. Jaoul.

Letter from Le Corbusier to André Jaoul, May 14, 1953. FLC G2 (14) 428.

—

Dear Friend,

I send you, along with this letter, my invoice, which I established in the following manner:

To begin with, I applied the minimum fee schedule due to the Architect (document drawn up by the Conseil Supérieur de l'Ordre des Architectes).

The anticipated percentages in this minimum scale allowed us to calculate the total fee corresponding to the complete work as originally proposed and studied by myself (house of Mr André Jaoul; house of Mr Michel Jaoul and common services below ground).

For the preliminary studies and preparation of construction files for this work, the portion of the fee due is equal to half the total fee thus calculated.

Regarding the part of my brief related to the building phase, it goes without saying that the figure indicated in the fee schedule will not be applied to the total until the construction work is concluded.

You will notice that I have not included any fees for the interior design work and decoration, even though the official fee schedule anticipates that such work will be paid separately; well, you know that such work constitutes, in effect, the largest part of the work that I must undertake.

I would be greatly obliged if you would kindly send me, at your earliest convenience, the total fee as calculated herein.

With my thanks, sincerely yours,

Le Corbusier

P.S. Concerning the construction of the temporary wood house based on the model called "3.66" I am in agreement with the Conseil Supérieur de l'Ordre minimal fee schedule, as per the main houses.

...I insist on making clear that I shall not ask for royalties on the patent application for the construction model called "3.66," it being understood that, in principle, royalties must be paid to me by the contractors applying for this patent.

L.C.

Letter from Michel Jaoul to Le Corbusier, December 1, 1953. FLC J1 (16) 472.

—

We're following the construction of our home very closely, and I must say that we're delighted by the atmosphere that already exists there. The vaults in particular are very beautiful and give an aspect of harmonious calm to the whole, which corresponds well to the ambiance that we were hoping for.

I send you this note because I dared not (since the departure of my Father) burden you with the details of our business, thus sparing your valuable time. You have surely heard from M[essieurs] Wogenscky or Michel about our financial worries in which we have been plunged as a result of the C.M.B. [Crédit mutuel du bâtiment] affair. This situation obliges us to reconsider the sequence of building operations at least until I am able to discuss with my Father alternative financial arrangements, if indeed there are any. The building contractors and your office collaborators have taken the necessary steps to limit the work provisionally to the structure and the damp proofing. Unfortunately, we shall no doubt be obliged as well, even if alternative financial means can be found, to reduce costs on the least significant jobs in the estimate, due to the losses that this sad affair has subjected us to. I cannot yet tell you in what measure we shall be able to cope, but I do know that I cannot commit myself to any other obligations beyond our present means. Michel [Jacques Michel, Le Corbusier's assistant] shared with us your ideas for the internal organization of the ground floor, and I must say that, apart from a few details, we are very enthusiastic. We particularly like the table. Unfortunately, I am afraid that I absolutely cannot countenance the cost of realizing it. I think that, although we may come back to this eventually, we can only consider furnishing our house with what we already own. Your ideas permeate us, my wife and I, like water through sand, but we regret that there are sordid and anti-progressive imperatives at play.

All this, I think, has direct consequences on the choice of the flooring. We very much like the combination of tiles and wood blocks that you propose, but it assumes a layout that we do not at the moment foresee. The end-grain wood alone must be very expensive. I think that it would be better to limit ourselves to a single surface finish, yet to be determined. It's a question of finding something that is easy to maintain and whose color and durability are acceptable. The ceramic tiles possess these qualities but we do not find them very exciting. The types of wooden flooring that I am aware of are not satisfactory. The cement tiles are very difficult to maintain and stain easily. This leaves various kinds of more or less durable stone among which we should be able to find the solution to our problem. For the first floor we are hesitating between wood or ceramic tiling with a preference for wood. As soon as we have a clearer picture of our financial problems, we shall inform you immediately and we could then recommence discussions in detail regarding all that concerns the interior design and that we would like to look at more closely. Right now, I should like to explain to you what might be the priorities for the work in the immediate future: floors, heating, etc.

Excuse me for having been so long-winded.

Again a word, despite all, to convey our admiration for your exhibition and to thank you once again for all the care you are taking to create a home for us.

Yours faithfully,
Michel Jaoul

Letter from Michel Jaoul to Charles Barberis, October 19, 1954. FLC J1 (16) 478.

—

Sir,

I have been notified by the Compagnie Générale Transatlantique that a delivery of 8 (eight) cases weighing in total 650 kg should be ready for me by the beginning of the month of October.

I want to call your attention to the fact that the transporters C.G.F.R. at 51, rue de Breteuil in Marseilles, the correspondent to the Compagnie Générale Transatlantique, did not complete this delivery until 16 October, that is, 17 days after the arrival notice in Marseilles and that, moreover, the delivery contained only 6 (six) cases weighing in total 430 kg. I leave it to you to ascertain with your expeditors whether an error or a loss has occurred.

I take this opportunity to express my total dissatisfaction over the unacceptable delay you incurred over fulfilling the order that you made with the Atelier Le Corbusier, with my agreement.

I should like to remind you that the sum of 660,000 francs *was transferred to your account on 31 March 1954, [and that] only during the month of July did I receive one part of the interior door and window frames of my house, then in October, a small portion of the exterior woodwork. Moreover, the installment of these interior frames was not carried out in the presence of your company representative, so that another contractor was obliged to assume the responsibility for this operation.*

In agreement with Le Corbusier's office, we had established the construction schedule so as to allow my moving into the house by October. In spite of my deploring a late delivery, I had then accepted the commitment you made with Le Corbusier's office to deliver the wainscoting that I had ordered at the end of the month of August.

At the end of August, I was informed that this delivery would be made only in the month of September. Here now, the 2nd or 3rd of the month of October has gone by and the deliveries made are once again incomplete.

Undoubtedly all this will push us into more than a three-month delay, wholly your fault. The trades that are obliged to follow your work, notably painting and electricity, have themselves been obliged to adjust their work schedule and thereby risk imposing additional delays on us as, in the meantime, they have taken on other job sites.

These delays entail major outlays or financial losses for us. In particular, the tax exemptions to which we have the right if we construct our house within a certain time frame will not, in all likelihood, be granted to us.

I understand that you let other orders take priority over mine. I do not know if this explains the reason for the delay that I have had to put up with: whatever the case, it remains that you have undermined the trust that Le Corbusier said we could place in you.

I ask that you inform me immediately, in the shortest delay possible, on what date you expect to complete the order corresponding to house B on the job site at 81, rue de Longchamp, as well as the date on which the installation of these various elements could be carried out.

I am sending M[onsieur] Le Corbusier a copy of this letter, in hopes that you commit yourself to making up for your own inadmissible delay in the execution of my order.

Michel Jaoul

Letter from Le Corbusier to Charles Barberis, October 21, 1954. FLC J1 (16) 243.

—

Dear Monsieur Barberis,

M[onsieur] Michel Jaoul sent me a copy of the letter that he addressed to you on 19 October.

What can I add to the grievances of this client? I am dumbfounded! I am very saddened over what has happened here. In your letter of 20 September 1954, you had given me explanations. I had sent a copy of this letter to my client so that he would understand the disappointing facts of life. However, it seems to me that you have not stuck to the promises that you made from this point onwards. I am very upset over this. I had considered our relationship to be one based on amicable trust and I think, therefore, that you will appreciate the urgency in doing the necessary so that this trust does not erode.

Sincerely yours,

Le Corbusier

NOTES

Introduction

1. Alice T. Friedman has discussed various examples of conflictual relations between architects and their clients. In the case of the Jaoul houses, even if the process of design and execution encountered some tense moments, the Jaouls expressed great satisfaction in having lived over thirty years in their Le Corbusier-designed houses. See Alice T. Friedman, "Being Modern Together: Le Corbusier's Villa Stein-de Monzie," in *Women and the Making of the Modern House: A Social and Architectural History* (New York: Harry N. Abrams, 1998), 92–125.

2. Works on the "*critique génétique* (genetic criticism)" of literary works taken up by Pierre-Marc de Biasi, Michel Contat, Daniel Ferrer, and Almuth Grésillon, among other researchers, has stimulated the adaption of this theoretical methodology to an analysis of the architectural profession. See "Architecture," Pierre-Marc de Biasi and Réjean Legault, eds., *Genesis* 14 (September 2000), a special issue dedicated specifically to this field of enquiry.

3. James Stirling, "Garches to Jaoul: Le Corbusier as Domestic Architect in 1927 and 1953," *The Architectural Review* 118 (September 1955): 145–51, reprinted in *The Le Corbusier Archive*, vol. 20 (Garland, NY), 9–12.

4. Letter from Le Corbusier to M. Errazuris, dated April 24, 1930, cited by Bruno Reichlin, "'Cette belle pierre de Provence.' La Villa de Mandrot," in *Le Corbusier et la Méditerranée* (Marseille: Parenthèses, 1987), 131. The Errazuris project was never executed. For an analysis of this house, see Christiane Collins, "Le Corbusier's Maison Errazuris," *The Harvard Architectural Review* 6 (1987): 38–53.

5. See Francesco Passanti, "The Vernacular, Modernism and Le Corbusier," *Journal of the Society of Architectural Historians* (December 1997): 438–51; Jean-Claude Vigato, "Régionalisme," in *Le Corbusier. Une encyclopédie*, ed. Jacques Lucan (Paris: Centre Georges Pompidou, 1987), 342–43; and Adolf Max Vogt, *Le Corbusier, the Noble Savage: Toward an Archaeology of Modernism* (Cambridge, Mass.: MIT Press, 1998).

6. Willy Boesiger, ed., *Le Corbusier et Pierre Jeanneret. Œuvre complète 1929–1934* (Zurich: Éditions Girsberger, 1964 [1935]), 48.

7. Interest in the regional aspects of modern architecture—and not only the international ones—was also apparent in the United States. Thus, after the International Style exhibition of 1932, the Museum of Modern Art organized a series of shows demonstrating the impact of regional traditions on American architecture, such as the wood-and-stone farmhouses in Pennsylvania or the white-painted wood clapboard houses. It was not so much the picturesque details that attracted attention, but rather the use of diverse materials and their subtle adaptation to local climate and topography. See Elizabeth Mock, *Built in USA, 1932–1944* (New York: Museum of Modern Art, 1944); also, for a summary of this dialogue, Nicholas Bullock, *Building the Post-War World: Modern Architecture and Reconstruction in Britain* (London, New York: Routledge, 2002), 31.

8. Regarding the evolution of discussions on 1950s and 1960s architecture, see Sarah Goldhagen and Réjean Legault, *Anxious Modernisms: Experimentation in Postwar Architectural Culture* (Cambridge, Mass.: MIT Press, 2000).

9. Letter from Jean-Jacques Duval, the director of a textile factory at Saint-Dié, to Le Corbusier, March 25, 1955.

10. For a close analysis of Le Corbusier's vocabulary and forms initiated in the 1930s, as distinct from his work in the 1920s, consult Kenneth Frampton, *L'Architecture moderne : une histoire critique*, especially chapter 15 "Le Corbusier et la monumentalisation du vernaculaire (1930–1960)," (Paris: Philippe Sers, 1985), 195–200.

11. By contrast, see the article by William Curtis, "Le moderne et l'archaïque, ou les dernières œuvres," in *Le Corbusier*, ed. Jacques Lucan, 246–49.

12. Tim Benton, "Six Houses. Maisons Jaoul, Neuilly-sur-Seine," *Le Corbusier: Architect of the Century*, (London: Arts Council of Great Britain, 1987), 67–68.

13. Six boxes, classified under J1 (12)–J1 (17), contain consecutively numbered written documents, along with a series of contact sheets by Lucien Hervé, illustrating various phases of construction. These items have since been reclassified according to a new system. In order to facilitate their identification, now only accessible through the FLC digital system, I have here identified each item by date(s), name of author, and name of recipient, following existing FLC reference codes.

The Promenade

1. "Polychromie architecturale—étude faite par un architecte (mêlé d'ailleurs à l'aventure de la peinture contemporaine) pour les architects (Architectural polychromy—study for architects by an architect [involved, by the way, in the adventure of contemporary painting])," manuscript, B1 (18) FLC, 1931. Text published in Arthur Rüegg, ed., *Polychromie architecturale. Les claviers de couleurs de Le Corbusier de 1931 et de 1959* [Architectural Polychromy. Le Corbusier's Keyboard of Colors from 1931 and 1959] (Basel, Boston, Berlin: Birkhäuser, 1997).

2. Interview by Le Corbusier with the rector Robert Mallet, 1951 (extract from *Entretiens. Le Corbusier* [Interviews. Le Corbusier], INA archives, cassette, Editions Didaklée/INA, 1987) in Gilles Ragot and Mathilde Dion, *Le Corbusier en France: projets et réalisations* [Le Corbusier in France: Projects and Built Works] (Paris: Le Moniteur, 1997), 175. Le Corbusier developed his thoughts on the role of polychromy in Paul Damaz, *Art in European Architecture/Synthèse des arts* [Synthesis of the Arts] (New York: Reinhold Publishing Corporation, 1956), vii–xii.

Chapter 1

1. André Jaoul died on November 12, 1954 in New York, when the houses were still under construction. "André Jaoul Dead; Paris Sales Aide, 60," Obituary, *New York Times*, November 13, 1954.

2. Interview with Michel Jaoul, April 11, 2001.

3. Le Corbusier, *Quand les cathédrales étaient blanches. Voyage au pays des timides* (Paris: Plon, 1937). Translated as *When the Cathedrals Were White. A Journey to the Country of Timid People* (New York: Reynald & Hitchcock, 1947).

4. Letter from André Jaoul to Le Corbusier, February 6, 1937, FLC B1(14)350.

5. For more details on the meetings between Le Corbusier and André Jaoul, see Mardges Bacon, *Le Corbusier in America. Travels in the Land of the Timid* (Cambridge, Mass.: MIT Press, 2001), 184–86, 211.

6. Willy Boesiger, ed. *Le Corbusier: Œuvre complète 1938–1946* (Zurich: Girsberger, 1946), 12.

7. Gilles Ragot and Mathilde Dion, *Le Corbusier en France: réalisations et projets* [Le Corbusier in France: built works and projects], 258–60 and 265–66. These houses were covered by a double-pitch roof sloped toward the center.

8. On Le Corbusier's wartime activities, consult Rémi Baudoui, "L'attitude de Le Corbusier pendant la guerre [Le Corbusier's standpoint during the war]," in *Le Corbusier*, ed. Jacques Lucan, 455–59. André Jaoul and Le Corbusier kept up a written correspondence during the year 1940 as witnessed by a series of letters in the Fondation Le Corbusier archive (FLC E2 (5) 106–14). For the chronology, see Luca Sampo, *La Maison Jaoul de Le Corbusier. La casa nomade e la città contemporanea* [Le Corbusier's Jaoul House (*sic*)]. Master's thesis (Rome: University La Sapienza, 2003).

9. Le Corbusier, *Les Trois Établissements humains* [Three Human Settlements] (Paris: Denoël, 1945). On December 26, 1945, he received a letter of payment to the sum of 5,000 French francs from the Société Ugine, covering his December honorarium fees. Another letter from March 1946 informed him of a stoppage to this salary.

10. Le Corbusier, *Le Modulor* (Boulogne: Editions de L'Architecture d'aujourd'hui, 1950), 60.

11. Letter from Michel Jaoul to the author, December 17, 2003.

12. Contract letters between Drouin and Le Corbusier dated July 26, 1944 and August 15, 1944. For the circumstances surrounding the breaking of the contract, see Le Corbusier's letter of discontent, Fondation Le Corbusier, dated April 8, 1946, followed by a second letter addressed to René Drouin on July 31, 1946. Le Corbusier would, ultimately, be largely represented by Galerie Louis Carré.

13. Galerie René Drouin mounted an exhibition of Fautrier's work entitled *Les Otages* [The Hostages] in October 1945, and an exhibition of Wols's drawings in December 1948.

14. Frances Morris, ed. *Paris Post War: Art and Existentialism, 1945–55* (London: Tate Gallery, 1993), 21.

15. Jean Dubuffet, "L'Auteur répond à quelques objections [The author responds to a few objections]" in *Mirobolus, Macadam et Cie: Hautes Pâtes de J. Dubuffet* [Fantastic, Macadam and Co.: Thick Paste Works of J. Dubuffet], in Michel Tapié, exhibition brochure, Galerie René Drouin, May 3–June 1, 1946.

16. Cf. Max Loreau, *Catalogue des travaux de Jean Dubuffet. Marionnettes de la ville et de la campagne* [Catalogue of works by Jean Dubuffet. Puppets of the city and country] (Paris: Jean-Jacques Pauvert, 1966), 18.

17. So emphasized by Lorenza Trucchi, "Dubuffet, Bacon, Giacometti: la vérité du portrait [Dubuffet, Bacon, Giacometti: candidness in portraiture]," in *Dubuffet*, ed. Daniel Abadie (Paris: Centre Pompidou, 2001), 20.

18. Paul Budry (1883–1949) was the founder of *Cahiers Vaudois* [Vaudois Notebooks]. He also maintained relations with Le Corbusier for the edition of *L'Esprit nouveau* [The New Spirit] from 1923 to 1924. Dubuffet stayed for an extended visit at Paul Budry's house in Lausanne during 1925. It is worth noting that Dubuffet was in contact with Max Jacob as well as Amédée Ozenfant.

19. Painted in February 1943, this work was entitled *Sauteuse de corde* [Girl Skipping Rope] by Dubuffet (in his letter to Le Corbusier, February 1, 1954), but called *Danseuse de corde* [Dancer Skipping Rope] by François Mathey (FLC C2 [5] 140, October 11, 1960).

20. Dubuffet, cited in *Dubuffet*, Daniel Abadie ed., 359.

21. Letter from Jean Dubuffet to Le Corbusier, FLC E1 (19) 263. The letter was not dated, but one can surmise that it was from 1946, as Dubuffet refers to his show at the Galerie René Drouin. Dubuffet continues his letter by mentioning the painting that he had received from Le Corbusier, "Since you showed such enormous generosity in offering me, in turn, a painting in exchange for mine, and I am embarrassed by this, because there is no rapport between the two, because my painting has no commercial value whatsoever."

22. Jean Paulhan thus describes the escapade of July 1945 in the *Guide d'un petit voyage en Suisse* [Guide to a short journey through Switzerland]: "Limérique runs in the local lunatic asylums. Auxionnaz gives lectures. As for me—as well as the studies that I mentioned—I make various visits." Jean Paulhan, *Guide d'un petit voyage en Suisse.* (Paris: Gallimard, 1947). Reprint.

23. See Hervé Gaucille and Valère Novarina, *Louis Soutter. Si le soleil me revenait* [Louis Soutter: If only the sun were to come back to me again] (Paris: Adam Biro, 1997).

24. Le Corbusier, "Louis Sutter [*sic*]. L'inconnu de la soixantaine [Louis Sutter (*sic*). Unknown at sixty]" *Le Minotaure* [The Minotaur] n° 9 (1936). The article was reprinted in *Louis Soutter* (Arles: Actes Sud, 1987).

25. Dubuffet cited by Mirella Bandini, "Michel Tapié de Paris à Turin [Michel Tapié, from Paris to Torino]," in *Tapié. Un art autre* [Tapié. A different art] (Turin: Edizioni d'Arte Fratelli Pozzo, 1997), 22.

26. Jean Dubuffet, *Prospectus aux amateurs de tout genre* [Leaflet for all types of amateurs] (Paris: Gallimard, 1946), 64.

27. Sarah Wilson, "From the Asylum to the Museum: Marginal Art in Paris and New York, 1938–68," in *Parallel Visions: Modern Artists and Outsider Art*, eds. Maurice Tuchman and Carol S. Eliel (Los Angeles/New York: Los Angeles County Museum of Art/Princeton University Press, 1992), 128–29.

28. It is quite possible that Dubuffet had not read Sartre's *L'Être et le Néant* [Being and Nothingness]. Nonetheless, during the summer of 1946, the artist had discussed with Paulhan his great interest in Existentialism. See Sarah Wilson, "From the Asylum to the Museum," in *Parallel Visions*, note 42, 146.

29. Sarah Goldhagen, "Freedom's Domiciles," in *Anxious Modernisms: Experimentation in Postwar Architectural Culture*, eds. Sarah Goldhagen and Réjean Legault (Montréal/Cambridge, Mass.: Canadian Centre for Architecture/MIT Press, 2000), 75–95. The importance of Existentialist thought on the intellectual and architectural milieu of the 1940s and 1950s is discussed by these authors, 79–83.

30. Le Corbusier's pictorial output has its own originality, but here the emphasis is placed on the Jaouls' interest in Dubuffet. On the subject of the role of objects for Charlotte Perriand, Fernand Léger, and Le Corbusier, consult Joan Ockman, "Lessons from Objects: Perriand from the Pioneer Years to the 'Epoch of Realities'" in *Charlotte Perriand: An Art of Living*, ed. Mary C. McLeod (New York: Harry Abrams, 2003), 154–81.

31. See Richard Ingersoll, ed., *Le Corbusier. A Marriage of Contours* (New York: Princeton Architectural Press, 1990), 7–16.

32. See Arnoldo Rivkin, "Synthèse des arts. Un double paradoxe [Synthesis of the arts. A double paradox]," in *Le Corbusier*, ed. Jacques Lucan, 386–91.

33. For sustained research on the development of the concept of the "synthesis of the arts" in the work of Le Corbusier, see Christopher Pearson, "Integrations of Art and Architecture in the Work of Le Corbusier: Theory and Practice from Ornamentalism to the 'Synthesis of the Major Arts,'" (PhD diss., Stanford University, 1995).

34. Regarding Jean Crotti (1878–1958) and Suzanne Duchamp (1889–1963), see

William A. Camfield and Jean-Hubert Martin, *Tabu Dada : Jean Crotti & Suzanne Duchamp, 1915-1922*. Bern : Die Kunsthalle, 1983).

35. Letter from Michel Jaoul to the author, December 17, 2003.

36. Tim Benton, *The Villas of Le Corbusier, 1920–1930* (New Haven and London: Yale University Press, 1987), 143.

37. Interview with Michel Jaoul, March 1, 2001.

38. Among others works, Notre-Dame du Haut, Ronchamp (1950–55), the master plan and Capitol, High Court (1951–55), Palace of Assembly (1951–62) and Secretariat (1951–58) in Chandigarh, as well as the Villa Sarabhai and Villa Shodhan (1951–56) in Ahmedabad. In 1953, Le Corbusier began research for the Monastery of Sainte-Marie de La Tourette (1953–59).

39. See also, *L'Architecture d'aujourd'hui* n° 33 (December 1950–January 1951), dedicated to urban planning in Latin America with an introductory article written by P. L. Wiener and J. L. Sert, followed by their proposals for four master plans for South American cities in Colombia and Peru. Their proposals for temporary housing units to lodge poor emigrants recall the simplicity of the longitudinal solution adopted for the Jaoul houses.

40. See Morgen Krustrup, "Poème de l'angle droit [Poem of the right angle]," *Arkitekten* n° 92 (1990): 422–32. For an analysis of the alchemy symbols discussed in this book and references to works by Kurt Seligmann and Carl Gustav Jung, see Simon Richards, *Le Corbusier and the Concept of Self* (New Haven/London: Yale University Press, 2003) , specifically "Wisdom Builds Its Own House," 137–70. For a more specific reading on the representation of women in Le Corbusier's works, refer to Flora Samuel, *Le Corbusier: Architect and Feminist* (Chichester: Wiley-Academy, 2004), 93–103.

41. Interview with Michel Jaoul, April 11, 2001.

42. Solicited in 1953 by the *Daily Mail Exhibition* to design a house, Entwistle made contact with Le Corbusier. Their proposal was presented as a collaborative work in the "Ideal Home" show (FLC I1 (18) 98 27).

43. Le Corbusier, *Concerning Town Planning* (New Haven: Yale University Press, 1948). Entwistle also translated the texts that accompanied Le Corbusier's sketches in the work produced with François de Pierrefeu, entitled *The Home of Man* (London: The Architectural Press, 1948), for which Entwistle also wrote the introduction. For a discussion of this book, see Simon Richards, *Le Corbusier and the Concept of Self*, 54–65.

44. Plans FLC 10076–10079 and plans 10043–10044. Entwistle had designed a gridded structure of metal columns with 9.8 feet between the axes. One of these plans (FLC 10044, dated June 28, 1951) in the Fondation Le Corbusier archives carries the double initials "C.E." and "M.J." (Clive Entwistle and Michel Jaoul).

45. Diary of Le Corbusier, June 1951, FLC. Le Corbusier also paid a visit to Sert on June 6 in his house on Long Island before returning to Paris on June 8, 1951.

46. According to Salvatore Bertocchi's recollections (in an interview with the author on April 26, 1986), the masonry contractor collaborated with Le Corbusier from 1950 to 1960.

47. On July 23, 1951, Jaoul decided to confer the task of executing the two dwellings to Le Corbusier, writing the following note to Entwistle, "Le Corbusier led me to understand that it would undoubtedly be possible to circumnavigate certain easement rules, which would permit our construction to increase in size" and added that he had been assured that "your relations with Le Corbusier would not seem to be compromised by these circumstances." (André Jaoul to Clive Entwistle, July 23, 1951, Jaoul archives). It nevertheless seems evident that the relationship between the two architects had indeed been affected based on the letter that Entwistle addressed to Le Corbusier on April 26, 1961, FLC E2 (1) 204. On his role in the building of the Swiss Pavilion at the Cité universitaire in Paris, consult Ivan Žaknić, *Le Corbusier, Pavillon Suisse: The Biography of a Building* (Basel: Birkhäuser, 2004).

48. Letter from Le Corbusier to Professor Fueter, March 17, 1950, FLC G3 (15) 291.

49. Interview with Domènec Escorsa, Barcelona, August 1986.

50. Stanislaus von Moos, *Le Corbusier. L'architecte et son mythe* [Le Corbusier. The architect and his myth] (Paris: Horizons de France, 1971), 125–26.

51. On the artist's house, see Willy Boesiger and Oscar Stonorov, eds., *Le Corbusier and Pierre Jeanneret. Œuvre complète 1910–1929*, op. cit., 53. During his trip to Barcelona, he also drew the vaults of the school at the Sagrada Familia designed by Antonio Gaudí. FLC Sketchbook C11, sheet 700.

52. Willy Boesiger, ed. *Le Corbusier. Œuvre complète 1946–1952*, 54.

53. In reference to the Peons' housing at Chandigarh. "By placing all the families side by side, they are completely separated and have absolute privacy. It is the same principle which was employed in the large apartment blocks... where on 17 stories, the apartments are contiguous and of the same lay-out," in Willy Boesiger, ed. *Le Corbusier*, vol. 5, 158. The type B Peon family dwellings contains 360.89 square feet (including the garden), composed of one 7.4-foot bay and one 9.67-foot bay.

54. The May 1951 special issue of *L'Architecture d'aujourd'hui* on Morocco featured a country house with Catalan vaults, designed by the architect E. Azagury; 25.

55. Willy Boesiger, ed. *Le Corbusier. Œuvre complète 1946–1952*, 173.

56. The Land Use Plan is located in the house building permit files in the Archives municipales de Neuilly. The bylaw concerns not only the implantation of built works, but also the proportional ratios to be respected between the constructed parts and the green space. In effect 80 percent of the unbuilt land surface area had to be planted and to contain at least one tall tree per 328 square feet of bare land; the imposed setback margins and those proposed in the plan had to be planted on at least 80 percent of the surface area. It seems that this obligation to plant rendered it difficult to find a location for the garage, according to evidence in numerous atelier drawings. The property limits were themselves regulated: a fence, made up of an arched side wall of a maximum height of 2.62 feet, surmounted by an open-work fence, was to be placed along the property line. It was stipulated that party walls were to be 4.26-foot-high fences hidden between two hedge rows.

57. Françoise de Franclieu, ed. *Le Corbusier Sketchbooks*, vol. 2, 1950–1954 (New York/Cambridge, Mass.: Architectural History Foundation/MIT Press, 1981). Sketchbook E22, sheets 549–553. The sketch on sheet 576 in the same sketchbook E22 shows a façade of Jaoul House B, dated late February–March 1952. Entwistle's plans from June 28, 1951, confirm that Le Corbusier's drawings were executed after this date.

58. Willy Boesiger, ed. *Le Corbusier. Œuvre complète 1946–1952*, 173.

59. See Tim Benton, *The Villas of Le Corbusier*, 131.

60. Le Corbusier. Sketchbook I D15, sheets 82–85, September 1950.

61. Le Corbusier. Sketchbook E21, sheets 512 and 513, July 1951.

62. The eighth International Congress of Modern Architecture (CIAM) was held at Hoddesdon from July 7–14, 1951, taking the "Core" as its theme, homonym for the social body and the heart, as well as socialization spaces. T. J. Tyrwhitt, J. L. Sert, E. N. Rogers, eds., *CIAM 8: The Heart of the City: Towards the Humanisation of Urban Life* (New York: Pellegrini and Cudahy, 1952). The larger discussion focused on uncontrolled urban spread and the means to counteract this phenomenon.

63. In *Josep Luis Sert: 1901–1983* (Milan: Electa, 2000), 234, Josep M. Rovira attributes this sketch to Sert. If this is the case, the handwriting, however, can be positively identified as that of Le Corbusier.

64. Letter from Le Corbusier to Escorsa,

July 26, 1951, FLC G2 (11) 756.

65. Ibid.

66. Ibid.

67. Joseph Abram, *L'Architecture moderne en France* [Modern architecture in France], vol. 2 (Paris: Picard, 1999), 68.

68. Willy Boesiger, ed. *Le Corbusier. Œuvre complète 1946–1952*, 173.

69. Born in Bogotá, Colombia in 1924, Germàn Samper obtained his architecture degree in 1947. Having decided to travel in Europe, he worked in Le Corbusier's atelier from 1948 to 1954, occupied mainly with the town-planning study for Bogotá and master plan for Chandigarh. See Germàn Samper Gnecco, *La Arquitectura y la ciudad. Apuntes de Viaje* (Bogotá: Fonda Editorial Escala, 1986).

70. Born in Poona, India in 1927, Balkrishna Doshi studied at Sir J. J. College of Architecture in Bombay, from 1947 onwards. During his study program, he left for London in 1951, then started working in the Rue de Sèvres atelier in Paris after having met Le Corbusier at Hoddesdon in July 1951. He remained in Paris for four years, working on the High Court, Governor's Palace, and Peons' housing in Chandigarh, and the Shodhan house and Mill-Owners' Association building in Ahmedabad. In 1955, Doshi returned to India to direct Le Corbusier's jobsites in Ahmedabad. See William Curtis, *Balkrishna Doshi. An Architecture for India* (New York: Rizzoli, 1988), 12.

71. Rogelio Salmona was born in France in 1933 to a French mother and Spanish father who emigrated to Colombia in 1933. He encountered Le Corbusier in Bogotá in 1947, serving as his translator. Concerned over political violence in Colombia during 1948, his father encouraged him to continue his architectural training in France, specifically with Le Corbusier. He was to remain in the atelier until 1957 where he collaborated on the town-planning study for Bogotá as well as "Marseille-Veyre," followed by the "Roq et Rob," Sarabhai, and Jaoul project developments. He later worked for Jean Prouvé, Bernard Zehrfuss, and J. de Mailly in Paris, before finally returning to Colombia in 1958. In his Casa de Huéspedes in Cartegean, he used the Catalan vault, this house restoration and extension dating from 1980 to 1986. See German Tellez, *Rogelio Salmona. Arquitectura y poetica del lugar* (Bogotá: Fonda Editorial Escala, 1991); also Ricardo L. Castro, *Rogelio Salmona* (Bogotá: Villegas Editores, 1998).

72. A preliminary version of this part of the text was published by the author under the title "Les maisons Jaoul de Le Corbusier [Le Corbusier's Maisons Jaoul]," in *Histoire de l'art* [History of art] n° 1–2, (1988): 75–86; a second version appeared under the title "'Regarder dehors pourquoi?' Les maisons Jaoul entre modernité et art de vivre ['Why look outside?' The Jaoul houses, between modernity and the art of living]," *Massilia, Annuaire d'études corbuséennes* [Yearbook of Corbusian Studies] (2003): 152–61.

73. Among others, the sections and plans FLC 10315–10321.

74. The sketches are not dated, but one might surmise that Samper had traveled to the Dordogne in early 1952. He commented on his trip as follows, "And in the Dordogne, peasant houses, with ramps to take produce up to the second floor, reminded me how in Ibiza vernacular architecture creates prototypes naturally which define for neighboring regions those in which the principle of variety within unity is applied." ["Y en Dordogne, las casas campesinas, con rampas para subir productos al 2° ; piso, me recordaron, como in Ibiza, que la arquitectura popular crea prototipos en forma natural que definen por regiones conjunctos en los que se aplica el principio de la variedad dentro de la unidad."] Germàn Samper Gnecco, *La Arquitectura y la ciudad. Apuntes de Viaje*, 40.

75. Jacques Lucan, "Nécessités de la clôture, ou la vision sédentaire de l'architecture [Necessities for an enclosure, or the non-nomad view of architecture]," *Matières* 3 (1999): 26.

76. Consult, among other drawings, FLC 9904 from March 14, 1952 and 10051 from March 12, 1952 corrected in August 1952.

77. Édith Girard, "La genèse du projet en situation de concours [The elaboration of a project during real competition conditions]" (interview with Pierre-Marc de Biasi), *Genesis* n° 14 (September 2000): 194.

78. See drawing FLC 10114, September 26, 1951.

79. Interview with Le Corbusier and the rector Robert Mallet, 1951, in Gilles Ragot and Mathilde Dion, *Le Corbusier en France* [Le Corbusier in France], 175.

80. Letter from Le Corbusier to André Jaoul, July 10, 1952, FLC G2 (13) 43.

81. Consult Judi Loach, "Les chantiers comme laboratoire—La démarche de Le Corbusier après la guerre [Building sites as laboratory—Le Corbusier's postwar approach]," FLC E2 (3) 52.

82. Cf. chapter 4, "*Fortuna Critica of the Maisons Jaoul.*"

83. Agenda of Le Corbusier, 1951, FLC F3 (9) 8.

84. Letter from Le Corbusier to Muncha Sert, October 24, 1951. FLC R3 (3) 310.

85. Letter from Le Corbusier to Muncha Sert, October 25, 1951. FLC R3 (3) 311.

86. Letter from J. L. Sert to Le Corbusier, November 16, 1951, FLC R3 (3) 313.

87. The ground-floor plan of Sert's house was reproduced in Josep Maria Rovira, *Josep Luis Sert*, 302.

88. Charlotte Perriand, *Un art de vivre* (Paris: Musée des Arts décoratifs, 1985), 45.

89. For the fitting-out of kitchens in Marseilles, see Ruggero Tropeano, "Intérieur (Aménagement). Unité d'habitation de Marseille [Interior (arrangement). The Marseilles Block], 1946–1952," in *Le Corbusier*, ed. Jacques Lucan, 200–206. For a history of the evolution of kitchens in the twentieth century, consult Catherine Clarisse, *Cuisine, recettes d'architecture* [Kitchen, recipes for architecture] (Paris: Éditions de l'Imprimeur, 2004).

90. Photothèque FLC L1 (13) 208.

91. In an interview with the author on April 11, 2001, Michel Jaoul added the following detail, "The proposal did not meet with the approval of the city planning department. It took the intervention of the Corsican carpenter, Charles Barberis, with the mayor of Neuilly, Achille Peretti, himself a Corsican, too, to ensure that the building permit was ultimately delivered."

92. The estimate of costs significantly exceeded this sum. The estimate dated June 10, 1952, quoted 36,495,000 French francs.

93. Letter from A. Wogenscky to Charles Barberis, December 16, 1952, FLC E3 (2) 390.

94. Cf. Benton, *The Villas of Le Corbusier.*

95. Letter from Le Corbusier to E. Claudius-Petit, July 26, 1952, FLC E1 (16) 222.

96. In reference to Claudius-Petit as reported by André Wogenscky to André Jaoul, July 26, 1952.*

97. Letter from Fernand Gardien to André Jaoul, June 24, 1953. FLC J1 (16) 82.

98. Honorarium fee n° 5 from July 12, 1955.

99. "I was totally dumbfounded when you told me that you were counting on finding your building underway upon your return. There was never any question of that being the case. Now you tell me that you are determined to construct no matter what the final decision over the subsidy and the loan. I take note of all this with pleasure, but allow me to remind you that this is the first time that you have openly declared your intentions to me." Letter from André Wogenscky to André Jaoul, dated June 6, 1952, FLC E3 (1) 288.

100. Letter from Le Corbusier to André Jaoul, January 22, 1952, FLC G2 (12) 87.

101. The official plan of the commune stipulated that the distance between the built work and the rear property line had to be equal to the height of the building divided by two. If this margin could not be respected, an agreement over the common court could be established between the neighboring proprietors. Archives municipales de Neuilly-sur-Seine.

102. Letter from Le Corbusier to André Jaoul, July 10, 1952, FLC G2 (13) 43.

103. The final plans are dated October 23, 1952; construction began in June 1953.

104. Interview with Salvatore Bertocchi, April 23, 1986.

Chapter 2

1. A first version of this chapter was published under the title "Artisanat et petites entreprises dans l'activité parisienne de Le Corbusier à Paris [Artisan trades and small enterprises involved in the Parisian activity of Le Corbusier in Paris]," in *Le Corbusier et Paris* [Le Corbusier and Paris] (Paris: Fondation Le Corbusier, 2001), 83–94.

2. "You will ask Wogenscky, Gardien, Le Marchand and Andréini who are the ones responsible at the atelier for estimates and contacts with the contractors." Letter from Le Corbusier to André Jaoul, July 10, 1952, FLC G2 (13) 45.

3. After a written text by Judi Loach, based on an interview with Fernand Gardien "Les chantiers comme laboratoire—La démarche de Le Corbusier après la guerre [Building sites as laboratory—Le Corbusier's postwar approach]," FLC E2 (3) 52 . See also Judi Loach, "L'atelier de Le Corbusier: un centre européen d'échanges [Le Corbusier's studio: a European center of exchanges]," *Monuments historiques* n° 180 (March–April 1992): 49–52.

4. After his experience at Le Corbusier's studio when still a non-registered architect, Jacques Michel (born in 1925) left for the United States in 1957 to enroll in the Masters of Architecture degree program at Harvard University. Le Corbusier wrote to his friend Sert, then the director of the Graduate School of Design, "I think that he's got the right idea as this [program] will allow him to obtain a degree from Harvard, which is valid in France. Here he would never manage to get a French degree requiring many years of study. The real reason for his trip there is to bring back a degree, to familiarize himself a little bit with the Americans and to learn English, which is very useful. He couldn't do better than your school." Letter from Le Corbusier to Sert, March 13, 1956, FLC G2 (20) 272.

5. Only the Bertocchi company, fluctuating between four to nine workmen, could qualify as a "small enterprise." The others employed more than ten workmen and were thus classified as middle-size or artisan-industrial companies.

6. Jean Petit, ed. *Le Corbusier, Architecture du bonheur. L'urbanisme est une clef* [Le Corbusier, Architecture of happiness. Urbanism is the key] (Paris: Cahiers Forces vives, Les Presses d'Île-de-France, 1955).

7. Benton, *The Villas of Le Corbusier*, 13.

8. Le Corbusier's esteem for these contractors and collaborators is confirmed by a project he wanted to create in 1956, called the "Atelier d'architecture de Paris [Architecture Studio of Paris]," for which he had drawn up a list of potential instructors, "Wog (Wogenscky), Charlotte (Perriand), Prouvé, Aujame, Martin, house painter, Alazard, glazier, Missenard, a man of science (or someone more modest), Cujex, acoustics expert, X [undecided], reinforced concrete." F. de Franclieu, ed. *Le Corbusier. Sketchbooks*, vol. 3, 1954–1957, Sketchbook K43, sheet 674.

9. Pascal Aumasson, "Le Corbusier-Savina, des intuitions spatiales à la forme sculptée [Le Corbusier-Savina, from spatial intuitions to sculptural form]," in *Le Corbusier et la Bretagne* [Le Corbusier and Brittany] (Brest/Quimper: Éditions Nouvelles du Finistère, 1996), 57–73.

10. Costantino Nivola (1911–1988) describes his encounter with Le Corbusier in "Le Corbusier in New York," in *Le Corbusier. A Marriage of Contours*, ed. Richard Ingersoll, 3–6.

11. Le Corbusier wrote to Nivola on July 3, 1951 asking for some photographs of his sculptures (FLC G2 (11) 684). According to Christopher Pearson, Le Corbusier had executed two relief sculptures of this type, which played a major role in the architect's work of the 1950s; see *Integrations of Art and Architecture*, op. cit., 380–384.

12. Willy Boesiger, ed. *Le Corbusier: Œuvre complète*, vol. 5, 1946–52, 227.

13. See Giuseppe Nieddu, "Les Sardes en Île-de-France. Histoire de vie [Sardinians in the Île-de-France region. A biographical history]" (Master's Thesis, La Sorbonne, Paris IV, 1986).

14. Willy Boesiger, ed. *Le Corbusier: Œuvre complète*, vol. 5, 1946–1952, 191.

15. Interview with Salvatore Bertocchi, April 26, 1986.

16. "He [the architect] has learned how to draw, and he could do this as he could not learn anything else. This, the craftsman cannot do. His hand has become leaden." Adolf Loos, "Architecture" (1910), in *The Architecture of Adolf Loos*, eds. Yehuda Safran and Wilfried Wang. (London: Arts Council of Great Britain, 1985, 105).

17. Le Corbusier, Sketchbook I D15. Sheets 83 to 85 have already been discussed in chapter 1.

18. Willy Boesiger, ed. *Le Corbusier: Œuvre complète*, vol. 5, 1946–1952, 191.

19. Zurich professor Rudolph Fueter was president of the committee of Swiss dignitaries and university members responsible for overseeing works taken on by the Confédération pour le Pavillon Suisse at the Cité Universitaire, Paris. It was he who commissioned Le Corbusier in 1948 to execute the mural painting, replacing the wall of photographs that had been dismounted in the early 1940s. See Le Corbusier, *Creation is a Patient Search* (New York: Frederick Praeger, 1960).

20. Letter from Le Corbusier to G. P. Dubois, the young architect in charge of overseeing the construction of Professor Fueter's house, November 14, 1949, FLC I2 (7) 138.

21. Jean Dubuffet, *Prospectus aux amateurs de tout genre* [Leaflet for all types of amateurs] (Paris: Gallimard, 1946), 64.

22. Letter from Le Corbusier to Salvatore Bertocchi, May 7, 1953, FLC J1 (16) 71.

23. Interview by Le Corbusier with Robert Mallet, 1951, in Gilles Ragot and Mathilde Dion, *Le Corbusier en France*, 174.

24. Interview with Salvatore Bertocchi, April 26, 1986.

25. Nonetheless, he had promoted his Pavillon de l'Esprit nouveau as a potential building prototype for the suburbs.

26. Blaise Cendrars, *La Banlieue de Paris* [The Suburbs of Paris] (Paris: Editions Seghers, 1949). Reprint Paris: Editions Seghers, 1966), 36–37, cited by Tim Benton, "La maison de week-end dans le paysage parisien [The weekend house in the Paris landscape]," *Le Corbusier et Paris* [Le Corbusier and Paris] (Paris: Fondation Le Corbusier, 2001), 101.

27. Jean Dubuffet, *Prospectus aux amateurs de tout genre*, 63.

28. Ibid.

29. Le Corbusier, *Les Constructions "Murondins"* [The "Murondins" buildings] (Paris/Clermont-Ferrand: Étienne Chiron, 1942). This 36-page booklet, published under the auspices of the Secretary-General of Youth under the Vichy government, was presented in the form of a technical manual aimed at assisting young people to construct their own building premises.

30. Le Corbusier, "Éléments modernes d'une communauté villageoise [Modern elements for a village community]," *Agriculture et communauté* [Agriculture and Community] (Paris: Librairie de Médicis, 1943), 102–103. The passage was underlined by Le Corbusier.

31. Mary C. McLeod, Urbanism and Utopia: Le Corbusier from Regional Syndicalism to Vichy (PhD diss., Princeton University, 1985), 420–22.

32. Le Corbusier, copyright invention, 1951. FLC T2 (7) 12.

33. Consult Tim Benton, "Pessac and Lège revisited: standards, dimensions and failures," *Massilia, Annuaire d'études corbuséennes* [Yearbook of Corbusean Studies] (2004), 64–99.

34. Cited by Danièle Pauly in *Ronchamp, lecture d'une architecture* [Ronchamp, an architectural reading] (Strasbourg/Paris: Ophrys, 1980), 58.

35. Regarding his research under the heading "Maisons rurales ou logis paysan [Rural houses or peasant lodgings]" (1955–1956), Le Corbusier mentions two specialists: Prouvé, who designed houses entirely in metal, and Barberis, who built only in wood. In this way, he sought to implement "hybrid metal-wood" projects like the Dry-Mounted Houses (1955–57), taking up a type already developed during the 1930s. The interior of his Cabanon at Cap-Martin (1951–52) was executed with wood panels and furnished with prefabricated pieces made by an artisan in Ajaccio, later assembled in place. To extend his Cabanon experiment, Le Corbusier asked Barberis to study the possibilities of fabricating a series of independent structures called "espace libre [free space]," and a 12-foot cellular unit with sliding Modulor windows (27.5 x 27.5 in) installed like "automobile windows in a metal building." Note written by Le Corbusier, n.d., FLC M2 (9).

36. Extract from a letter of recommendation dated March 14, 1964: "The Barberis Company has executed *pans de verre*, special types of exterior casement windows, door units, façade panels for 321 apartment units in Marseille, 290 apartment units in Nantes, 339 apartment units in Briey, 100 rooms at the Maison du Brésil. It has also collaborated on 855 apartment units in Bobigny with Aillaud and Vedres (arch.), 790 apartment units in Pantin with Aillaud and 100 apartment units at Asnières with Vedres." FLC. Barberis file.

37. Adolf Loos, "Architecture" (1910), in *The Architecture of Adolf Loos*, eds. Yehuda Safran and Wilfried Wang.

38. Jules Alazard and Jean-Pierre Hébert, *De la fenêtre au pan de verre dans l'œuvre de Le Corbusier* [From the window to the *pan de verre* in the work of Le Corbusier] (Paris: Dunod, 1961).

39. Françoise de Franclieu, ed. *Le Corbusier Sketchbooks*, vol. 3, 1954–1957, sheet 674.

40. Statement by Le Corbusier, May 22, 1964, FLC U3 (9) 303.

41. Le Corbusier, *Modulor 2*, (Boulogne: Éditions de L'Architecture d'aujourd'hui, 1955), 192–94.

42. Painting estimate furnished by Établissement Jean Martin, April 15, 1953, FLC J1 (14) 487.

43. Letter from Le Corbusier to Levaillant, June 7, 1956, cited by Arthur Rüegg, "Marcel Levaillant and 'La question du mobilier [The question of furniture],'" in *Le Corbusier before Le Corbusier*, eds. Stanislaus von Moos and Arthur Rüegg (New Haven: Yale University Press, 2002), 130. Despite Le Corbusier's confidence in Matroil paints, in 1957 the Jaouls complained to his atelier and the painter about the poor performance of these paints, the difficulties with the colors, and their upkeep.

44. André Missenard's publications, including *L'Homme et le climat* [Man and Climate] (Paris: Plon, 1937); *À la recherche du temps et du rythme* [In Search of Time and Rhythm] (Paris: Plon, 1940), are found in the collection of the Conservatoire national des arts et métiers.

45. André Missenard, "Préface. Civilisation et climat [Preface. Civilization and Climate]," *Techniques et Architecture* [Techniques and Architecture] n° 7–8 (1950),: 35–37. From Missenard's research emerged a wide range of arguments on the potential effects of the physical environment on the improvement of social conditions.

46. Letter from Michel Jaoul to Le Corbusier, December 1, 1953, FLC J1 (16) 472.

47. Note addressed to Wogenscky dictated by Le Corbusier, June 17, 1954, FLC.

48. Letter from Jacques Michel to Entreprise Allard, October 12, 1953, FLC J1 (15) 49.

49. Letter from Jacques Michel to Entreprise Allard, October 29, 1953, FLC J1 (15) 52.

50. Interview with Salvatore Bertocchi, April 26, 1986.

51. Letter from the expert appraiser Jean Faury to the Le Corbusier atelier, dated April 22, 1961, FLC J1 (13) 44.

52. Report by Jean Faury addressed to the Société Mutuelle des Architectes, dated December 11, 1961, FLC J1 (13) 117.

53. Letter from Entreprise Allard to Fernand Gardien, November 7, 1961, FLC J1 (13) 113.

54. Letter from Domènec Escorsa to Pierre Jeanneret, February 23, 1953, cited by Fernando Marza and Esteve Roca, "La boveda catalana en la obra de Le Corbusier [The Catalan vault in the work of Le Corbusier]," *Le Corbusier i Barcelona* [Le Corbusier and Barcelona] (Barcelona: Fundacio Caixa de Catalunya, 1988), 112.

55. Sketch of a Catalan vault and its principles of construction, July 1951. Françoise de Franclieu, ed., *Le Corbusier Sketchbooks*, vol. 2, 1950–1954, Sketchbook E21, sheets 512 and 513.

56. Interview with Salvatore Bertocchi, April 26, 1986.

57. During an interview with the author on March 1, 2001, Michel Jaoul recalled that, "because of the three-month standstill in construction, the vaults executed in House B were exposed to rain. The cement cast and the plastering on the bricks remained as they were. A Swiss company later came to see what could be done to clean the brick slip, but the job was too expensive."

58. Domènec Escorsa, Catalan engineer-architect exiled in France, was associated with Pierre Jeanneret from 1949 onwards. They collaborated on the study proposal for the technical *lycée* at Béziers from 1950 to 1955.

59. Letter from Jacques Michel to Domènec Escorsa, September 17, 1953, FLC J1 (16).

60. Letter from Domènec Escorsa to Jacques Michel, September 28, 1953, FLC J1 (16) 1.

61. Letter from Charles Barberis to Le Corbusier, September 20, 1954, FLC J1 (16) 499.

62. Letter from Le Corbusier to Charles Barberis, October 1, 1954, FLC J1 (14) 374.

63. Letter from Le Corbusier to Michel Jaoul, October 1, 1954, FLC J1 (17) 28.

64. Letter from Michel Jaoul to Charles Barberis, October 19, 1954, FLC J1 (16) 478.

65. Letter from Michel Jaoul to Le Corbusier, November 30, 1954, FLC J1 (17) 31.

66. Letter from Fernand Gardien to Michel Jaoul, December 2, 1954, FLC J1 (17) 34.

67. Financial statement of work carried out up to November 15 sent by André Wogenscky to Michel Jaoul, December 31, 1954, FLC J1 (17) 34.

68. A letter from Michel Jaoul to Fernand Gardien, dated April 16, 1955, confirms that he "wanted work to be followed up as rapidly as possible by the various companies involved and that, with this goal in mind, all operations or necessary orders be issued, within the terms of estimates already established." FLC J1 (17) 59.

69. Letter from Michel Jaoul to Le Corbusier, September 30, 1955, FLC J1 (16) 487.

70. Letter from Le Corbusier to Michel Jaoul, March 13, 1956, FLC J1 (16) 425.

71. Letter from Jacques Michel to Entreprise Allard, February 25, 1954, FLC J1 (15) 63.

72. Note from Jacques Michel to Le Corbusier, November 19, 1953, FLC J1 (16) 115.

73. Cook file, December 11, 1926, cited by Tim Benton, *The Villas of Le Corbusier*, 159.

74. Ibid, 158.

75. Letter from Le Corbusier to Salvatore Bertocchi, February 25, 1953, FLC J1 (16) 65.

Chapter 3

1. Letter from Le Corbusier to members of CIAM, Chandigarh, June 1953, Records of the CIAM Belgian section, Acc. no. 850865. CIAM Box 8, folder 7, Getty Research Center, Special Collections and Visual Resources, Los Angeles.

2. The CIAM conference, held at Aix-en-Provence in July 1953, was devoted to the Chart of Habitat. Five hundred members from twenty-one countries took part. This was the last conference in which Le Corbusier and Gropius participated. See Eric Mumford, *The CIAM Discourse on*

Urbanism, 1928–1960 (Cambridge, Mass.: MIT Press, 2000), 225–38. See also "CIAM 9, Aix-en-Provence, juillet 1953," *L'Architecture d'aujourd'hui* 9 (October 1953).

3. Witold Rybczynski, *Home: A Short History of an Idea* (New York: Penguin, 1986), 188.

4. Le Corbusier, *L'Almanach d'architecture moderne* (Paris: Crès, 1926; Paris: Connivence, 1975), 5.

5. Christopher Reed, ed., *Not at Home: The Suppression of Domesticity in Modern Art and Architecture* (New York: Thames and Hudson,1996), 9.

6. Beatriz Colomina, *Privacy and Publicity: Modern Architecture as Mass Media* (Cambridge, Mass.: MIT Press, 1994).

7. Alice T. Friedman, "People Who Live in Glass Houses: Edith Farnsworth, Ludwig Mies van der Rohe, and Philip Johnson," in *Women and the Making of the Modern House: A Social and Architectural History* (New York: Harry N . Abrams, 1998), 127–59.

8. Jean Petit, ed., *Le Corbusier: L'architecture du bonheur: L'urbanisme est une clef* (Paris: Les Presses d'Ile de France, 1955), back cover.

9. Willy Boesiger, ed., *Le Corbusier: Œuvre complète 1952–1957*, vol. 6 (Zurich: Girsberger, 1957), 208.

10. Le Corbusier, "L'Aventure du mobilier," in *Précisions sur un état présent de l'architecture et de l'urbanisme* (Paris: Crès, 1930; repr. Paris, 1960), 111.

11. Ibid., 115.

12. "Le problème du mobilier n'a pas été abordé." Boesiger, ed., *Le Corbusier: Œuvre complète 1952–57* (Zurich: Girsberger, 1957) 6: 208.

13. Michel Jaoul to Le Corbusier, April 20, 1953, (FLC), J1 (16) 468.

14. Letter from Michel Jaoul to Le Corbusier, December 1, 1953, FLC J1 (16) 472.

15. Michel Jaoul, conversation with the author, December 26, 2003.

16. E-mail from Michel Jaoul to the author, December 17, 2003.

17. Françoise Choay, *Le Corbusier* (New York: George Braziller, 1960), 29, n. 31.

18. Letter from Le Corbusier to Françoise Choay, September 21, 1961, Michel and Nadine Jaouls' private papers, Neuilly-sur-Seine.

19. Choay, *Le Corbusier*, 29.

20. "Les pionniers du rangement, Charlotte Perriand," *Maison Française* (February 1952), press clipping, FLC X1 (18) 175.

21. Charlotte Perriand, "L'art d'habiter," *Techniques & Architecture* 9-10 (September–October 1950): 33.

22. Letter from Michel Jaoul to Jacques Michel, March 2, 1955, FLC J1 (17) 52. In June 2001, Michel Jaoul recounted that he continued to apply himself to the task of storage and that he designed furniture for his house following the lead of Le Corbusier's office. He also worked on the lighting arrangements in the living room of House B, purchasing wall fittings from the Steph Simon Gallery. Le Corbusier had specified so little artificial illumination that the clients were forced to remedy the situation themselves.

23. Michel Jaoul drew up a list of fitted furniture for Houses A and B. Letter from Michel Jaoul to Jacques Michel, March 2, 1955, FLC J1 (17) 52. This document was followed by a list of this furniture to be used in Houses A and B (FLC J1 (16) 122–125). A number of letters followed, tracking the progressive reduction of this commission and the frustration caused by the workmen's delays.

24. Letter from Michel Jaoul to the Atelier Le Corbusier, April 7, 1955. FLC J1 (14) 420–22.

25. "Récapitulatif commande menuiserie Jaoul maison B," April 1955. This document was sent by the Atelier Le Corbusier to Charles Barberis, FLC J1 (16) 123–24.

26. Ibid.

27. Nadine Jaoul, conversation with the author, June 8, 2004.

28. "Poliban," *L'Architecture d'aujourd'hui* 34 (March 1951): n.p.

29. *L'Architecture d'aujourd'hui* 34 (March 1951): n.p.

30. Concerning the furniture, see Roger Aujame, "A Synthesis of the Arts: The Collaborations of Charlotte Perriand and Jean Prouvé," in *Charlotte Perriand, An Art of Living*, ed. Mary McLeod (New York: H.N. Abrams, 2003), 145.

31. See Reed, ed., *Not at Home*, 10.

32. In a plan letter to the contractor, Mr. Espinasse, Jacques Michel asked for the same tiles. Postscript from Jacques Michel sent to Mr. Espinasse, November 16, 1953, FLC J1 (16) 113.

33. Le Corbusier interviewed by Robert Mallet (1951), in Gilles Ragot and Mathilde Dion, *Le Corbusier en France: projets et réalisations* (Paris: Moniteur, 1997), 177.

34 Note from Le Corbusier to Jacques Michel, April 8, 1954, FLC J1 (16) 169.

35. Letter from Michel Jaoul to Le Corbusier, December 1, 1953, FLC J1 (16) 472.

36. Ibid.

37. Letter from Jacques Michel to Jean Martin, May 27, 1955, FLC J1 (15) 526.

38. Gillian Naylor, "Modernism and Memory: Leaving Traces," in *Material Memories*, ed. Marius Kwint, Christopher Breward, and Jeremy Aynsley (Oxford and New York: Berg, 1999), 91–106. For a discussion of crafts and the personalization and humanization of Modernist interiors in the Eames House (1945–1949), see Pat Kirkham, *Charles and Ray Eames: Designers of the Twentieth Century* (Cambridge, Mass.: MIT Press, 1995).

39. Concerning the fireplace in House B, see the dictated note from Le Corbusier to Rogelio Salmona, February 9, 1953: "See if we can devise for Jaoul junior a lowered fireplace like that at Erazeuris (sic)." FLC J1 (14) 554.

40. Following a list established by Michel Jaoul and sent to the author, December 17, 2003.

41. The collection included some Picasso engravings, an oil painting by Hans Reichel, and another by Wols; a canvas by Henri Rousseau ("le Douanier"); a painting by Gaston Chaissac and one by Alexander Calder; and a painting on wood by André Bauchant. The last, which had belonged to Le Corbusier, was given to Madame Jaoul, probably as a token of gratitude for the financial support that André Jaoul had provided the architect during the war. Le Corbusier had helped to establish a circle of loyal art lovers around Bauchant, consisting of avant-garde artists and well-informed collectors.

42. Naylor, "Modernism and Memory," 94.

43. Le Corbusier, interviewed by Robert Mallet (1951), in Ragot and Dion, *Le Corbusier en France*, 176.

44. Ibid.

45. Letter from Michel Jaoul to Le Corbusier, October 5, 1955, FLC J1 (16) 489.

46. François Barré, "Les maisons de l'enfance: La maison Jaoul," (conversation with Marie Jaoul), *L'Architecture d'aujourd'hui*, no. 204 (March 1979): 85–88.

47. Ibid.

48. Rolf Lemoine, "Les permis de construire assortis de dérogation abusive se multiplient," *Le Figaro*, July 13, 1970.

49. Achille Peretti, "Aucune dérogation aux règles du permis de construction n'a jamais été accordée à Neuilly," *Le Figaro*, July 17, 1970.

Chapter 4

1. Roland Barthes, *Criticism and Truth*, translated and edited by Katrine Pilcher Keuneman (London and New York: Continuum, 2007), 25, originally published as *Critique et Vérité* (Paris: Seuil, 1966), 50.

2. Reyner Banham, *The New Brutalism. Ethic or Aesthetic?* (London: Architectural Press, 1966).

3. Paul Chemetov, Jean Deroche, Pierre Riboulet, Jean Renaudie, Gérard Thurnauer, Jean-Louis Véret, and Roland Simounet.

4. Christian Devillers, "Les derniers puritains [The Last Puritans]," *AMC* n° 11 (April 1986): 118.

5. This remark takes up categories suggested by H. R. Jauss: "In the communicational activity of society, the

specific role that falls to the aesthetic experience may thus turn on three distinct functions: preformation of attitudes or transmission of the norm; motivation or creation of the norm; transformation or rupture of the norm," in Hans Robert Jauss, *Pour une esthétique de la réception* (Paris, Gallimard, 1978), 261.

6. Paradoxically, in relation to these questionings, it must be pointed out that in England, most postwar architects designed load-bearing wall constructions rather than post-and-beam structures.

7. Nikolaus Pevsner, "The Return of Historicism," in *Studies in Art, Architecture and Design*, 2 (London: Thames & Hudson, 1968), 242–359.

8. James Stirling, "Garches to Jaoul. Le Corbusier as Domestic Architect in 1927 and 1953," *The Architectural Review* N°118 (September 1955): 145–51.

9. James Stirling, "Ronchamp: Le Corbusier's Chapel and the Crisis of Rationalism," *The Architectural Review* (March 1956): 155–61.

10. James Stirling, "Garches to Jaoul," 146.

11. Ibid, 149.

12. Ibid, 149.

13. Ibid, 146, 148.

14. Ibid, 149.

15. Kenneth Frampton, "The Other Le Corbusier: Primitive Form and the Linear City 1929–52," in *Le Corbusier Architect of the Century*, ed. Tim Benton (London: Arts Council of Great Britain, 1987), 31. It is important to note that Frampton's criticism arrived within a more complex intellectual environment, enriched by Colin Rowe's pointed criticisms, among others.

16. James Stirling, "Garches to Jaoul," 146.

17. Reyner Banham, *The New Brutalism, Ethic or Aesthetic?*, 86.

18. James Stirling, "Garches to Jaoul," 146.

19. Reyner Banham, *The New Brutalism, Ethic* or *Aesthetic?*, 86.

20. Michel Thévoz, "Plaidoyer pour la haine de l'art: l'invention de 'l'art des fous' [Plea for hatred in art: the invention of 'art of the insane']," in *Où en est l'interprétation de l'œuvre d'art* [Where is interpretation in the work of art?], ed. Régis Michel (Paris: Ensba, 2000), 111.

21. Ibid.

22. James Stirling quoted in *Architecture Culture: 1943–1968. A Documentary Anthology*, eds. Joan Ockman and Edward Eigen (New York: Columbia University, Graduate School of Architecture, Planning and Preservation/Rizzoli, 1993), 242.

23. Quoted by Adrian Forty, "Le Corbusier's British Reputation," in *Le Corbusier Architect of the Century*, ed. Tim Benton (London: Arts Council of Great Britain, 1987), 38.

24. Robert Maxwell, *James Stirling* (London: Architectural Design Profile, 1982).

25. James Stirling, "Regionalism and Modern Architecture," *Architects' Year Book 8*, 1957, 62–68. The article is reprinted in Joan Ockman and Edward Eigen, eds. *Architecture Culture: 1943–1968*, 243–48, without the photographs of the Liverpool warehouses.

26. Reyner Banham, *The New Brutalism*, 1970.

27. Ibid, 85.

28. The international group of CIAM architects, responsible for the program of the 10th congress in Dubrovnik in 1956: Jacob Bakema, Georges Candilis, Rolf Gutmann, William Howell, Alison and Peter Smithson, Aldo van Eyck, John Voelker and Shadrach Woods. Cf. Eric Mumford, *The CIAM Discourse in Urbanism.*

29. Jean Dubuffet, *Place à l'incivisme*, 1967, quoted by Michel Thévoz, in "Plaidoyer pour la haine de l'art: l'invention de 'l'art des fous' [Plea for hatred in art: the invention of 'art of the insane'], *Où en est l'interprétation de l'œuvre d'art* [Where is interpretation in the work of art?], ed. Régis Michel (Paris: Ensba, 2000), 112.

30. Reyner Banham, *The New Brutalism*, 85.

31. See Jacques Lucan, *France Architecture 1965–1988* (Milan/Paris: Electa/Moniteur, 1989), 10–17.

32. Reyner Banham, *The New Brutalism*, 89, 126–127.

33. Letter from Le Corbusier to Madame André Jaoul, March 15, 1962, FLC J1 (16) 465. This extension proposal was developed by Jacques Michel and Jean Prouvé after Le Corbusier's death. See "Extension des maisons Jaoul à Neuilly," *L'Architecture d'aujourd'hui* (June–July 1970): 13; "Avant-projet d'extension des maisons Jaoul de Le Corbusier," *Techniques & architecture* (October 1970): 72–73.

34. John Winter, "Le Corbusier's Technological Dilemma," in *The Open Hand: Essays on Le Corbusier*, ed. Russell Walden (Cambridge, Mass.: MIT Press, 1977), 323–45.

35. Sketch FLC 10051 is erroneously dated March 12, 1952, to August 15, 1952, in the Garland edition. The plan clearly indicates "du 12 et du 15 mars 1962 [from 12 to 15 March 1962]." Josefina Gonzalez Cubero incorrectly interprets this drawing as a study sketch for the placement of a pedestrian ramp along the northwest property line. See Josefina Gonzalez Cubero, "La arquitectura del suelo: las casas Jaoul en Neuilly-sur-Seine," *Massilia, Annuaire de recherches corbuséennes* (2003): 170.

36. Letter from Michel Jaoul to Jules Alazard, March 11, 1965, FLC J1 (13) 228–29.

37. In the late 1960s, Lord Palumbo had proposed that Mies van der Rohe design a skyscraper in London. After protests from neighboring residents, the tower was not built. Purchased by Palumbo in 1968, in December 2003 the Farnsworth house was put up for auction in New York by the National Trust for Historic Preservation. It fetched $7.5 million. Cf. Carol Vogel, "Landmark Mies House Goes to Preservationists," *The New York Times*, 13 December 2003, A17.

38. Marie-Jeanne Dumont, "La restauration des maisons Jaoul [The restoration of the Maisons Jaoul]," *L'Architecture d'aujourd'hui* n° 275 (June 1991): 141–44.

Conclusion

1. Le Corbusier, *L'Almanach d'architecture moderne* [Almanac of modern architecture] (Paris: Crès et Cie, 1926), 5.

2. Manfredo Tafuri, "Machine et mémoire: la ville dans l'œuvre de Le Corbusier [Machine and memory: the city in the work of Le Corbusier]," in *Le Corbusier. Une encyclopédie*, ed. Jacques Lucan, 464.

3. Letter from Jean-Jacques Duval to Le Corbusier, originally mailed to the Jaoul family on April 25, 1955, FLC J1 (16) 329–31.

BIBLIOGRAPHY

The main primary sources are correspondence, iconography, and oral history, obtained directly from Michel and Nadine Jaoul, and consulted at the Fondation Le Corbusier when the original documents could still be inspected before digitization of the archives. The documents were kept in boxes J1 (12) to J1 (17). Today the documents can be consulted in digital form under the class mark J1 (12) to J1 (17), J3 (17), L2 (3) 23 to 68, E2 (5) 102–127, E2 (5) 353. The photographic records were identified at the Fondation Le Corbusier, many of them belonging at the Lucien Hervé archive which is now held at the Getty Research Institute (Los Angeles). I carried out a number of interviews in 1986–1987 and in 2002–2003: Michel and Nadine Jaoul, André Wogenscky, Jean-Louis Véret, Jacques Michel, Roger Aujame, Domènec Escorsa, Salvatore Bertocchi, Rogelio Salmona. I made extensive use of the journals *L'Architecture aujourd'hui*, *Techniques et Architecture* and *The Architectural Review* in order to set the architectural scene of the 1950s and 1960s.

Books and articles from Le Corbusier (selection)

Le Corbusier. *L'Almanach d'architecture moderne* [The almanac of modern architecture]. Paris: Crès et Cie, 1926.

Le Corbusier. "Louis Sutter [*sic*]. L'inconnu de la soixantaine. [Louis Sutter (*sic*). Unknown at Sixty]." *Le Minotaure* 9 (1936). Reprinted in *Louis Soutter*. Arles: Actes Sud, 1987.

Le Corbusier. *Quand les cathédrales étaient blanches. Voyage au pays des timides*. Paris: Plon, 1937. Translated as *When the cathedrals were white. A journey to the country of timid people*. New York: Reynald & Hitchcock, 1947.

Le Corbusier. *Les Constructions "Murondins."* Paris/Clermont-Ferrand: Étienne Chiron, 1942.

Le Corbusier. "Éléments modernes d'une communauté villageoise. [Modern Elements for a Village Community]." In *Agriculture et communauté*. Paris: Librairie de Médicis, 1943.

Le Corbusier. *Les Trois Etablissements humains* [The Three Human Establishments]. Paris: Denoël, 1945.

Le Corbusier. *New World of Space*. New York: Reynald & Hitchcock, 1948.

Le Corbusier. *Propos d'urbanisme*. Paris: Bourrelier et Cie, 1946. Translated by Clive Entwistle as *Concerning Town Planning*. New Haven: Yale University Press, 1948.

Le Corbusier. *Le Modulor*. Boulogne: Editions de L'Architecture d'aujourd'hui, 1950. Translated as *The Modulor*. Cambridge, Mass., 1954.

Le Corbusier. *Le Modulor 2*. Boulogne: Editions de L'Architecture d'aujourd'hui, 1955. Translated as *The Modulor 2*. Cambridge, Mass., 1958.

Le Corbusier. *L'Unité d'habitation de Marseille*. Mulhouse: Souillac, 1950. Translated as *The Marseilles Block*. London: Harvill Press, 1953.

Le Corbusier. *Une petite maison* [A small house]. Zurich: Girsberger, 1954.

Le Corbusier. *Le Poème de l'angle droit* [The poem of the right angle]. Paris: Verve, 1955.

Le Corbusier. *Claviers de couleurs Salubra* [Salubra Color Keyboards]. Bale: Salubra, 1959.

Le Corbusier. *L'Atelier de la recherche patiente*. Paris: Vincent, Fréal & Cie, 1960. Translated by James Palmes as *Creation is a Patient Search*. New York: Frederick Praeger, 1960.

Le Corbusier. "Preface." In *Art in European Architecture / Synthèse des arts*, ed. Paul Damaz, vii–xii. New York: Reinhold Publishing Corporation, 1956.

Correspondence

Le Corbusier: choix de lettres [Le Corbusier: A Selection of Letters], ed. Jean Jenger. Basel: Birkhäuser, 2002.

Le Corbusier, lettres à Auguste Perret, ed. Marie-Jeanne Dumont. Paris: Editions du Linteau, 2002.

Published documentary sources

Bill, Max, ed. *Le Corbusier and Pierre Jeanneret. Œuvre complète 1934–1938*. Zurich: Girsberger, 1939.

Boesiger, Willy, and Oscar Stonorov, eds. *Le Corbusier and Pierre Jeanneret. Œuvre complète 1910–1929*. Zurich: Girsberger, 1930.

Boesiger, Willy, ed. *Le Corbusier and Pierre Jeanneret. Œuvre complète 1929–1934*. Zurich: Girsberger. 1935.

Boesiger, Willy, ed. *Le Corbusier. Œuvre complète 1938–1946*. Zurich: Girsberger, 1946.

Boesiger, Willy, ed. *Le Corbusier. Œuvre complète 1946–1952*. Zurich: Girsberger, 1953.

Boesiger, Willy, ed. *Le Corbusier. Œuvre complète 1952–1957*. Zurich: Girsberger, 1957.

Brooks, H. Allen, ed. *The Le Corbusier Archive*. 32 vols. New York/Paris: Garland/Fondation Le Corbusier, 1984.

Franclieu, Françoise de, ed. *Le Corbusier Sketchbooks*. 4 vols. New York/ Cambridge, Mass.: Architectural History Foundation/MIT Press, 1981–1982.

Monographic studies, reference works, other works

Abadie, Daniel, ed. *Dubuffet*. Paris: Centre Pompidou, 2001.

Abram, Joseph. *L'Architecture moderne en France 2*. Paris: Picard, 1999.

Alazard, Jules, and Jean-Pierre Hébert. *De la fenêtre au pan de verre dans l'œuvre de Le Corbusier* [From the Window to the *pan de verre* in the Work of Le Corbusier]. Paris: Dunod, 1961.

Bacon, Mardges. *Le Corbusier in America: Travels in the Land of the Timid*. Cambridge, Mass.: MIT Press, 2001.

Baker, Geoffrey Howard. *Le Corbusier. An Analysis of Form*. New York/London: Van Nostrand Reinhold, 1985.

Banham, Reyner. *The New Brutalism, Ethic or Aesthetic?* London: Architectural Press, 1966.

Barthes, Roland. *Criticism and Truth*. Translated and edited by Katrine Pilcher Keuneman. London/New York: Continuum, 2007. Originally published as *Critique et Vérité*. Paris: Seuil, 1966.

Benton, Tim. ed. *Le Corbusier. Architect of the Century*. London: Arts Council of Great Britain, 1987.

Benton, Tim. *The Villas de Le Corbusier, 1920–1930*. New Haven /London: Yale University Press, 1987.

Bullock, Nicholas. *Building the Post-War World: Modern Architecture and*

Reconstruction in Britain. London/New York: Routledge, 2002.
Castro, Ricardo L. *Rogelio Salmona*. Bogotá: Villegas Editores, 1998.
Camfield, William A., and Jean-Hubert Martin. *Tabu Dada : Jean Crotti & Suzanne Duchamp, 1915-1922*. Bern: Die Kunsthalle, 1983.
Cendrars, Blaise. *La Banlieue de Paris*. Paris: Editions Seghers, 1949. Reprint Paris: Editions Seghers, 1966.
Chiambretto, Bruno. *Le Corbusier à Cap-Martin*. Marseilles: Parenthèses, 1988.
Choay, Françoise. *Le Corbusier*. New York: George Braziller, 1960.
Clarisse, Catherine. *Cuisine, recettes d'architecture* [Kitchen, Recipes for Architecture]. Paris: Éditions de l'Imprimeur, 2004.
Colomina, Beatriz. *Privacy and publicity: modern architecture as mass media*. Cambridge, Mass.: MIT Press, 1994.
Curtis, William. *Le Corbusier: Ideas and Forms*. Oxford: Phaidon, 1986.
Curtis, William. *Balkrishna Doshi. An Architecture for India*. New York: Rizzoli, 1988.
Dubuffet, Jean. *Prospectus aux amateurs de tout genre* [Leaflet for all Types of Amateurs]. Paris: Gallimard, 1946.
Ferro, Sergio, and Cherif Kebbal, Philippe Potié, and Cyrille Simonnet. *Le Corbusier: Le couvent de La Tourette*. Marseille: Parenthèses, 1988.
Frampton, Kenneth. *Le Corbusier: Architect and Visionary*. London: Thames & Hudson, 2001.
Gaucille, Hervé, and Valère Novarina. *Louis Soutter. Si le soleil me revenait* [Louis Soutter: If only the Sun were to Come Back to Me Again]. Paris: Adam Biro, 1997.
Golan, Romy. *Modernity and Nostalgia: Art and Politics between the Wars*. New Haven/London: Yale University Press, 1995.
Goldhagen, Sarah, and Réjean Legault. *Anxious Modernisms. Experimentation in Postwar Architectural Culture*. Montréal/Cambridge, Mass.: Canadian Centre for Architecture/MIT Press, 2000.
Guiheux, Alain. *L'Ordre de la brique* [The order of brick]. Bruxelles: Mardaga, 1985.
Ingersoll, Richard, ed. *Le Corbusier. A Marriage of Contours*. New York: Princeton Architectural Press, 1990.
Jauss, Hans Robert. *Pour une esthétique de la réception* [Toward an Aesthetic of Reception]. Paris: Gallimard, 1978.
Jencks, Charles. *Le Corbusier and the Continual Revolution in Architecture*. New York: Monacelli Press, 2000.
Jeong, Jinkouk. "L'Œil et le mur. L'origine de la polychromie architecturale de Le Corbusier 1923–1931 [The Eye and the Wall. The Origin of Le Corbusier's Architectural Polychromy 1923-1931.]" Ph.D. dissertation, École des hautes études en sciences sociales, 1993.
Kirkham, Pat. *Charles and Ray Eames: Designers of the Twentieth Century*. Cambridge, Mass.: MIT Press, 1995.
Lapunzina, Alejandro. *Le Corbusier's Maison Curutchet*. New York: Princeton Architectural Press, 1997.
Lavolé, Dominique. "La Paroi au-delà de la forme: la matière, élément signifiant dans l'architecture moderne [The Wall Beyond Form: Texture, a Defining Element in Modern Architecture]" Master's thesis, UPA 8, 1982.
Loreau, Max. *Catalogue des travaux de Jean Dubuffet. Marionnettes de la ville et de la campagne* [Catalogue of Works by Jean Dubuffet. Puppets of the City and the Country]. Paris: Jean-Jacques Pauvert, 1966.
Lucan, Jacques, ed. *Le Corbusier. Une encyclopédie*. Paris: CCL/Centre Georges Pompidou, 1987.
Lucan, Jacques. *France Architecture 1965–1988*. Milan/Paris: Electa/Moniteur, 1989.
Marcus, George H. *Le Corbusier: Inside the Machine for Living*. New York: Monacelli Press, 2000.
McLeod, Mary C. "Urbanism and Utopia: Le Corbusier from Regional syndicalism to Vichy." Ph.D. dissertation, Princeton University, 1985.
McLeod, Mary C., ed. *Charlotte Perriand. An Art of Living*. New York: Harry N. Abrams, 2003.
Missenard, André. *L'Homme et le climat* [Man and Climate]. Paris: Plon, 1937.
Missenard, André. *À la recherche du temps et du rythme* [In Search of Time and Rhythm]. Paris: Plon, 1940.
Moos, Stanislaus von. *Le Corbusier: l'architecte et son mythe* [Le Corbusier : the architect and his myth]. Paris: Horizons de France, 1971.
Morris, Frances, ed. *Paris Post War: Art and Existentialism, 1945-55*. London: Tate Gallery, 1993.
Mumford, Eric. *The CIAM Discourse on Urbanism, 1928–1960*. Cambridge. Mass.: MIT Press, 2000.
Nieddu, Giuseppe. "Les Sardes en Île-de-France. Histoire de vie [Sardinians in the Île-de-France Region. A Biographical History]." Master's thesis, La Sorbonne, Paris IV, 1986.
Ockman, Joan, and Edward Eigen, eds. *Architecture Culture: 1943–1968. A Documentary Anthology*. New York: Columbia University, Graduate School of Architecture, Planning and Preservation/Rizzoli, 1993.
Paulhan, Jean. *Guide d'un petit voyage en Suisse* [Guide to a Short Journey through Switzerland]. Paris: Gallimard, 1947. Reprint Paris: Gallimard, 1974.
Pauly, Danièle. *Ronchamp, lecture d'une architecture* [Ronchamp, an Architectural Reading]. Strasbourg/Paris : Ophrys, 1980.
Pearson, Christopher. "Integrations of Art and Architecture in the Work of Le Corbusier: Theory and Practice from Ornamentalism to the 'Synthesis of the Major Arts.'" Ph.D. dissertation, Stanford University, 1995.
Perriand, Charlotte. *Un art de vivre* [An Art of Living]. Paris: Musée des Arts décoratifs, 1985.
Petit, Jean, ed. *Le Corbusier, Architecture du bonheur. L'urbanisme est une clef.* [Le Corbusier, Architecture of Happiness. Urban Planning is Key.]. Paris: Cahiers Forces vives, Les Presses d'Île-de-France, 1955.
Petit, Jean. *Le Corbusier lui-même* [Le Corbusier himself]. Geneva: Éditions Rousseau, 1970.
Pierrefeu, François de, and Le Corbusier. *The Home of Man*. London: The Architectural Press, 1948.
Ragot, Gilles, and Mathilde Dion. *Le Corbusier en France: projets et réalisations*. Paris: Moniteur, 1997 (2nd ed.).
Reed, Christopher, ed. *Not at Home: The Suppression of Domesticity in Modern Art and Architecture*. London: Thames & Hudson, 1996.
Richards, Simon. *Le Corbusier and the Concept of Self*. New Haven/London: Yale University Press, 2003.
Rovira, Josep Maria. *Jose Luis Sert 1901–1983*. Milan: Electa, 2000.
Rüegg, Arthur, ed. *Polychromie architecturale* [Architectural Polychromy]*: Farbenklaviaturen von 1931 und 1959*. [Color keyboards from 1931 and 1959]. *Les claviers de couleurs de 1931 et de 1959*. Basel: Birkhäuser, 1997.
Rybczynski, Witold. *Home: A Short History of an Idea*. New York: Viking Penguin, 1986.
Saddy, Pierre, ed. *Le Corbusier. Le Passé à réaction poétique* [Le Corbusier. The Past as Poetic Stimulation]. Exhibition catalogue. Paris: Hôtel de Sully, Caisse nationale des Monuments historiques et des Sites, 1988.
Samper Gnecco, Germàn. *La Arquitectura y la ciudad. Apuntes de Viaje* [Architecture and the City. Travel Sketches.] Bogotá: Fonda Editorial Escala, 1986.
Samuel, Flora. *Le Corbusier Architect and Feminist*. Chichester: Wiley-Academy, 2004.
Sarkis, Hashim, ed. *Le Corbusier's Venice Hospital and the Mat Building Revival*. Cambridge, Mass./Munich: Harvard Design School/Prestel, 2001.
Sekler, Eduard and William Curtis. *Le Corbusier at Work: the Genesis of the Carpenter Center for the Visual Arts*.

Cambridge, Mass.: Harvard University Press, 1978.
Tellez, German. *Rogelio Salmona. Arquitectura y poetica del lugar* [Rogelio Salmona. Architecture and Poetics of Place]. Bogotá: Fonda Editorial Escala, 1991.
Tyrwhitt, Jacqueline, José Luis Sert, and Ernest Nathan Rogers, eds. *CIAM 8, the Heart of the City: Towards the Humanization of Urban Life*. New York: Pellegrini and Cudahy, 1952.
Viatte, Germain and Danièle Pauly, eds. *Le Corbusier et la Méditerranée*. Marseille: Parenthèses, 1987.
Vogt, Adolf Max. *Le Corbusier, the Noble Savage: Toward an Archaeology of Modernism*. Cambridge, Mass.: MIT Press, 1998.
Žaknić, Ivan. *Le Corbusier, Pavillon Suisse: The biography of a building*. Basel: Birkhäuser, 2004.

Articles

"La première résidence créée par Le Corbusier depuis 1935." *Maison & Jardin* [House & Garden] 34 (February 1956).
Aujame, Roger. "A Synthesis of the Arts: The Collaborations of Charlotte Perriand and Jean Prouvé," in *Charlotte Perriand, An Art of Living*, ed. Mary McLeod, 130-153. New York: H.N. Abrams, 2003.
Aumasson, Pascal. "Le Corbusier-Savina, des intuitions spatiales à la forme sculptée [Le Corbusier-Savina, from spatial intuitions to sculptural form]," in *Le Corbusier et la Bretagne* [Le Corbusier and Brittany], 57-73. Brest/Quimper: Éditions Nouvelles du Finistère, 1996.
Bandini, Mirella. "Michel Tapié de Paris à Turin," in *Tapié. Un art autre* [Tapié. A Different Art]. Turin: Edizioni d'Arte Fratelli Pozzo, 1997.
Banham, Reyner. "The New Brutalism." *The Architectural Review* 708 (1955), 354-361.
Barré, François. "Les maisons de l'enfance : la maison Jaoul." (conversation with Marie Jaoul), *L'Architecture d'aujourd'hui* 204 (1979): 85–88.
Benton, Tim. "Six Houses," in *Le Corbusier. Architect of the Century*, ed. Tim Benton, 44–70. London: Arts Council of Great Britain, 1987.
Benton, Tim. "La maison de week-end dans le paysage parisien [The Weekend House in the Parisian Landscape]," in *Le Corbusier et Paris*, 95-111. Paris: Fondation Le Corbusier, 2001.
Benton, Tim. "Pessac and Lège revisited: standards, dimensions and failures." *Massilia, Annuaire d'études corbuséennes* [Yearbook of Corbusean Studies], (Barcelona, 2004), 64–99.
Biasi, Pierre-Marc de. "Pour une approche génétique de l'architecture. [For a Genetic Approach to Architecture]." *Genesis* 14 (September 2000): 13–65.
Candela Suarez, Maria. "Sobre la villa Hutheesing-Shodhan: pormenores de un encargo." *Massilia, Annuaire d'études corbuséennes* [Yearbook of Corbusean Studies] (Barcelona, 2004), 200–225.
Collins, Christiane. "Le Corbusier's Maison Errazuris." *The Harvard Architectural Review* 6 (1987): 38–53.
Croset, Pierre Alain. "La questione del cliente." [The Question of the Client] *Rassegna* 3 (July 1980): 5–6.
Devillers, Christian. "Les derniers puritains," *AMC* 11 (April 1986): 118–129.
Dubuffet, Jean. "L'Auteur répond à quelques objections [The Author Responds to a Few Objections]," in Michel Tapié, *Mirobolus Macadam et Cie: Hautes Pâtes de J. Dubuffet* [Fantastic Macadam and Co.: Thick Paste Works of J. Dubuffet]. Paris : René Drouin, 1946.
Dumont, Marie-Jeanne. "La restauration des maisons Jaoul." *L'Architecture d'aujourd'hui* 275 (June 1991): 141–144.
Forty, Alan. "Le Corbusier's British Reputation," in *Le Corbusier. Architect of the Century*. ed. Tim Benton, 35–41. London: Arts Council of Great Britain, 1987.
Frampton, Kenneth. "Le Corbusier et la monumentalisation du vernaculaire (1930–1960) [Le Corbusier and the Monumentalization of the Vernacular (1930-1960)]," in *L'Architecture moderne: une histoire critique* [Modern Architecture : A Critical History], 195–200. Paris: Philippe Sers, 1985.
Frampton, Kenneth. "The Other Le Corbusier: Primitive Form and the Linear City, 1929–52," in *Le Corbusier. Architect of the Century*, ed. Tim Benton, 29–35. London: Arts Council of Great Britain, 1987.
Franclieu, Françoise de. "Savina (Joseph)," in *Le Corbusier. Une encyclopédie*, ed. Jacques Lucan, 364–365. Paris: Centre Pompidou, 1987.
Girard, Edith. "La genèse du projet en situation de concours. [The Genesis of the Project for Competition]" *Genesis* 14 (September 2000): 179–201.
Goldhagen, Sarah. "Freedom's Domiciles," in *Anxious Modernisms. Experimentation in Postwar Architectural Culture*, eds. Sarah Goldhagen and Réjean Legault, 75–95. Montréal/Cambridge, Mass.: Canadian Centre for Architecture/MIT Press, 2000.
Gonzalez Cubero, Josefina. "La arquitectura del suelo: las casas Jaoul en Neuilly-sur-Seine [The Architecture of the Ground: The Jaoul Houses in Neuilly-sur-Seine]." *Massilia, Annuaire d'études corbuséennes* [Yearbook of Corbusean Studies] (Barcelone, 2004), 162–177.
Krustrup, Morgen. "Poème de l'angle droit [Poeme of the right angle]." *Arkitekten* 92 (1990), 422-32.
Loach, Judi. "L'atelier de Le Corbusier: un centre européen d'échanges. [Le Corbusier's Studio: a European Center of Exchanges]" *Monuments historiques* 180 (March–April 1992): 49–52.
Loos, Adolf. "Architecture," in *The Architecture of Adolf Loos*, eds. Yehuda Safran and Wilfried Wang, 104–109. London: Arts Council of Great Britain, 1985.
Maniaque, Caroline. "Les maisons Jaoul de Le Corbusier." *Histoire de l'art* 1–2 (1988): 75–86.
Maniaque, Caroline. "Lettres aux clients, lettres aux artisans: le cas des maisons Jaoul [Letters to Clients, Letters to Artisans: The Case of the Jaoul Houses]," in *Le Corbusier et l'écriture*, 55–65. Rencontres de la Fondation Le Corbusier, 1993.
Maniaque, Caroline. "Artisanat et petites entreprises dans l'activité parisienne de Le Corbusier à Paris [Artisan Trades and Small Enterprises Involved in the Parisian Activity of Le Corbusier in Paris]," in *Le Corbusier et Paris*, 81–94. Rencontres de la Fondation Le Corbusier, 2001.
Maniaque, Caroline. "Réception écrite et réception construite: le cas des maisons Jaoul dans la critique anglo-saxonne [Written Reception and Built Reception: The Case of the Jaoul Houses in Anglo-Saxon Criticism]," in *Cahiers thématiques 2*, Lille/Paris: EAL/ Jean-Michel Place (2002), 101–113.
Maniaque, Caroline. "'Regarder dehors pourquoi ?' Les maisons Jaoul entre modernité et art de vivre ['Why look outside?' The Jaoul Houses, Between Modernity and the Art of Living]" *Massilia, Annuaire d'études corbuséennes* (Barcelona, 2004), 152–161.
Marza, Fernando, and Esteve Roca. "La boveda catalana en la obra de Le Corbusier [The Catalan Vault in the Work of Le Corbusier]." *Le Corbusier i Barcelona* [Le Corbusier and Barcelona]. Barcelona: Fundacio Caixa de Catalunya (1988), 105–114.
Maxwell, Robert. "The architect as artist," in *James Stirling, Architectural Design Profile*, 218–226. London: Academy Editions/St.Martin 's Press, 1987.
Missenard, André. "Préface. Civilisation et climat." *Techniques et Architecture* 7–8 (1950): 35–37.
Munoz, Maria Tereza. "Il dilemma delle case Jaoul [The Dilemma of the Jaoul Houses]," in *La Casa di Le Corbusier*, eds. Antonio Alfani, Manuela Canestrari, and Alberto Samonà. Roma: Officina Edizioni, 1987.

Naylor, Gilian. "Modernism and Memory: Leaving Traces," in *Material Memories*, eds. Marius Kwint, Christopher Breward, and Jeremy Aynsley, 91–106. Oxford/New York: Berg, 1999.

Ockman, Joan. "Lessons from Objects: Perriand from the Pioneer Years to the 'Epoch of Realities'," in *Charlotte Perriand: An Art of Living*, ed. Mary C. McLeod, 154–81. New York: Harry N. Abrams, 2003.

Passanti, Francesco. "The Vernacular, Modernism and Le Corbusier." *Journal of the Society of Architectural Historians* (December 1997): 438–51.

Perriand, Charlotte. "L'Art d'habiter [The art of living]." *Techniques et Architecture* 9–10 (1950).

Pevsner, Nikolaus. "The Return of Historicism," in *Studies in Art, Architecture and Design*, 2: 242–359. London: Thames & Hudson, 1968.

Rüegg, Arthur. "Marcel Levaillant and 'La question du mobilier,'" in *Le Corbusier before Le Corbusier: applied arts, architecture, painting, photography, 1907-1922*, ed. Stanislaus von Moos and Arthur Rüegg, 108–131. New Haven: Yale University Press, 2002.

Spiegel, Herman. "Site visits: an engineer reads Le Corbusier's villas." *Perspecta* 31 (2000): 86–95.

Stirling, James. "Ronchamp. Le Corbusier's Chapel and the Crisis of Rationalism." *The Architectural Review* (March 1956): 155–61.

Stirling, James. "Garches to Jaoul: Le Corbusier as Domestic Architect in 1927 and 1953." *The Architectural Review* (September 1955): 145–151. Reprint in *The Le Corbusier Archive*, 10: ix. New York: Garland, 1983.

Stirling, James. "Regionalism and Modern Architecture," in *Architects' Year Book 8* (1957): 62–68.

Tafuri, Manfredo. "Machine et mémoire: la ville dans l'œuvre de Le Corbusier [Machine and Memory: the City in the Work of Le Corbusier]," in *Le Corbusier. Une encyclopédie*, ed. Jacques Lucan, 460–469. Paris: Centre Pompidou, 1987.

Thévoz, Michel. "Plaidoyer pour la haine de l'art: l'invention de 'l'art des fous' [Plea for Hatred in Art: the Invention of 'art of the insane']," in *Où en est l'interprétation de l'œuvre d'art* [Where is the Interpretation of the Work of Art], ed. Régis Michel. Paris: Ensba, 2000.

Wilson, Sarah. "From the Asylum to the Museum: Marginal Art in Paris and New York, 1938–68," in *Parallel Visions: Modern Artists and Outsider Art*, ed. Maurice Tuchman and Carol S. Eliel, 128–29. Los Angeles/New York: Los Angeles County Museum of Art/Princeton University Press, 1992.

Winter, John. "Le Corbusier's Technological Dilemma," in *The Open Hand: Essays on Le Corbusier*, ed. Russell Walden, 323–345. Cambridge, Mass.: MIT Press, 1977.

Worbs, Dietrich. "Die Jaoul-Hauser." *Bauwelt* (October 1987): 1459–1462.

INDEX

CREDITS

Architect's Journal: fig. 211
The Architectural Review: figs. 201, 202, 203, 207 (W. J. Toomey)
Tim Benton: figs. 17, 22, 29, 30, 59, 125, 126, 136, 160, 177, 183, 184, 189, 192
Manuel Bougot: figs. 1, 5
CNAC/MNAM, Pierre Joly/Vera Cardot: fig. 210
Dubuffet/ADAGP Foundation: figs. 44, 45, 48, 187
FLC/ADAGP: figs. 2 (André Martin), 7, 15, 25, 39, 40, 41, 42, 56, 57, 58, 61, 62, 63, 64, 65, 66, 67, 68, 69, 70, 71, 72, 73, 74, 75, 76, 77, 79, 80, 81 (Match/Rizzo), 82, 83, 84, 85, 86, 87, 88, 90, 91, 92, 93, 94, 95, 96, 97, 98, 99, 100, 101, 102, 103, 104 (Michel Sima), 105, 106, 108, 109, 110, 111, 112, 113, 114, 115, 116, 117, 119, 121, 123, 127, 128, 129, 130, 131, 132, 137, 138, 139, 140, 141, 142, 143, 144, 145, 146, 150, 152, 156, 159, 161, 164, 167, 173, 174, 175, 176, 180, 181, 186, 197 (André Steiner)
Getty Research Institute for the History of Art and the Humanities, Los Angeles: figs. 28, 149
Pierre Henon (drawings): figs. 9, 10, 11, 12, 13, 14, 21, 34
Lucien Hervé: figs. 16a, 16b, 16c, 107, 124, 133, 134, 135, 148, 154, 155, 157, 158, 163, 166, 185, 205, 206
James Stirling Archives: fig. 209
Jaoul/Clichés Tim Benton Archives: figs. 34, 35, 36, 37, 42, 43, 46, 47, 52, 53, 54, 55, 60, 153, 162, 165, 179, 188, 191, 194, 195, 196, 200, 213
Jean-Pierre Jornod: fig. 190
L'Architecture d'aujourd'hui: figs. 49, 50, 51, 78, 178
Maison & Jardin: figs. 198, 199
Caroline Maniaque Benton: figs., 8, 18, 19, 23, 24, 26, 27, 30, 33, 59, 120, 147, 151, 193, 220
The New Brutalism: figs. 208, 212
Charlotte Perriand/ADAGP: figs. 170, 171, 172
Jean-Christophe Pratt/Doris Pries: figs. 6, 20, 31, 32, 118, 182, 204, 216, 218, 219
Paolo Rosselli: figs. 168, 169
German Samper: fig. 89
Techniques et Architecture: figs. 170, 217